A Kaleidoscope of Stories

A KALEIDOSCOPE OF STORIES

MUSLIM VOICES IN CONTEMPORARY POETRY

First published 2020 by Lote Tree Press

www.lotetreepress.com

ISBN 978-1-9162488-0-9 in paperback print format

A CIP catalogue record for this book is available from the British Library

In Memory

Daniel Abdal-Hayy Moore
1940 – 2016

Abdalhamid Evans
1951 – 2018

Omar John Nemeth
1998 – 2018

Shahbano Aliani
1967 – 2019

From The Soft Rope We Are

Daniel Abdal-Hayy Moore

9/5/2013 (from *The Soul's Home*)

From the soft rope we are
from the jagged tear in a canvas we are

from the wrecked and twisted bicycle we are
from the lengthy shadow of a lost world we are

from flickers at the edge of a dark wood we are
from an echoing empty stadium at midnight we are

from crumbs left for birds on a windowsill we are
from the signal sent from a ship's fo'c'sle we are

From land sighted and land ignored we are
from polished silver laid out perfectly we are

From a peak wreathed in roseate cloud we are
from a low-lying hamlet under brown smoke we are

From rows of burgeoning grape-trellises we are
from a sunny valley between green hills we are

From the spontaneous defenses of our sovereignty we are
from silence in the midst of chaos we are

From dust flakes falling down an endless chute we are
from an abrupt announcement at the table we are

From a door slammed and a door left open we are
From blue fog suddenly filling a deep canyon we are

From no one left in the meeting hall but us we are
from just one more face in the billowing crowd we are

From oft-blessed in abundance from we know not where we are
from bereft never knowingly visited by angels we are

From fervent supplications each dawn religiously we are
from the last whispered breath of prayer when we die we are

when even stillness stands still
right where we are

O God in Your Magnificence and Glory
Who moves us and moves in us

without Whom we would not be
whoever and wherever we are

Bring out from us what light You will
and quench us with every breath

in Your only existence
when no more than a shadow of a shadow of a shadow we are

Small flickering light in Your window we are
tiny birdsong of distant jubilant whistling

heard near and far
we are

Contents

Preface

The Islamic world is steeped in poetry. The rich tapestry of poetic traditions within it encompasses the pre-Islamic *Mu'allaqāt* odes of the Arabian desert, the mysticism of Rumi and Yunus Emre, court poetry from across the Islamic world, the treatises of polymaths, the ascetic devotional poems of Rabia al-Adawiyya, and much besides.

It seems in the traditional Islamic world everyone was writing poetry, from the beggar in the market to the Caliph in his palace. Official documents, sermons, excuses, insults and love letters were all written in verse. Need to ask a ruler to save your island, like the 9th century al-Zahra al-Soqotriyya? Just send them a good poem explaining the problem, as she did, with troops being quickly dispatched to her aid in response. Or perhaps you have a land dispute - why not compose some verses to defend your position like the 18th century Fatima al-Adiniyya successfully did? Want to express your undying love for someone, or perhaps pen a witty prologue to your latest masterpiece - all of these could be done in verse, and if you demonstrated your skill as a wordsmith and delighted the intended recipient with your eloquence, then you were more likely to get a favourable outcome.

This collection of contemporary Muslim poetry draws on a wealth of these poetic traditions, together with Western traditions of poetry which have, through processes of colonisation and globalisation, spread throughout the world. The poetry in this anthology ranges from a few more formal compositions, adhering to rules of metre and rhyme, to free verse, making up most of the poems in the collection, and spoken word pieces that represent a new, popular revival of poetry, mirroring the oral poetic traditions that have flourished through the ages. Some of the poems included are polished, while others are more raw - like pebbles on the beach, both have their attraction.

The multigenerational poets in the anthology come from and have ancestral roots in countries across the Middle East, Asia, Africa, Europe, North and South America and Australasia, and often come from a combination of backgrounds, forming the complex multicultural identities of the modern world. This anthology is a space to celebrate our daily lives and spirituality, and it is hoped it will serve as an antidote to the one dimensional presentation of Muslims as the maligned Other that the media so often presents us with.

Initially the poems were grouped into chapters covering subjects such as loss, love, or the relationship with the Divine, but this approach seemed not to reflect the dynamic flux of real life, which is more a succession of expansions and contractions, moments of elation and disaster, and everyday pleasures and challenges. Therefore, a more organic approach was settled upon, which might at first appear somewhat arbitrary. The hope is that this arrangement will produce more of a patchwork effect, varied but with repeated motifs, reflecting the diversity of voices and experiences of the poets in the anthology, with one poem flowing into another, not necessarily on the same subject or written in the same tone or style, but hopefully mirroring the astonishing way life can surprise us in its constantly evolving kaleidoscopic dance.

R.S Spiker
April 2020

Dada Agnes
Rakaya Esime Fetuga

The mother of our four generations
steps out onto the orange path
as herons grace lagoons spilled with
sunset.
She carries decades of wisdom in her patterned drapery
looking in her eyes is looking into me
don't cry, she says, just pray
every day could be the last day
and we live breathing in the echo of the words we say.
She takes my hand
though she must not remember me
a child of Elsie's Elsie
but I love her through the ropes of
legacy, I love her
like the song of destiny has
called me here
to her line.
Mourn quick then smile because the
slot for life is fine
time
pockets our chances with every beat of a heart
we might drop out of this world before
we learn who we are.
Our mother shines, our mother knows
we are vast and holy homes
and there are diamonds in
the floorboards of our souls.

What it is
Khadijah Lacina

you want
to talk
of love
i can do
that love
is a cool
hand on hot
forehead
the door
ajar the
hallway
light on
a gift
wrapped
under
colored
strands of
light with
your name
on it
love is
linked
pinkies in
the back
of the bus
notes left
in a hollow
tree a game
thrown
because
winning
we know
is not
everything
love
is the

chance
look over
a shared
plate of
spaghetti
that ends
in belly
deep
laughter
in a dim
lit room
the hot
mound
of flesh
that draws
you a bee
to honey
the soft
whisper
and moan
of firelit
night the
caress of
you belong
here with
me there
is nowhere
else i would
ever want
to be
love is the
absence of
moondrawn
cycle the
first faint
stirring of
are you in
there are
you real

are you
you? the
flutter of
barefeet
against
beating
heart the
first stab
of pain
that builds
to a final
agonized
push the
hardest
thing we
have ever
done we
did it
together
love is small
wonder
curled
tight chest
to breast
first full
body smile
joy too big
to live in
such a tiny
body the
first steps
to, then
away love
pulled tight
pushed to
the breaking
point healed
let go yet
held close

love is
forever
in a world
where
nothing is
forever
a promise
between
sun and moon
earth and wind
you and i and
always opening
expanding
to let one
more in or
let one more
out love is
the knowing
of time
a shadow
stretched
across
heavens
the stars
awaiting
the day
they hear
me call
your
name

guardian trees
Idris Mears

whether the tree was planted
and staked with intention
or whether it was a wild sapling
destiny pushed through
the undergrowth of the norwich cemetery
i don't know
but God knew and God knows
the branches spread a shade
of peace over my companions
and God knows us each
and our resting places
and i hope to lie under it too
or under another of the guardian
trees of paradise
in paris or constantia or abu ayyub
or on the mountain top
under the cork oak beside the great *qutb*

trees watered by the mercy of centuries
as in my short time i have been rained on
by the blessing of the water
I drank at the breaking of the fast
the joy of the water I swam in
the cleansing of the water
I used to prepare for prayer
and in course the water used
to wash me for the grave

Wishes for Friends
Yasmine Ahmed-Lea

Yes we got married
In my living room
Lavender and peonies
Everywhere everywhere
My mother was
The real queen
No her knight
In shining armour
Was not there
His face reflected
In the rose water and candles
Glittering before me
Whilst I wept
Silent tears of
Everything everything
Into the pool
No I did not know him
For years and years
Even on that day
My acceptance was silent
A mere nod in the direction
Of a council
Of elders
But they say souls meet
Light miles before time
Where we were all together
In the covenant of promises
That can never be broken
By solid gold hearts
Yes only my beloveds
Were there
Both fortunate and
Less of fortune
Those who had lost all
But had still
Everything everything

Shared with me
In that day
Of course I wish
I could see all of you
My soul mates digital
And my soul mates far beyond
The borders
Of my mind
No I didn't
Spend the wealth of
Countries and pearls
Unwilling to buy myself
Into happiness
Everything everything
Went according to His plan
All I wish now
Is that for my fellow human
That your feet be wed
In garlands of lotus
And saffron
And the perfume
Of companionship
Be it this world
Or the next

And often we cry and argue
And often we shout and sigh
And often we walk apart
But
everyday everyday
I still call him
My best friend

Shukr bil-Lisan (Thankfulness of the Tongue)
Rashida James-Saadiya

In the middle of the night
when you need God most
may the sky unfold and pull you closer

May the ache of uncertainty drift away
and the ocean within your chest, spill from your eyes
For wherever there is darkness
there is light and wherever there is light
there are angels waiting patiently to hold your hand

So that you may know
the beauty of heaven and earth
the tenderness of wisdom

By the moon which brightens
and the pen that shall record
Let it be written in bone and marrow
stitched in the breath of patience and prayer
be certain of nothing except the existence of God
For every star is a prophecy

May you become a descendant of light
May the thread of faith run through your hands
May your prayers be heard
and your voice raised in gratitude
May your feet be planted firmly
and guided only by the way of love
May you walk with those who embody grace
and whenever you are lost may this path
bring you home, again and again

In the middle of the night
when you need God most
may the sky unfold and pull you closer

Thunder Afternoon during Ramadan
Paul Abdul Wadud Sutherland

to honour my wife who took a
vow of silence as part of her fast.

You won't eat - to rest
and cleanse the stomach, or talk
to soothe, clean your tongue.

You let the phone blare -
you put your hand on your heart
and I turn speechless

like a sounding box
every passing sound vibrates
in your day's silence.

Now, in loud meadows
far beyond the cricket grounds
by the River Rase

a queen settles on
her cushioned throne – a bee lands
on purple knapweed

I make quick *wudu*
catching first drops from deluge
in cupped crinkled hands

the cooling storm swirls
like arrows in a vortex
thin sun-blond grasses

fast from onyx ranks -
topaz, ruby, beryl - a half
rainbow gems the east

for your afternoon
swifts, pulsing and screeching,
abstain from our sky

between thunder-shocks
my dripping shifty shadow
is a missing friend.

My heart takes the vow
to listen more. Mallards swim
pleased their path's refreshed.

I pick goose-weed burrs
off my clothes – then lift the latch
to your calm garden.

So much sorrow dis-
appears, without a comeback
in our un-telling.

The Oasis
Nimah Ismail Nawwab

Alone in a crowd
  the pull of isolation
       seeps   in
The need to move on
   feel the stretch of the earth
      the cresting of endless, welcoming waves
        heed the silence of forests
          the utter quiet of the unrushed

     To let thoughts form without intent
            words leap in a ballet of ecstasy
               unleash a heart and soul seeking light

        And begin
          surging
         toward
            the Oasis of Serenity

Hilal
Ray Lacina

The sky cracks
just a little
and light
the Light
pours in,
pours down
and we with cupped hands catch it,
and all the month
is a held breath.

Life as an underground nymph

Rabea Benhalim

Today I dream of being buried under the leaves,
A cicadian hibernation.
An obliviousness to anything other than the gentle hum of the earth
composting her matter.
I long for the gentle envelopment of soil on skin.
A time to rest
before emerging
And taking flight.

I love you
Miroku Nemeth

Omar, when I kissed your forehead for the last time,
It was your forehead, my son, though it seemed cold.
Your eyes were still your eyes.
Even though they were closed,
And the doctors and nurses said you were dead.
Your hair was still your lion's hair,
Your dreadlocks soft and beautiful.
I stroked them again and again,
In the endless two minutes they allowed us,
Like I stroked your soft head, new to the world,
As a baby, putting you to sleep or just loveholding
You in my proudfatherarms.
You were still perfect.
You were still beautiful.
Even with the blood from the tracheotomy,
Even with the blood in your nose and mouth,
Your perfect mouth that only truly spoke
In broad smiles, or grins that said I love you,
Or in poetry or to condemn injustice,
Or to say clearly like your true last words to me,
"I love you, Baba".
You were still perfect with your Nubian mother
Praying in Arabic and crying over you,
Her firstborn son's blood forever unwiped from her cheek.
You were still beautiful while I continued to stroke
Your lion's mane with my left hand, and for the last time,
Ran my right hand gently (O gentle boy, O kind man),
Over your head, your cheeks, your chin, down your neck,
Down to your warrior shoulder (O warrior, I heard your deathsong),
Caressing your warrior arm only as the father of a warrior
Mourning mourning before he carried you in your burial shroud,
Mourning mourning but touching you for the last time,
Letting my hand travel down your forearm,
That strong forearm of an Eskrimador,
Until I reached your hand, Omar,
Measured it against my hand,

Father. Son. Hand touching hand for the last time.
And your hand was mine, but so much bigger,
And so much more perfect.

I Don't Know Any Other Way
Shahbano Aliani

i love You
like a sky full of monsoon clouds
loves the earth

with abundance
with abandon
without reserve

and like
the sky full of monsoon clouds
i want to become
a million
tiny
glistening
tear drop
stars
of water

that pour
day after day
night after night
without pause
without fear

until the very last drop
is dissolved
and obliterated
in the ground
of Your Being,

has become
pure, silent,
emptiness

i love You like this
because like the sky

and its monsoon clouds
i don't know
any. other. way.

Haikus for the Divine

Tazmin H. Uddin

I.
You are the Writer
of my being. Teach me to read
Your signs around me.

II.
Your name to me is
an elixir of love. It
seeks to consume me.

Arrivals
Yahia Lababidi

I don't quite know how it occurred
that this great fish has appeared
almost fully-formed, it seemed
to crowd out all else in my aquarium

Perhaps, this creature of the depths
always was, just out of sight
secretly feeding on hidden longing
and now demands acknowledging

With the swish of a majestic tail
it's upset my incidental decor -
gone the rubber diver and plastic treasure.
The glass frame itself can't be far behind...

Fajr Mornings
Muneera Pilgrim

This morning I woke up missing the taste of you
the fragrance of you
the sight I imagine, heavenly that is the view of you
the sweetness of your features,
if I could somehow run my coarse fingers across the expanse of your
remoteness, clutch your coco lined hands and dance into the darkness
then into the lightness, until we emerge as one likeness
the fusion of painted blues and reds across your *fajr* horizon
or the bursting banks of your bride - The Nile - as they surround Tuti
Island
I was so blessed to kiss you, love you, hug you and now miss you
I'll sing a blues for you
 a gold tainted blues
you without me is abuse
lament on the many ways we made love, made life, made meaning,
made pain go away and breathing fair seeming, made *dhikr* way into
the night, passion filled lovers
lips wet forsaking our covers, awaiting the moment, that moment
when the heavens open like a bolt of thunder
Rahma is her reign
The trumpeter starts to blow time itself slows
down foretasting the approaching
shh!!
seconds of silence... A solitary sound germinates the night's skies
ricocheting like pinballs and shooting stars until all you hear is the
repetition of Allah Allah, *Allahu akbar*, a crescendo sung by the
heavenly host
the night is in a frenzy
dear Creation, prayer is better than sleep, prayer is better than sleep
coming from all directions
it's infectious
and then it evaporates and turns into dust, almost as if it was a figment
of my longing heart, a metaphor for feeling parched.
Ya Sudan this morning I awoke missing you, the taste of you, the feel
of you, your *fajr* mornings, oh how I adore them.

Linguistics and Lost Languages
Mariam Akhtar

we're discussing dates
(not the failed ones
and not the sweet ones either)
my aunt pronounces - note not mispronounces
calendar as calundhur
and as her young daughter mocks her
my heart stutters and stirs with anger
I ask her how many languages she can speak
she replies one
but is blessed to be able to understand two
I remind her of how beautiful her mama's brain is
this magic that occurs
where she can switch
between two sets of letters and sounds
and maybe sometimes in the transition of translation
her mouth may soften
and what comes out may be rounder than intended
because she's a woman with a hard face but a soft heart
from a culture and a long line of tradition
that feeds people endlessly and selflessly
all the irony in the world is not lost
on a family of a lost language
one that's invisibility manifests its presence
in conversations like this

Ṭalaʿa l-Badru ʿAlaynā
The Full Moon Rose Over Us
Efemeral

Years ago, I walked East
along Broadway
from where the hospital revives
the city's wounded
towards the mural of la Virgen,
her prayer full hands clasped
to serve you,
the best tacos my city has to offer.

Past purpose is now purposeless
for memory's sake
I no longer remember
what I was walking from,
where I was going,

only that every Eastbound step
was a sinking into
viscous
viscid
visceral

Light

poured
forth
flowing
from
every
single
face
that I passed,
years ago, as I walked East
along Broadway.

Enveloped in cityscape

I submerged synesthesious
in a Light
somewhere in
between olive oil and sweet honey.

Light shone, unearthly
from those moon faces -
some perhaps more full than others,
but all
I knew
was the light in every phase.

Years ago, I walked East
along Broadway
yearning,
I suppose,

to one day drown
in the brilliant bright flood of
perfectly reflected
Illumination.

Us

Asma Khan

Subtle, hidden, this stream of molten gold
this essence, this bond that ties us two
lying beneath our day of heavy illusion.
I turn and catch you looking unaware
That pure, teasing, elusive gaze
holding me in the lightest of embrace
No longing or possession.
just a secret truth
that takes my breath away

hi

Jessica Mathieu

hi.
i see you there, you shine.
if i joined you,
would you mind?
hand in hand, let's fly.
side by side,
let's ride the crest of time,
explore the secret gardens
in our hearts we hide.
let's stroll together
the wild forests of our minds.

hi.

i see you there, you shine,
and i know you know what i mean
when i say, you can See.
so let's Captain Cook the frequencies,
you and me.
do you think we can circumnavigate a heart?
let's embark!
oh, these seas!
on a journey no ear can hear
no eye can see.
i know you know what i mean.
you and i,
we are flutes carved from the same reed.

i've been drawing a map of my heart
only you can read.
are you ready?
the moment is waiting!
it sparkles with the dust of heaven
falling so heavily
i think i'm going to sneeze!

my curmudgeonly heart is bursting
in a tender, riotous bloom
do you see the colors?
they are for you.
it's a symphony in every hue.

hi.

i see you there, you shine.
may i walk with you
til the end of time,
seeking all that's Pure and True,
dissolving in the Source of Love,
your hand in mine
hearts combined
learning to dance the Dance
of the Flutist Divine?

together,
let's learn to be beautiful
to His Holy Eyes,
as we dance
the way two galaxies collide
and then circle each other
til the end of time.

hi.

you shine.

would you Walk with me,
your hand in mine
til the end of time?

Silence
Eisha Basit

The needles of the pine trees
Swayed in worship,
The mountains were hewed,
Sheer-faced in worship,
The sky spilled colours,
Red-gold in worship,
A full silence over the scenery,
The lull a worship,
For so long, I thought
This love for God
Was a riddle
Waiting to be solved,
But now I stand,
A fool in awe,
Open-mouthed,
Bewildered,
Amazed in worship

My Father's Tongue
Amal Kassir

I once asked my father
what language he dreams in
and he did not know the answer to this question.
In fact,
the question startled him.
He's spent more of his life here in America
than in his motherland -
and here he is,
a man who's mastered both languages,
not sure which he dreams in.

I remember the only time I saw my father stutter-
it was in a crowded grocery parking lot.
He was taken aback,
& did not have enough stripes or stars on his tongue
to muster a response to the bigot
who called him something with an f word,
an n word -
a terrorist.

It's like my father did not have the tongue to respond -
Imagine, a man without a tongue--
he was tripping over his own voice
like it was like a herd of wild horses
he could not tame

I could see the heat in his body from this powerlessness,
Nothing will render a person more powerless
then their voice escaping them.

This man,
My Baba,
Speechless?
He is the son of a poet,
the child of a mother of fourteen,
He is an Arab,

From *Lughat Aḍ-ḍād*
He possesses letters
Not found in any other dialect on the planet

A man whose own sister was deaf,
That he helped create her language.
A man who has memorized so many chapters in the Quran
with *tajweed,*

One who has managed to make friends
From El Salvador to Togo,
Using his English or his Arabic
or his etiquette or whatever else he can find -
one who can tell a joke in two languages.

My father,
A man so well-versed in this world,
And still he did not have the tongue to respond
to the bigot at the grocery store

I ask my father what language he dreams in
And he does not know the answer to this question.
He's spent more of his life here in America
Than in his motherland -
a man whose mastered both languages,
unsure of which he dreams in,

because he probably dreams in both -

My father gets his livelihood from feeding people food,
From catering to their taste buds,
Whatever culture they may come from.

Baba couldn't pick one country
so he put his motherland into restaurants
so that everyone could have it on their tongue -
so everyone knew what tabbouleh tastes like,
so that the English language could transliterate it well enough
to settle in their mouth

So that even the bigots who walked into our restaurant
would find out that the American dream
was dreamt up in **another** language.

He would spend 5 minutes at a table
teaching customers the correct pronunciation
of the foods on our menus,
of our hellos and goodbyes,
& 'peace be upon you's

My father was not the type of man who stuttered,
he was never speechless -
he's got a story for every word you give him,
he's got a *hadith* for any piece of advice you need.

I think God decided that a man whose tongue is this holy
shouldn't even bother responding.

I Too Want to Be a Poet
Sukina Pilgrim

I too want to be a poet
To live a virtuous life
Away from the poverty of the mind
And the starvation of spirit.
I too want to live in the liquid light
Of art making, all the time.
Always seeing the beauty
Always seeking the poetry
Smiling inwardly when poetry slips into domestic settings
And the mundane suddenly becomes a place of magic
Where those gifted with word crafting
Can cast spells over everyone
Even if only for one second -
In the kitchen
Or the community centre
Or the playground
In the council estates
Where even the tower blocks
Can become pillars of majesty
When the glow from the setting sun hits the windows
Even if only for one second
We desire to
Plant poetry where it's least expected
And watch it bear fruit.
I too want to find a way out
Of cycles of pain
And stifled potential
And the inability to fly
Because women who look like me
Are often born with clipped wings
And if we find our way out
We are seen as magical things
To be praised and petted
In all these foreign settings.
I too want to roar
My story

Into the vastness of the sky
Whilst the city is half asleep
And remind everyone that I am here
I want the butterflies in my stomach
To burst forth through my throat
And dance from my tongue
And land in the space between
You and me
Our garden of poetry.
I am worthy
To be heard
And held
And I too
Can chase rainbows
And pursue my dreams
And swallow them
Until they can be seen in my eyes
And heard in my voice
And felt when I place my hand on yours

one without an other
Yohosame Cameron

a hawk soars directly overhead -
rodent in talons, glorious in its rapture
reminding me that
i am a high mountain dweller,
a descendant of highland warriors -
a fierce lineage pounding at the door

it's clear the hawk isn't fasting.
it was not prescribed for one
composed of pure *taqwa*...

even the earth herself
will bear witness
on the Day when all
are brought forth

to testify

yes, the *quran al takwini*,
the holy unwritten book of nature -
(complete with signs on the horizons
and within one Self)

has always been an open surah
for my being to read, freeing indeed,
a most exquisite
reminder that i too
long to be (and am) as pure
(when 'i' is removed from the equation)

inhale a new pace of *tawba* acquired through
the absorption of no 'thing' in particular (fast!)

'the circle around the zero'
as i heard word of a rumi once said

ah, and there he is...
...khidr come again

shamz clad in green, his *nur* blinding to the eye,
with a wild beard and a natty dread locked *tasbih*
consciousness that overflows and overtakes my
cautious demeanor, spilling all of the skeletal
hidings out and about in purgative antiquity~
a cathartic shedding of dead skin~

a telling of the tale that is
echoing in a vacant chamber (a *qalbin salim*)
as one rhythm keeps rolling over the tongue
(created for its perfected enunciation)

la illaha il Allaaaaaah.

hawk and i are One!

Balsam
Fatima's Hand

Accompany my thoughts
In the mountain cave
With Rabia's longing,
And Rumi's nay,
Give me the treasure
Of the sunlit stone,
Of a fountain sacred
And the hermit alone,
Give me the scents of
Amber and musk,
The cricket's love song
On twilight's cusp,
Let me kiss that
Hair of the blackest *layl*,
Give me Jonah's prayer
In the belly of the whale,
Gift me the hope
Of lucid dawns
Bring me that balsam
For a heart forlorn,
Sing me the garden
That I cannot forget,
The garden, the garden
Where we lovers met

The Confluence of the Birds
Peter Dziedzic

The conference of the birds
   renews
      in each age as
                  the hoopoe's cry rings
                     in each ear,
                     each heartbeat.

       Though quiet, though
     drowned in the swell of
infinite manifestation,
     atoms moan and
       yearn with
    that great
        aching outstretched plea for
         fullness
           and wholeness
            and clarity,
the seal
  of a primal covenant
            |Am I not your Lord?[1]
known by its dancing shadows
  upon spirits' eyes.
We are told:
             |Read![2]
     Read
       everything upon the land
       and seas and skies
       and in the depths of Heaven's vaults
       and the fiery firmaments adorned
     read
       and remember.
In the ever-stirring conference
  the confluence emerges
    seeking springs of wisdom
      pulsing, surging,

---

[1] Qur'an 7:172
[2] Qur'an 96:1

homecomings of
entangled roads revealing angels
   borne on each breath of
the blazing phoenix
      of the self-same flame as the
     rooted Cosmic Tree.
                   |*Read!*

    Read
        that the straight path
        is never straight
        but curves and bends, the Face
        and Names encountered ever anew
     read
        and remember.
The conference turns with
    the *Simorgh's* blazing body built
      in the swell of
        birds of paradise
as a song rises from the growing din
      and murmurs melt in unison
    when echoes of moonlight resound
      and the secrets of heart-caves whisper
        and the chants of ancestral forest-halls recall:

the ways of God are many
within this Sea of Mercy.

              |*Read!*
    Read:
        all the sages and their
                  journeys of life-giving taste
        as the confluence rises, one
        with the spinning cosmic spheres
     read
        and remember.

Supplicate - 25 Ramadan 1440
Saraiya Bah

weeping willows
bow but never break.
as do these sisters
who never break
as they bow to
their Maker.
their concern is
the here and now.
the moment where
fears, desires and dreams
crystallise into deeds.
supplications scooped
in henna tinted hands
made to The One
who commands us
to yield to His Oneness.
Who weathers storms
to strengthen the roots
of those who bow.
their branches graze
the masjid floor.
create ripples in Persian rugs.
their *duas* rustle wordlessly
to frolic in the domes covered
in sacred geometry.
how glorious that
devotions can manifest
in a multitude of ways.
how glorious is Al Musawwir
to fashion mercy in these
precious days.
they never take a break
as they bow.
they alternate from
prostration to circumnavigation
of their *tasbih*.

at times, tears carve tracks
on cheeks the hue of mahogany.
shoulders shudder from
swallowed grief.
not wanting to wail
as they weep.
yet they still don't break.
just supplicate.
and bow.
and wait.
and bow.
wow.

Fatima's Children
Mai Sartawi

Yumma's dementia glitches
recollect Fatima's children

"My children,
 where are they?!"

"Yumma, we are here..
         not in Iraq..
look we are in peace."

perhaps seen from the sky
the murderers outside
holders of inner snipers
now nearing Yemen's border
still striking her kids out of site

her frightened voice escalates:
"MY CHILDREN WHERE ARE THEY?
WHY ARE YOU NOT LOOKING?"

a forsaken fragrance funnels
forward into the gulf sea
did she come atop the roof?
to see heirs' corpses diced
dissolved in rivers red?

Mama said [1]:
Bushra Mustafa-Dunne

home is
a blazing tree
behind my sister

Burning stars I could touch if
I reached out my hand
then found
– closing dreamed-up fingers to catch –
I was one of them

home is watermelon:
رقَّي[3]
green skin suspended in the Tigris
White water

home
is broken pomegranate husk,
red, red رمَّان[4]
under my nails

in a place I don't know, a house left with the stove on
door open.

Sky me,
because home on earth
is rubble

---

[3] Watermelon, pronounced *reggi* in Iraqi Arabic
[4] Pomegranate, pronounced *rummān* in Arabic

For Mother
Aasifa Usmani

In our transient worlds
my homeland, Kashmir often caught into segments of wars
Mother, I could not reach or comfort,
I wanted to cherish that one last glance of your grace, wrinkles of your
fragility, whispers of your
last, living, beautiful, painful breath:
Mother, my first pulsating, fulfilling, pouring strength.

A pilgrim enmeshed in shrouds of grief's revelations
your existence survives in recitations,
like the *tasbih* enveloping your fingers
like radiance emanating from repentant hands lifted for *duas,*
like the breath in fulfilment of *sujoods*:
And solace when inside my soul your favourite prayer reverberates-
salaamun qawlan mirrabbin rahim
"Peace. A word (of salutation) from a Lord Most Merciful."

Line...up
Jamila Fitzgerald

I became a Geometer of sorts
Though 10th grade geometry: D
Algebra: D, I hate to admit.
Fascinated to no fastening,
In free fall, where do I stand
In this? And why?
Same thing in Philosophy...
I WOULD fall, but there's no
Gravity out here in pure space.

Then came the Christians with
A pair of...WINGS...at least.
Wait! How? What's that
Falling
Feeling?
You'd have to laugh (if it weren't
Your NECK!)

Next in, Zen in-- Zen out,
"Just contemplate the V O I D."

Third time God chooses me
To sign on the dotted line...
...to marry this TRUE MAN...
comma
...become a Muslim...

Mohamed, peace on him and us,
Stood on this earth
And heard what he heard across
The universe;
Five times a day a chance
To wash off my load
And lay it before the Lord;
Spill it...
Help!

Where do I put my feet?
On the straight path!
Say:
"GUIDE ME"

The triangle on the pool table
Aligns, rounds up the spheres
For my shot at Salvation.

No god but God
No *dhikr* without Islam
Squared first.
From my mess
To sweet remembrance
Is not a straight shot.
In the geometry of the thing,
The shortest distance is
through the Message Written.

The Grace Note of Remembering
ALLAH
A sweet taste, gone in a thrice,
Any fool can-- Who wouldn't?
But the beads are numberless
They move through time, only
Time after time,
Is sweetness squared.

You have touched me

Joel Hayward

I could boil an egg in my hand
and melt asphalt with footsteps
as I walk to You, O Lord

O I will run

I am aflame

I have seen Your kingdom
in a bright blue dream
in sagging clouds before rain
in the slippery birth of a foal
in the eyes of mercy

My heart is aflame

I heard You call
in breaking waves
in the wide ocean's silence
in the cry of gulls

in an echo in my heart

Ready for Ramadan
Mohja Kahf

My palette now so overloaded,
tongue so freighted, forgetting
its four basic tastes, corroded
and lolling in fullness, letting

the ease of receiving the blessing
lull me in the sleep of the sated:
I am ready for the Ramadan vetting
Oversugared, oversalted, weighted

by undigested angers, the burn
of the sour encounter, I steady
for lessons at the desk of the stern
schoolmistress, hunger. Time to return

to the Ramadan table, tidy and spare
as the bone of my need made bare

Jean

Hanan Issa

'You are Welsh first!' my nan always says,
though she can't speak a word of it.
Kids in her school got a rap on the knuckles
for every 'll' caught whispered in the playground.

Growing up, it was Rosie stories at bedtime,
sinking into her softly warmed marshmallow divan.
We woke to grateful chirps outside the window
since Nan always left out bread for the birds.

She liked bringing us breakfast in bed.
Doorstop toast, butter sliced thick like cheese,
cut into not-quite-triangle shapes
'cause she nibbled the burnt edges first.

Cheeky kids – we still mimic her Valleys voice,
tricking her into saying the *shahadah*
or asking her to call my dad a *kalb*.
She swears she has no idea what it means.

Nan prayed with us once. In a room full of women
wrapped in susurrant cotton and prayers.
She stood next to me, head bowed,
enamoured of the quiet loyalty of another tongue.

Turkish Bath

H I Cosar

I had always imagined him
On a war horse
Carrying a sickle
Ready to harvest
His new found seeds
For the after life

Face to face
He is more like
A Zen master
On an Arab Stallion!
Powerful
Peaceful

One winter's night
(The coldest in fifty one years
Temperature minus eighteen degrees
Snow crawling up to our knees)
He knocked on our door
Unannounced
Carrying my sister

Death, does its duty
It does not have a say
But if my sister's corpse could speak –
I wondered what she would say

She would want **me**
To tell mum and dad
'Inna lillahi wa inna ilayhi rajiun'
To God we belong and to God we will return
To hold them
As I hold back my own grief
And repeat each time dad says
'what do you mean'

She would want me to wash her
One last time
There will be no fuss no fun
Of our childhood baths
No fat lady giving us a massage

As she lay on the Stone Table
She might - sense my hesitation as I struggle with
A forgotten wire in her knee
(Residue of doctors' futile attempt to make her whole)
She might feel my trepidation
When I see her Frankenstein stitches
(Stitches that stretch from the end of her chin to the top of her pelvis
Stitches that bear more questions than answers
Stitches that almost undo me)
She might notice my apprehension
As I gently clean them
And surprise me with her dark humour
'Dude- I'm already dead- it doesn't hurt'

If my sister could speak
She would ask me to plait her long black hair
And add some red to her lips
(love can be found in the most unexpected places)
She may not want poppy seeds or rose petals
But I'll sprinkle them anyway
In the folds of her death dress

If my sister could speak
Maybe she would say
'Thanks *Abla**, see you later'
As I lay her near grandma.

March-15
*Abla is big sister in Turkish.

69

Alive
Murtaza Humayun Saeed

Take me there where the sun does not shine on steel and concrete
Where the paint still cracks in the heat
Where strangers still invite you in for lunch
Where people gather around tea and sweets
Where everywhere you look
Is touched by the work of hands
Where the furniture is still made of wood
Where the hearts are alive
Where people rise and sleep with the sun
Where rain means blessings
And God is mentioned before you eat

My Children, will my efforts be enough?
Toneya Sarwar

When I ask you to be mindful of the food you eat, not to waste and to consider those who are hungry while our own bellies are full...
When I tell you that to give is better than to receive and I encourage you to show generosity at every opportunity, as it presents itself...
When I teach you that our Prophet advised us to visit the sick and take care of the needy

When I encourage you to be part of this wonderful human race and to see good in everyone regardless of race, religion or colour

When I show you that success lies in hard-work, honesty and humility

I do all of the above, because that's what it means to be Muslim.
I am sorry that when you watch the news you are confused. You see and hear messages that contradict the above
I hope and pray that my efforts will be enough and that you and the rest of the world see that an extremist minority does not speak or act for the majority.

Hot Coals
Abdalhamid Evans

I took a nugget from a raging river
   A big gold nugget, and it shone like the sun
      I took a nugget from a raging river
      I brought it home and gave it to my son

I got turquoise on a high wild mountain
   Deep blue blue, like the ocean water
      I got turquoise on a high wild mountain
      I brought it home and gave it to my daughter

Hot coals, hot coals deep in the ground
   Hot coals, hot coals won't you pass them around
Hot coals, hot coals all across the land
   Hot coals, hot coals in the palm of my hand

I took a ruby from a deep dark mine
   Deep blood red, it was like no other
      I took a ruby from a deep dark mine
      I brought it back and gave it to my brother

I saw an emerald in a tall green jungle
   Bright green, and I could not resist her
      I saw an emerald in a tall green jungle
      And I took it home and gave it to my sister

I took a diamond from a baking desert
   Bright, so bright it nearly came to life
      I took a diamond from a baking desert
      I brought it home and gave it to my wife

I bit a bullet in a raging battle
   A bullet, to keep me safe from danger
      I bit a bullet in a raging battle
      I held it in my hand and gave it to a stranger

A heard a secret in a cool dry cavern

A secret that struck me like an arrow
    I took a drink in a distant tavern
And it quenched my thirst, deep down in my marrow

I saw signs on the far horizon
    Visions clear and clean like the sun
        In myself and on the far horizon
        So keep them safe to give to everyone

Hot coals, from the fires of deep devotion
    Hot coals, hot coals won't you pass them around
Hot coals, on the land and in the ocean
    Hot coals, hot coals in the palm of my hand

Halfway Through the Fast

Daniel Abdal-Hayy Moore
- from the poetry collection Ramadan is Burnished Sunlight

Halfway through the fast
is it a giant granite stone we shoulder

uphill in a boiling sun?

Or pool after reflective shady
pool in fragrant afternoons that

flow everywhere?

Is it coming face to face with
ourselves holding an empty

walnut shell in a
cubicle of mirrors

or suddenly relieved of the
anatomical discomforts of our

egos' slouches and shrugs we think
define us

now we sit as easy as
weightless jockeys on

horses of burnished silver
for the race to the finish?

The universe surrounds us with a
personable hug

that with days of
gastronomical emptiness we sense the

deft butterfly touch that actually

makes up its doings and

goings

Allah's subtlety in the
interconnectedness of all things

as our beings move forward while others
sail past in the opposite

way but go to the exact
same place in His dazzling

geometrical perfection

these close-ups of shattered and
reshaped patterns pouring their

diamond endlessness all around us
Light upon

irrefutable
Light

"Human Beings"
Abbas Mohamed

The best thing we can do
(for ourselves)
is be

The best thing we can be
(for our souls)
is empty

To allow Divine Breath
to fill in the empty spaces

to remember us
to express us
to speak to us
to create us

to annihilate us
to speak through us
to express through us
to remember Him
through us

till we are empty spaces
and all that is left is the Divine Breath

The best thing
for us to be
is everything

The best thing
for us to do
is nothing

Regularcillo[5]

Medina Tenour Whiteman

I saw him hovering by the organic shop
hands in pockets, no basket in sight
and I asked how he was
though I could see the state of him

'*Regularcillo*' he replied

I asked why even though I knew the answer:
I'd seen them parting
at the door of their son's music school one day
her striding, determined
him standing, crumbling

I recognised that look
like the Angel of Death brushed you
aiming for someone else
a little death that keeps you only just alive
to notice the gap in your chest
that lets every wind whistle through
without cooling the ragged ring
a death that keeps you dying just enough
to watch your child (your, plural)
grow with a rift down their middle
extending in each of your directions
(your, plural)
now you are plural, apart

What is the pronoun for
previously together?
How to bind that separation into your language
(your, singular)
mark your words so that no one will need to ask
the obvious, searing question
make it normal as I and You and We?

---

[5] an Andaluz expression meaning 'pretty ordinary'.

We the rent asunder
We the formerly
We who are no longer
We the dead that breathe

I saw him hovering by the organic shop
and I noticed the green bean seeds they had for sale
asked him between hugs if they had
started looking for separate homes
how they would shuttle the child between them
–he said he needed beaches,
she wanted to stay in the mountains–
asked how the kid was taking it
as he, the younger,
(third person, singular)
knelt impishly on a cork chair
seeming quite alright, actually
in spite of my practical questions
foreseeing the continuing grief
of separation after separation
of kids heartbroken after every holiday with dad
of the logistics of this limping along
once the first incandescence of pain subsides
once you are used to the bereavement
of your defunct marriage
though you have nothing to bury
and when his eyes recovered their whites
I broke off to greet a Swedish carpenteress
I hadn't seen for months
and he drifted away

This is a death I've learned to live with
and I no longer limp
merely waking in the night
grieving for a unity I once believed in
a fragile faith that fell through
when I put my weight on it

By day I swing forward
buoyed by this knowledge
of coexisting with loss
growing though cleft by a
slow lightning strike
treasuring this new chance
of a love that might
stand my weight

Soulmates

Jessica Daqamsseh

When I was a dream of my Lord's making
and you were a thought unborn.
Did our souls engage in discord
or were we luminaries
awaiting earthly descendance
to reignite our love once more?

Separate Ways - *extract*
I.AM.SHAHEED

My eyes burn. My tear ducts are salty
The redness. The soreness. Grief most gorgeous

The walk away blows all talk away
It's enormous inside where the war is

Crack the kernel. The heart is a beautiful bruise of purple
What are we for? What could be more?

Than disregard, not to be considered
Not to be valued. Spirit so withered

This love's a killer. Potential undelivered
Looking in the mirror. Doubt is a silverback

Second guess myself, second stress myself
So pissed in my abyss every depth is felt

Bloodstains the glass whenever we pelt stone
Speak no sunrise. Ain't for want of trying

Deficit desires
The long ting of offspring

A hollow house furnished in finality
Withdraw to corners. Gulf grows gradually

Aggressive passively. Affections are AWOL
Pantomime make pretend, disgraceful

The felony of infidelity. A shameful label
No one cares how we got to the point that we came to

Beautiful Disaster

Yusuf Abdalwadud Adams

I've come here seeking sanctuary
It's better to go within these walls
Than ricochet around the streets
Hungry eyed and hollow chested
It's better to call out a name and
Hear birdsong as the only wisdom
Available for longing so strung twelve
Strings tuned low to a 'D' felt in the
Chest where the rest is scatter pattern
Meridians better to close the door
Glimpsing oblivion as a blink of an eye
Never longer just the wink of existence
And non-existence just like love or falling
The same as the song the blackbird riffs
Gifted far beyond the hands of a man
Whose skin should be brown from the field
Worn from the felled tree gently smoking
The honey bees away to tease out the comb
Shaking infinitesimal India ink in bowl and
Dry brush to define figures from mountains
And clouds rooting out the knot on your
Shoulder bare and knowing the hope and
Spark and tiredness there and reaching for
A rope that pulls the sail tight to the wind
Yes traveling true to far off kin and knowing
Sovereignty and being true from this earth sky
Standing beneath a darkest blue night and
Moon the garden humming the heat knowing
The wax and wane of the day and the beard
Turning grey and the measure of magic you
Only glimpse as a gift as you sift through
Memory and contemplate what beautiful
Disaster left you like this.

Tajalli
Wajiha Khalil

The dyes of pre-eternity synchronise to call you Nur
Peace be upon you echo the angels
Your notes hold a thousand frequencies unnoticed
Exchange between channels purified from ocean to ocean
The lote tree shook and confounded the inhabitants
As you bloomed within the seed infinite petals rejoiced
Small innocent hands of fireflies caught a glimpse but kept the secret
The flashes told the heart's eyes how to sing
Snowflakes became sunbeams awakening to Spring
Emerald, diamond and ruby pledged to serve you
Rainbows veiled their hues to shine sheer
Coal simmered in obedience as stone listened
Swaying palm trees confessed and wheels praised every turn
Corners sacrificed meeting to honor sacred space
Winds harmonised to carry the glad tidings on invisible wings
Crystals absorbed energy to beam until al-Mahdi
Cotton learned soft and silk slipped into smooth
Eyes blinked absent of darkness because of the radiance of the light
Each particle testifies to its purpose
As every wave gives up its life
These are the cloaks that cover
The traveler on the road to God

Kaleidoscope
Nura Tarmann

Beautiful patterns form in a kaleidoscope of stories interconnected.
Creating beautiful patterns, and like a child looking through its toys,
we
search for the light to illuminate the pages of our lives
We sing and hold hands and raise our arms to heaven
You are an essential part of the collective experience
Your story running like a thread in the material of consciousness
The history of fathers finding expression in the songs of their sons
An old man contemplating his story intertwined in ancient
cobblestones.
Head bent, shuffling along a path trodden for centuries.
His feet have walked so many miles across the pavements of continents
Now he is alone in the alleys of his mind, replaying old melodies
Young men scratching the old records of memory, the old stories of
antiquity
Give them a new spin, telling a different story, yet always the same
enemy
Dark and cruel, there outside, lurking in the shadows of false identities
The others have returned like chickens coming home to roost
Now they live next door and the scent of strangeness becomes familiar
And the eye of every enemy becomes a mirror in which we see our
own imperfections
History with its funny way of stammering and, repeating sentences
Finds re-interpretations of events that light up the kaleidoscope
Now faith is analyzed in labs by men in white coats claiming
credentials,
yet lacking the most basic necessity, manipulating minds steaming
with sensitivity,
telling us that progress can only be achieved by ruthlessness
But now we learn to deflect the evil eye with faith in its goodness,
and evil spells become nothing more than ineffectual mumblings
in whose faces we hurl loving brilliance, and the frequency of our
songs
resonate harmoniously, ascending and descending truthfully in love

Painted toe nails
Hina Jabeen-Aslam

I got my toe nails painted on the day I knew you were there
In celebration of my new love affair
I painted my toes red, all I did was stare
Positive, two to three weeks it was so amazing to me
A lifelong love affair is what anticipated me

I finally understood why I craved tabasco on everything and why my
moods would swing as high as the storms which break the wind

I told your grandmother first, and for the first time in years we
embraced, a real chesty embrace where we both for the first time in
our history shared a feeling of earth and space

I told your father second, and the look on his face filled my heart with
the faith that brings me the knowledge that you were loved from the
moment those words left my face

I took you to Paris, you went up the Eiffel Tower and to the Louvre
Tasted some French macaroons which I know u loved because you
made me eat lots!
We spent a lot of time with your Aunty Aisha and we followed on to
Barcelona where I felt at peace with you.

We sat in la Sagrada Familia and cried, it may have been the scale of
the beauty around me or the hormone imbalances that left me teary
perhaps I felt unknowingly wary

After ten days of being away, we came home to an immaculate space,
daddy had been cleaning
with pride on his face welcomed us with his warm embrace

Kissed me on my tummy and said salaam peanut, that was to you

10 weeks on and you are gone
Allah had a plan for you and this was not it, your heart only beat just
for a little bit

Your tiny body was not any bigger than a date, it comforts me to
know that you did not feel any hate
The world can be bitter and a sad place
But know that it's better for you to be in Allah's embrace
I hope to see you at the gates of heaven when my time comes to see
your face

You are loved and my heart will always have space
For you my peanut

My toenails are still painted, I'm just not ready to take off that red

What Endures
Tasnim McCormick Benhalim

Do not think me distant or grieve when I am gone
for my soul has danced with light streams
and taken such delight in the whisper fine breath of air that holds
this life afloat and soars through blues of sky cascading pinks and
deep rich greens and browns rolling colors interplay that
have been my intimate companions and deepest teachers
heart soul deep preceding and transcending language
before I could speak

Surely this will carry and continue long after I am asleep
For the love endures as it always has
each and each and each
timeless in the dancing and embrace.

Punctured Sighs
Yasin Chines

Of the human fabric,
there is something oddly musical
about whimpered words
on the prayer mat,
near to or indeed accompanied by
an apocalyptic flood of tears.
An agony, raking at sweetness
with each punctured sigh

Truly Falling
Sabila Raza

The way you smile
The way you laugh
You sparkle - completely,
In pure happiness
It is not just a part of you
It is who you are
A joke found in anything
In the simple, ordinary and unexpected
All those around instantly enveloped
In the energy of your joyful innocence
Why was I so taken?
Without needing to think
You made my soul smile
An inner glow overwhelmed
Soothing reminding... reminders
In how small-singular-moments- connect
Living life
Meant finding,
My peace

My acceptance
Hope is always there if you can just see it
Like everyone else
I know your life was never perfect
You had your
Share of traumas and pain
Oppression was deeply planted
Well before eyes could open
But you still
Chose to smile
Chose to laugh
Whenever the chance
I can easily see spending year after year like this,
With you
I would never tire
All those things that guarded my heart
Without realization
Vanished

Is it that simple
When destiny gives you permission

glass heart
Malika Meddings

Thank you for my glass heart
This is where my life will start
Be broken shattered torn apart
Thank you for my glass heart

See right through to the centre place
All my tears are falling grace
Now you witness my clean face
I thank you for my glass heart

A glass heart to hold you bright
Shine right through original light
Light upon the dust - shadows
Light upon the rust - shadows

See right through back to the start

No more acting no more face
No more lying to misplace
The fear you give me from disgrace that
Dusted up my glass heart
The lies I told to save my face
The fears I told to fall from grace
The boasts I made to make a place that
Rusted up my glass heart

Shine right through now no more face
Tears can glow to save the grace
No more lying no more boasting
No more hiding glass heart
Shine right through me, now I start
To
Thank you for my glass heart

The City
Asiya Sian Davidson

In the city I walk entranced
I hear the hammer on the anvil
I press crushed petals to my lips
and every door holds the image of a sacred map
radiating circles and diamonds and stars
every house opens onto a
wellspring

in my room at night
I feel the pull of my heart
rise through the roof
and flow out through the
Cosmos

the ceiling is twenty metres high
I inhale with the *fuqara*
who gathering
in the garden of oranges
at that very minute
chant of
Life

unable to get there by foot
in the night alleyways
I stay home
in the room
in the centre of the
Universe

the city is made of the pure heart
of Being
its labyrinth laneways
artisans and traders, men and women
have scaled the sky on the rope of God
and brought His vision back
so that it echoes in every
courtyard

the full moon
rising over the fountain at *fajr* time
and the *adhan* calls
echoes in the dark of the
universe city
the same *adhan* that calls in my own heart
five times a day

I am the qamariyya of Sana'a
I am the warm sand fashioned into mud in Tarim
I am the fountain sweeper calling
'*Marhaba Hajja*' astonishing me,
expanding me in welcome
the olives that grow before the rise of the Rif
seed bathed in the light of the first creation
I am that light too

it would be easy to
stay for several lifetimes
in the city in the heart of the universe
cradled by eternity
rolling over in love
each day and each minute
a portal to the
moment

and this is why
we must live somewhere else
so far away
in the city that is not a city
in the buildings that have no heart

post-structural distortions
whose curves give way to jagged
and disjointed brokenness
where flat streets call our souls into heedlessness
and to hear the *adhan*
requires a dedicated
will

House of Cards
Mohammad Durrani

You've been down many paths before
in this life, you can own a 100,000 worlds
or anything physical you can conceive
the novelty wears off
you always return lacking that something.

Stop building houses out of decks of cards
placed on top of paper bridges
you have traded a handful of dust
for a chance at the Hereafter, and
access to the Eternal Consciousness.

It is time to stop playing around now,
even children grow up from the breast
and move onto solid food, then wisdom food
and finally, they hunt for the Spirit Food.

Become a hunter, a seeker of the Invisible
all secrets are awaiting the sharpening
of the inner vision of eye and ear
which combine, shaping vision of the heart
leading to the mine of unimaginable treasures,
the trove of The Living One, attainable only by
following the Way of Light.

1.618
Fikasophy

Just like the Golden Ratio
Nothing is coincidental
Everything is God's Divine Intervention
"Kun fa yakun"

If tonight is the night,

I've mentioned your name for a thousand months

The universe echoes Your Name on my behalf for a lifetime.

You!

Hu!

Before
Novid Shaid

Before, I thought it all a hopeless mess
Imagined all a helpless cry of distress
Considered all a hapless guess
Rejected all a heartless process
Abandoned all, a homeless essence
Until I found it **All a h**idden blessing
Discovered **All a h**opeful beginning
Accepted **All a h**istory of genesis
Unveiled to **All a h**eavenly gnosis

Paradise
Alan ʿAbd al-Haqq Godlas

Paradise,
even more beauty,
more love,
more truth,
more justice,
more life,
more joy,
more blessedness,
than you can ever imagine!
Go for it,
now!

Deep down,
you have always hungered
to be filled,
to be bathed,
every fiber,
every cell of your being,
saturated with Paradise!

You who are God's
lowly
poor
servant,
you deserve nothing;
yet you do deserve Paradise!

Set the bar that high,
and higher still!

Reach for it
now,
since now
is the only time
you can choose
to reach for it!

94

But beware!
After the flood
of honeymoon awe
will come
the demons
of disappointments,
heartaches,
and broken trusts
of unmet yearnings past!

"Never again
will I open my heart
to such suffering,"
you said.

And so, you
resigned yourself,
you settled,
you contented yourself
with a shack
in the middle of the desert
of your life.

No running water of love,
only a few drops
here and there,
enough to get by;
but at least
the gaping wounds
were shut!

So many days went by,
so many years!

But now, your hovel,
scheduled for bulldozing,
perhaps today,

perhaps next month,
next year.

Do you remember
the nightingale?
Can you still hear its song?

You are no longer
the lost bleeding child
you once were,
alone, with just
the shards of your
shattered dreams
slicing through your heart.

Now you can see
that where what once
were only fragments of glass,
ripped flesh,
crimson corpuscles
and shrieks knifing through the darkness
has always been
your Beloved's face,
which even now
is your Beloved embracing you!

So, if you remember
even a note
of the nightingale's melody,
if you can still
taste the fragrance
of the rose
and the jasmine,
let them rekindle
the longing!

You are of age now,
you can come into this tavern,
the door is open wide!

You know
that you can sit at a well-worn corner
of the bar,
and sip
one drop, one ache, at a time.

You know,
there is nothing here,
but your Beloved,
inviting you
to this ancient tango,
inviting you
to Paradise!

Divine Love
Nile Mystic

My heart was a burning village,
thirsty for the Amazonian rains
The idols that dwelled within me consumed every drop of love
Causing the drought,
that sparked the fire
Clouds are gathering veiling my heart
Fog is forming around me like a whirling dervish
The wind is descending carrying water from Baab Al Rayan
Lightning is striking
The thunder shouts:
repeat after me
La Ilaha Illa Allah
La Ilaha Illa Allah
La Ilaha Illa Allah

A Forgotten Conference
Cherif Al-Islam Abou El Fadl

Baba, do you hear them singing?
Their cries of joy shake the dust in plumes
I am covered and two shades darker
The food and tables, covered
Nothing is safe from their holy explications
in a language I cannot understand
but feel in tremors under my skin

Baba! Plumes of dust!
mixed with blood from my fingers and toes
cuts from fumbling clumsiness
the aisles have grown so narrow
they cajole me to twist and turn dancing with them
pressed to my chest through clouds of dust!

Baba! They sing!
I can hear them sing!
in a language I don't understand
my tears tell me this is real
They sing of being touched by your gentle, appreciative hands
Their regality forgotten by other hands
They sing in rage at Muslims' failures
They sing in excitement for what is to come!

Baba, you once wrote
that you fear the Islamic civilization is dead
it is not dead, Baba
Muslims are dead
deaf and blind to the boundless glory bound between trees

Baba, my love for trees
my youth speaking with them
now feels a timid memory
compared to this choir chanting heavenly hymns
of rage and joy--of the secret of what the angels knew not
of a divine humanity!

Baba, how does the dust rise like this
when it has been caked on for years?
Plumes! Clouds rising and twirling!
Ethereal dervishes laughing in Love
and my constant coughing and dripping nose
all this dust

Do they sense you in my hands?
Do they sense that I know these two hands belong to them more than
they belong to me?

If only every bookcase was made of top shelves!
they are living, breathing royalty to be exalted!
they sing the Islamic civilization--the civilization of the book--
will never die

they never needed me to dust them after all
it is I who needs them

Bulrushes

Ron Geaves

Forests
of
feathered fronds
made
Rumi ponder
surrender.

White silk
     bends
in
daylight
     turns
purple
to
breathe sunset.
Higher
     than giants
heavy-headed
slender
     bow
to the wind
but
never broken.
Jalaluddin
     I am in
your dream
scent
the mystery
of breath.

Each Orphan Day
Ray Lacina

You wake in every orphan day, after
they've gone, and think to call them
remember
press feet to the cold floor
rise
and yes you still have
the ones who grew with you, still have
the ones who shelter with you now
brother, sister, wife, child
but when you wake each orphan day
there's an absence felt
since the day the call came
however long ago the call came and
the soil, to steal an old metaphor,
that fed your roots that you fought so hard
to push your green shoots through
to grow beyond
is left dry by a rainless summer
salted by some passing army
and no matter how long
they've been gone
you remember her laughing as she blew out smoke
the mad glint in his eye when he was about
to embarrass you
and when some sweetness comes you want to call
them and feel their pride in you and when
something breaks you want so much
for them to lift you
up, to
carry you up
into a day and a place
a house cupped in green hills
in the morning of the world
when you were small and they were giant
and somehow you knew as they held you
that they would always hold you

always carry you up, but
now you rise each orphan morning
and the phone's a dead useless thing when
you reach
for it
then remember
you can't call.

Universal Integrity
Flamur Vehapi

Even the brainless planets,
Particles in this galaxy,
Circle around humbly
In a slow and quiet motion
Floating in the universe
And never colliding
With one another.

Each time they pass by one another
They spin around, and smile,
And when they leave they weep
For their spinning lovers.

This should be a great example
For clashing humanity
As a way of moving together
Towards Great Universal Integrity.

81:26

Ayesha Ijaz

when you measure everything
as good or bad

when progress leaves
no time for gratitude

when you live
between fear and rage

when you build up a horde
to keep out the riff-raff

when you kindly mistreat
those who just-don't-get-it

when the title is more important
than 'stepping in it'

when you step over women
to get to the front

when you silence a child
to speak to God

when you beat your wife
but cry for Palestine

when you raise yourself
on the backs of the disenfranchised

when you silence your heart
so it's just you… and more you

when you only see ugliness
in a world of beauty

when productivity leaves
no time for joy

when you measure your worth
by profit or loss

when you cross-dress your ego
and call it your soul...

Reality,
slips out of the unseen,
puts her arm around my shoulders
and wonders out loud:

So... where are you going?

Pilgrimage
Nabila Jameel

The Clock Tower
is a cheap ornament,
the plastic kind that sits on nearly
every auntie's mantelpiece, collecting dust.
Crudely designed, it still seems to pull a crowd,
almost like a place of worship, but not quite.

They talk about how it used to be:
none of this was here, nor this, nor that.
I could be in Dubai, or New York when standing
with my back to the Kaaba. I could be anywhere.

It makes me wish I was here five hundred years ago,
when the walk between Safa and Marwa didn't feel
like dodging Sales victims in the Trafford Centre.
I find the rock, all glazed and frozen in time,
where Hajra walked and ran in the heat for water.

I wish I was here just fifty years ago,
so I could see the remaining few bricks from the house
where the prophet Mohammad (peace be upon him)
lived with his wife Khadija. Now that place is a toilet block.

The cranes are taller than the Kaaba,
it's an industrial site, it's growing bigger,
the Kaaba is shrinking. There are imitations
of the west – KFC, greasy eateries,
Starbucks and Pizzerias,
convenience and coffee.

The Kaaba is the object in selfies, with prolonged
standing and huddling together of groups,
glowing with pride. Some frustrated pilgrims deeply
absorbed in prayer, frown and shake their heads.

We could be at the Colosseum,
the Empire State Building,
or the Eiffel Tower.

106

Pure Love

Ahmad Ikhlas

Love flows through me like the red liquid which contains iron.
Love is stronger and weightier than the latter mentioned in its purest
form
Love descends on my being like falling H_2O when the sky's face
weeps.
Like the wind love is an entity intangible but yet it is felt by the whole
body
I have been created by the Creator of love, destined for the nation of
the beloved and in return I am a lover

Untitled
Marissa Diaz

I had a family once
They tattooed their names on my skin
They told me stories and showed me pictures of all the beautiful ones
who came before me
and said "see little pearl, you come from them."

They would look at me as though I were the mountains and the sky
precious as the whole world
They gave to me because they wanted to
Never because they had to
And through this taught me that giving is more valuable than gifts

I had a family once
The smell of corn reminds me
Of a nourishment deep in my bones
Of fire and smoke that stuck to my hair
and made me smile whenever I laid down
The smell of belonging
wrapped in the universe of my pillow

The sun reminds me of them
The heat and the sand
Braving the ocean
Not even the most mountainous waves could take my safety
The cold reminds me of them
small fingers tingling and numb
And then their breath broken by smiles
bringing my hands back to life

They became my warmth

The air reminds me of them
hair blowing around the most beautiful faces
Making me think that perhaps God was
A person
A place

A time
A moment
With them

I had a family once
they tattooed their names on my skin
And then as people do
sometimes too swiftly,
they became the clouds
the sky
the trees
the water
The same red earth I come from

I had a family once
They tattooed their names on my skin
So that when the time came
and I would no longer see them
I could stare into the sacred waters where I was born
and in seeing myself
know how to find them

The Phoenix

Marguerite Lake

Stirring from the blackly whitened ash of obliterated self
She turns again towards the rising sun, ruffles her plumes,
Unfolds and spreads her crumpled wings and falls upwards
Borne forever aloft, she soars towards the summit of creation

There, the beckoning Lord resurrects her in all His glory
Ignites her heart with flames, unveils her eyes, caresses her soul
Washes her stiffened spine with flood-waves of silent ecstasy
Rejoices in the mirrored vision of His own redeeming grace

Blinded by the bright vision of her own resplendent soul
She contemplates creation through darkly light-filled eyes
Consumed to dust and ash, scourged by heaven's flames
She bows her head in acknowledgement of her Creator

Quickened by an overwhelming surge of love from the Beloved
She plummets earthwards once more to the wild and precious
Cauldron of life called earth; destined to reflect the One reality
Through the moment by moment unfolding of truth from within

Your Unletteredness, His Perfect Tongue
Barbara Flaherty

Ya Muhammad, His Prophet,
you came reading the unseen
book of the heart
to all the shattered parts,
the scattered voices within.

We said, Where is the hiding place?
You said, There is no hiding place.
When you ran in terror
from the holy cave
the sky was still filled
with the angel's speaking presence.

The Sovereign of the universe
ripped open your heart from within,
made your unletteredness
His perfect tongue. Made your fear
His perfect nest of mercy.

A Good Word
Iljas Baker

We talked of trees
that morning
it was winter and the trees
were bare
it was cold outside
I said
(remembering Surah Ibrahim)
a good word is like
a good tree
with
firm roots
skyward branches
fruit bearing

later you almost wept
and inside I kept repeating
good words
Arabic words
and became firm
in faith in our mother's
winter journey from
this life to the next

Light
Vedad Grozdanic

Always, go gently, into the good night:
with goodly reminder, conclude the day.
The next life has promises, filled with light.

Reward for good deeds is described as "bright;"
a rainy April has a sunny May.
Always, go gently, into the good night.

Glory to Him, Who possesses all might:
He follows a raindrop with golden ray.
The next life has promises, filled with light.

The righteous will see Him, in open sight:
the truth, in splendor, has ultimate say.
Always, go gently, into the good night.

Bones will dissemble, and spirit feel fright –
yet His plan unfolds, in a perfect way.
The next life has promises, filled with light.

The end is not dark, for those who do right:
the Hereafter houses eternal play.
Always, go gently, into the good night –
the next life has promises, filled with light.

Insaan
Matthew Bain

we are the forgetting intimates of Allah,
the ignorant go-betweeners of creation,
would-be correlators of temporal with Divine.

Wisdom courses nature's veins,
now all but over
as we lay waste
to heather hives
with hegemonic heresies.

Mottled butterflies danced this year
with iridescent spasms
riddled with meaning,
but we have armoured ourselves
against nature
with stupidity.

Move over, mind-death
and let us grasp once more
the precious silken thread of memory
harking back to primal harmony -
Rabb reflected in all things
like mother's face in baby's tears.

Grief
Nargis Latif

Going through the chocolate box of grief
Which one will i choose?
Bereavement? loss? Disappointment? regret?
They all seem so attractive.
How long will I dwell on each flavour
Each with its own aftertaste?

Going through the washroom of sadness
Which ones do I wash myself of first?
The stains of emptiness? hollowed out-ness? Moments I should have
loved more-ness?
This wash will take some time
Each fabric is so heavily soiled.

Reading through my library of denial
Which versions of self will I read first?
The story of a forlorn child, the painfully long yarn of solitude, the
tragedy with no ending?
They feel so heavy in my hands
Each page weighing a stone.

Cry your tears child, till the vessel is empty
Then cry some more.
Give this world its story through the ink of your wet eyes
Surrender to its tempo
Relent to its haunting melody
Till the final symphony chimes.

ﺏ - Voyage of Recovery

Rabia Saida

I lost my smile between waves
Of worry and dismay
By pools of disappointment
And frustration overwhelmed.
I looked into the mirror pond
And saw that it was gone
And knew I had to find it
Because it looked so wrong.
I had to tread water -
Recover shipwrecked humour
And laugh out loud
At the place
My smile overturned.
Laugh at the girl who tried to sail
Aboard a capsized boat
That sunk
and ran ashore
Because
The smile keeps us afloat -
Bā ' [6] is for *basma* and *bismillah*
Bā' - the boat of recovery.

---

[6] The Arabic letter *bā'* ﺏ

Resting Place
Yahia Lababidi

There are no maps for the land
my mind's eye is fixed upon
Instead a trail of wrecked ships
mark this treacherous path

My guide, a mysterious star
whose light dims if, briefly,
I happen to turn away -
and which glows brighter
when my heart's aflame.

The Snatching

Abdul Kareem Stone

I have oceans and forests within me,
I have skies
And when I close my eyes
I can see falling from a web of stars
A luminous mist onto these woods within.
From its dark silence oozes
The sound of the owl
And down by the beach,
In flickers of silver,
Fish jump in succession
And try to reach the mist of light
Until in a moment
The might of the ocean pulls them back
Or until one is snatched by the claws of the fish owl.
As the owl, like a thread of silver, flies away
It pulls at the fabric of water and sea,
Draining it of all its might
The roots of ancient trees begin to glow.
A light that wakes the sleeping birds.
The birds pluck illuminated leaves
And form a shining murmuration.
One by one a bird leaves this spectacle
And drops a leaf upon a sloping ridge
A nest is formed shining without strain
Its light creates for the first time
A vista of my inner whole.
I can make out a bridge
That spans across to a distant shore
A place I never saw before

The Cloaked Lovers
Arthur Skip Maselli

Her eyes are
    knitting needles,
my heart
       Her design,
Her words are golden gossamer threads,
sewn into a cloak,
    as clandestine
invisible as a spider's web,
dusted with dew
    and tangled light
we slip away like moon and stars
as dawn arrives to restore our sight
And she reveals the secret,
He is in all ways everywhere,
wherever we always are.

Oh, faint fever,
feel this ever-curing bond with You...
the sinuous slips of aloeswood
the interlocking of imagined fingers...
the indentation of Your proximity upon my soul
'tis the tincture of oud.

This love is a crossroad between
long and distant highways
    unseen
You are always there... I,
sometimes here, with her, yet
love is where there is
    not a where...
of this, dear God,
    I have become aware.

Now, I sit in shadows
    and listen to lovers
speak of their encounters...

"He was touching me," she said.
   He says, "she kissed me...
      then we woke beneath sheets,
  I remained in bed,
she made tea in the low angle morning light..."
all this, I saw whilst
     out of sight."

These are simple tales and plaints
   But You and I Lord,
we speak poesies into the solitude,
   Lovers like these say,
     "I - you,
       touch your - my soul,
     You - I,
       kiss my - your heart,
     we - You,"
       wake in quiet moments,
  Sight lingers behind my eyes
     in shadows of truths
I dip this porous cup
   into the ocean of my heart...
  to where Your rivers flow
  carrying the sweetness in the sunlight
    through the valleys of the dark.
    spilling love along the path.
We sip tea, now just Mustafa and me, oh Beloved...
  We two speak poesies.

If there were but only one star
  in an empty night,
I'd be able to imagine it
  disappearing...
    I'd worry - but why?
For You are every star...in this
  star-filled sky
You are the arc of my eye's leap...
  from one star spire to the other.
    I'll navigate in infinite circles if I must.

But it will take a billion disappearing stars,
    one after another into dust,
for You to go dark
    but they are always in Your sight
       wherever they are.

Send my eyes to the gallows
    banish me from my city walls
Muhammad was left by flesh
    and angels alike
orphaned time again and again

The silk road of love
    travels away from the heart
    and yet this same road
    is the unpaved path going in and in
    and in.

What trail can the feet follow,
    when flesh is shed
    when the mother and father are dead
    when the uncle has left
    when the tribe is cleft
when from the cave you fled
    awaiting the message
       to follow what the messenger said

Taken in by gypsies, left for alms
bodies dance with open palms
one up, one down
I, the center axis
You, where all reality collapses
into a point, a single unity
of being.
Love is the synapsis.

This heart is a star in my Beloved's sky,
    not an earthbound beacon.
The former follows Her an eternity,

the latter eventually disappears.
    Love is all that's left of me
as my body is poisoned with death
it slips away
    like a shell
        with every soul dislodging breath,
ever more, ever more
within the extinguished body
is the spirit's secret cure.

Study of molluscs at sunset, in three parts
Bushra Mustafa-Dunne

i.

when sunset bitters
I walk through darkness to kneel
to no one
but The One

treading darkness
like my first swim, how
I didn't drown?
Met the sea as a stranger, now

we are intimate
lovers, the best of friends
- maghrib and I,
the perilous ocean that
saves me every night
from myself.

Many things in this way are oceanic
many men are oceans.

When I see The Name written

I see the legs that walk to bend
when sunset is still sweet.

ii.

High tide: two men search for
mussels in Asilah, it is neither sea nor sand.
How their fingers must taste like sea salt,
always. Searching for sunlight, gold,
pink, onyx. Turning sand over, turning it
into clouds.
and I want to shout down to them

"the sun is already set!
Search after *fajr* and you will swim in
gold"

iii.

we cannot speak of them now:
the hands that search for purple-
black shells in a serene sea,
it would be the inversion of sanctity.

here, in the city we turn over every
exhale

like searching for pearls among
pebbles, praying
that in the inversion
there is another chance for life; an
inhale
we have forgotten how to embrace,

a sanctuary to exist within us that
cannot exist without,
we yearn
for indispensability.

(how our hands must taste
like the searching!)

The Valley of Khayal
Wajiha Khalil

The valley of Khayal is a warm, womb-like basin
buoyant with bodies of meaning where inspirations
stack stanzas like spines and grow the flesh of words

Angels flock to this full bellied land
inscribing the decrees and destinies
while infinite possibilities and prospects compete
for the most auspicious potential

Here, kiss the tree of *kismet*
with *nur* kindled foliage
that reveal could-be possibilities
as the winds of wonder tickle the leaves
revealing new consequences in the combinations
of fortuity

Wonder beyond
where the river meets the creek
at the corner where the ruby rock reflects names
pull a puddle into your palm
one sip will fill your mouth with poetry
and quench the quest for art

Honoring horizons adorn heavenly hearts
As the Beloved said,
 "Reflect upon the horizons
and in yourselves
until you become sure of the truth"

Rest for a time
in the cave for *khalwa*
until you've harnessed that inner glow
that will speak on your behalf
silence is the speech of knowers

Khayal winds fill your lungs with scents

that dye with every breath
a new color of fragrance
that attunes you to the frequencies
of harmonious channels
to the Sacred Prophet ﷺ
the melody that never leaves you
more intimate than life itself

Pluck from the mango orchard
where the juice rhymes meters
of freshly squeezed illumination
get lost within the grape vineyards
crush them with your syllables
and intoxicate

There are landscapes
with padded moss between jagged jewels & rocks
the watery pools reflect the clouds
that cast shadows but create contrast
for the sun

There is a forest
few visit through its narrow path
of towering redwood trees
that can feel frightening
to the outsider
Instead, acquaint yourself
pass through with greetings
intertwine for a while
and salaam upon these friends

The meadow is ripe
with Birds of Paradise
and emerald colored grass stones
Animals speak various tongues
that translate through the grace of Khayal

The fresh scent of pine needles
undertones of jasmine flowers

soft whispers of lotus families
are always revealing new hymns
to those who venture here

Words are incubating
growing tempo & harmony
new poems are born every day
birthed in secret
in the valley of Khayal

an improv
Yohosame Cameron

salt & silver
pine sap blossom
i like my poetry dangerous
cream with my coffee
dhikr with my altitude
sickness

in repose: recite delight and delirium
death & the dream king sipping
rebel puehr tea and laughing
"she used to be delight"
now she blows bubbles
of different colored fish
that children see clearly
so speak dearly
and forever hold your Peace

i wrap my mᴜsˤħaf in a shawl
that used to wipe the sweat
from your blessed brow and now
i can still smell your oudh like essence
making me light... headed in the right direction
my reflection shimmering simmering
baking slowly and raw

edible night shade uni.verse
no rehears.al ~just dance with abandon
to find out what remains
truth stains of
trains bound for glory

cinnamon lick and smile
pools of perfect *sajdah*
signed sealed and delivered
between dawn & sunrise
she sighs and i recite delight
that used to be delirium

Stranger[7]

Toneya Sarwar

In a moment
Everything changed
The world shifted gears
While history was rewritten
Two buildings
Tall and proud
Crumbled like sandcastles
On a sandy beach
As they fell
Nations fell with them
Concrete and dust
Veiled stories and souls
hearts shake
Eyes weep
Heads turn and
Fingers point
Fear envelops me
My veil heavy like armour
Will the jury be
Executioner too?
The train is rush-hour full
But people feel alone
The silence is deafening
As revenge pollutes the air
Minutes feel like hours
A stranger in my homeland
Unrecognizable
Will I see him again?

In a moment
Everything changed
The world shifted gears
While history was rewritten

---

[7] September 11, 2001 is the day the earth stood still. It changed the narrative of Islamic and secular world relations. I was in my London office when the news broke. Fear of backlash immediately filled the air, and as a visible Muslim I was afraid of being an easy public target. It was the first time I thought about removing my headscarf. The 'him' refers to my husband who I was desperate to get home to.

American Culture

Rabea Benhalim

Fear has
acquired
Thickness.

Clogging our air,
Suffocating
ordinary spaces.

Children's bedrooms,
airplanes,
cafes.

Seeping into
the space between
old lovers.
Engulfing
the distance across
dining room tables.

So heavy
it confines some
to their beds.

How About We
Sukina Pilgrim

How about we tell stories so beautiful
That all illusion fades into darkness.
How about we tell stories of our truth
The beauty and the breaking
And how we're now
elevating like lotus flowers towards the sun
How about we tell stories
Of dignified defiance and triumph
Of fathers with hearts like lions
And mothers whose love
Could breathe life
To dead bones -
You know, I have a soft spot
For the oppressed ones
Those who found hope
When the tide was low
Let's talk of the ordinary hero
The everyday revolutionaries
Who will be forgotten by History
Not featured in documentaries
For newly woke folk
To quote on their insta-stories
No these, free women and free men
Gave life to children
Who could dream freely
And write light with a free pen
Let's speak then, of women
whose femininity
Did not hinder
the manifestation of their dreams
You know those queens
You find them in every nation
The brave ones
Often unnamed ones
Who cared not for ruptured reputations
Or the insults of weak men

Nothing could break them
Let's speak then
About the wonders
Of this journey called life.
Let's sing to the Earth
and tell our children
Stories of the universe
Plant seeds that invite them
To travel when they dream
to realms unseen
So they can see their reflection
In the stars, up close
How about we tell our stories so beautifully
That we allow beauty to be our reality
How about we own our narrative
So that we are not spoken about
But spoken to
How about I tell you
My story

Urban Mawlids
Wajiha Khalil

This evening
The old tray is showing use
The 'lemon, lavender, mint' organic tea
Was the chit chat
The elderly Arab woman & I
Indulged coffee
We desperately needed after
that Arabic poetry
She told us how
Her husband died on Hajj
And due to road closings
Was buried in the graveyard of martyrs
A circle of vulnerable hearts
We talked boundaries
Frequencies
service
Marifa
spiritual recourse
And secrets
One of them
She knew Allah as a child
Without any messenger
And would write him a letter
And place it in the Moonglow
To be read
I felt my heart open
Like a lotus flower
Even while the cake trays needed fixing
This evening
A night journey
Between the sacred precincts
Of my sisters' hearts

Qarawiyyin Song
Asiya Sian Davidson

sing me one of the old songs
from the days when the doors
were never shut
and when the water flowed
into every household
sing me your song

my mind has grown tired
wanting to know
all the while the breath tells
this silent expanse is growth

don't rush, watch how
uncle listens to the fountain
grandmother kisses your hand
a few dirhams are a paltry exchange
for the surrender in her gaze

sing me a song that we all remember
when time came down from above
and gnosis burned like an ember
in every chest
sing me your song of love

Red Sulphur
Nura Tarmann

Joy arose clamouring for something red
Like flowers greeting the sunshine
Red toenails
Lips leaving a red mark
Mother's cooking spoon
I remember red pomegranate seeds
Red beet salad
A red heart somewhere drawn small and delicate
Trying to convey
Drops of life
Blood dripping through a canister
Red
Life equating Love
Struggling to be passed on and on and on
Sitting and waiting
Incantations are repeated
The Red Sulphur prayer
"Pray" grandmother says
And hands me red prayer beads
A red turban
On the head of an old woman
Little red flowers on a child's dress
Mother's comforting arms
Red skies at dusk
Father gives me a red dress
How did this turn into a red tale?
Perhaps the message lies in the rubric cube
That is twisted round and round like
Red Rubaiyat tales repeated

Queens

Yasmine Ahmed-Lea

I don't want to
Slay every day
I don't want to
Slay anyone actually
I'm not okay with
Being Fierce
Or my own
Girlboss
Going out to get it
Being a
Get up and go kind
Where are the slogans
For the ones who want a quieter life
Why must we all be
On top of the game
Why do we all need to aspire to be
Yasss queens
Not even sure
What that really means
Some of us tread lightly
In this world full of
Loud and proud
Some don't want to be
Everything every day
In this world full of
All talk and
No action
Empowerment
Tastes differently
To me
I dream of silence
Women in market places
In Mauritania
Going about their day
Not looking to slay
Or Queen

Or Be
On Fire
Giving up dreams
Of owning Empires
Not watching our moves
Fingers on the pulse
They are the peacemakers
Walking graciously
By the light
Of the calming moon
Beams reflected
In their luminous smiles
Eyes in the stars in the stars
Hearts
Basking in grace.

Zaghareet
Efemeral

dedicated to the martyrs, the *kandakaat*[8] and the descendants of
diaspora
January 18th 2019

diaspora watches revolution
on mobile phones
watches their
crimson blood spill
on blank paper
emerald leaves unfurl
from cracks in the ebony asphalt

the *kezan*[9] runneth over
with blood

---

[8] Derived from a Nubian word meaning 'queen', used to describe contemporary Sudanese women revolutionaries. Historically, the women who ruled during the Kingdom of Kush.
[9] Term used to refer to the former president, his regime and those in military power

yesterday
today

the crowning bastard of empire
still rules
stillborn
his wizened frame
heaving

I have never been so certain
of his end
as when they imprisoned the *kandakaat*

only for *zaghareet*[10] to contract
through concrete and steel
out and into
the world anew

"*Hurriya,*
salaam,
wa 'adala"[11]
was carried
on every tongue

Moses' sister
went out and
into the crowds
brought her brother home alive

don't you know?
when women
zaghrit revolution
they have already seen
rebirth
they are celebrating
tomorrow

---

[10] *Zaghareet/Zaghrit:* ululations/ululate
[11] freedom, peace, justice

Peace Be Upon You

H I Cosar

Peace Be Upon You
O Prophet of Allah!
Blessings be upon you
Greetings upon you
Perfection of creation
Our Salvation
Each poem written for you is forever a draft
You - the final seal.

O Prophet of Allah!
Your birth made the abstract concrete
You brought the unreachable close
You the chosen one
Interpreter of the Universe
Mediator between
Slave and Master
The brightest star mirroring the Vastness

The humble river courting the Eternal Sea
The silk veil protecting Beauty
The echo of Earth's Harmony
The perfume of Heaven's serenity

O Prophet of Allah!
Beloved of Allah!
Flawless, perfect and complete one
The key to the door
Guarding the key to the Throne
You the crown of all metaphor
Peace be upon you O peace!

Muzdalifa
Abdalhamid Evans

You've drunk from the Fountain
   You have been on the Mountain
      Now don't get lost in Muzdalifa

You've kissed the Black Stone
   It's time to pick up stones
      Just don't get lost in Muzdalifa

It's just a stepping stone
   So go pick up your stones
      And don't get lost in Muzdalifa

You'll taste the Great Relief
   Can cut off all your grief
      Just don't get lost in Muzdalifa

Soon it will all be clear
   A stranger in the mirror
      Just don't get lost in Muzdalifa

Just make a rough bed
   Try and lay down your head
      And don't get lost in Muzdalifa

This night will go by
   Just get some shut-eye
      And don't get lost in Muzdalifa

You've nearly made it through
   To relief you never knew
      Just don't get lost in Muzdalifa

You called from the Great Plain
   Where the Mercy falls like rain
      Just don't get lost in Muzdalifa

There's knowledge in your bones
  Just go pick up your stones
And don't get lost in Muzdalifa

If Beginnings Can Be Holy
Murtaza Humayun Saeed

Leave me in a quiet place to pray
Where I can receive the energy
To face the new day
A place close to nature
Re-vi-tal-i-zing
Ox-y-gen-a-ting
Calm-ing
Leave me there early in the day
Leave me alone (if you can)
So I don't have to feel embarrassed
If I cry
Thinking about how hard it is
To remain in a calm place inside
Soon the traffic will start
The noise of business
Will burst the stillness
I don't mind the cold
Soon everything will be gold
Perhaps I'm too sensitive
But if beginnings can be holy
I can return to this quiet place inside
Re-vi-tal-i-zed
Ox-y-gen-a-ted
Calm-ed
So leave me here a while
So leave me here a while
Till I can feel the sun rise inside me.

Prior To Fajr (Kerala, S.W. India)
Paul Abdul Wadud Sutherland

Clingy night smothers every bird song.
A lorry's stretching moan on the empty road
honed-winged cicada subdued at this hour
a solo passenger jet ploughs the stars.

By the two-sided wide-open window
I'm sat, listening for the earliest crackle
from the yard a pre-dawn cockerel's call.
My bare feet settled on the shiny floor -
a natal coolness like a scent from nowhere
and floral gaps in high fronds stay in stasis.

The cockerel's, then the human-voiced *adhan*.
I wait and when I hear will go and shower off
this heat, dress and smooth on my white turban
prepared to sink my forehead at *fajr* prayer -
honour Muhammad in the month of his birth.

the watches of the night
Idris Mears

o Beloved!
Your troops have overrun
the defences of my heart
and chased sleep from the field

my petty loves are banished
from Your conquered realm
and i patrol the borders of my soul
in the watches of the night
to guard against their sneaking back

may my paces in the dark be counted

Heartbreak

Joel Hayward

Without a coat I'm drenched in the grief
that falls as a winter downpour

It drips from my nose and chin
and I shiver beneath stars that play deaf when I plead

I beg them to share the secret of where
the Angel of Death took her sweet soul

Their silence kills me

They know! They must!

A hollow quietness fills the space where we once walked
talking of a future that has become a beetle on its back

The conspiring earth holds her body
but offers no words of comfort

The earth has shaken down our city
yet now minds his business

I call down to my wife
knowing she can't hear

I ask that droopy moon if she's with Allah and happy

He just stares

I search inside myself
but I am as empty as my faith and prayers

for a while

Even Allah says nothing
that I can understand

I cannot find her and I cannot feel her
I trudge in winter rain and shiver

Things I didn't understand
Yasmine Ahmed-Lea

When you swirled your tea
In the porcelain saucer
Like worlds colliding
Milky ways immersing into you
And you drank
That smile on your face
At simple pleasures

I only understand it now

When you wore cool cotton
Bright colours enveloping
Your deep brown skin
And how free you looked
Wind billowing through your soul
I only understand it now
When you ate so wholeheartedly
Mmming to me about the lusciousness
Of the taste, the smell,
of the God-given blessing
Of senses

I only understand it now

When you left your hair long
In that perfect plait, sliding down your back
So elegant shining even without light
So unchanged, unscathed
Lace scarf covering your crown

I only understand it now

When you were you
Through and through
Every day
And even though I didn't think

144

You could leave
You did
Because you always do
What you want to do

I only understand it now.

I Want to Say Your Name
Shahbano Aliani

i want to say Your name
over and over again

over and over
and over again

in words carried by Love
rising like a spiral
from the core of all being
in my being

i want to say Your name
with heart-breaking tenderness
and call You by the million names
of endearment and beauty
ever uttered, by anyone

i want to say Your name
and tell you i love You
over and over again

over and over
and over again

until i have
spent all my words
all my tears

145

all my strength
all my breath

until i can
think no more,
say no more
breathe no more

be no more

and in that stillness
finally hear
walls, doors,
floors and ceilings
grains of sand,
blades of grass
sky, clouds,
trees and air
all speaking only
of You
and love for You

Knowledge That is Shy
Medina Tenour Whiteman

There is knowledge that is shy,
dodges knowledge vampires
with their ravenous jawed eyes
and colander stomachs.

This knowledge didn't listen at school,
doodled through every textbook
and watched the swallows
out of the science block window.

It waits for you while you stand
slack-mouthed, spaced out
by a fountain on a wooded hill
noticing only the quick undulations
on the green surface, the sludgy floor
before announcing itself: *Hi!*

This knowledge whistles casually
on the police taped edges
of disaster areas, sidling in between
the last phone call and the sigh
inserting itself, a comma, no argument.

Its footnotes kick up leaves,
stub their toes deliberately
on furniture it then
surreptitiously removes.

It doesn't build up, fact upon figure,
but peels off in archaeological layers
burns iron shapes in neat appearances
drops spiders down collars and
seats itself innocently in chairs
vacated by the shrieking pranked.

This knowledge is free but

still must be bought
no ads will defray its existence
and its scholars, its teachers, its institutions
won't make you cleverer
but wider
more swimmable
until you see it doesn't creep up on you at all
but chips away at the plaster
you hide your light behind
an inside job, a regular cat burglar
of personal hindrances
leaving only its own brilliance
reflected in your awe-struck face
a shine that cannot be caged in an image
and pinned down, struggling, to a scrolling screen
like sushi for bottomless information appetites
and most would not take it for knowledge but
acceptance, or forgiving, or longing, or love,
but it will know you from the inside out
until you know yourself.

This knowledge will not give you riches
it will prove that you are gold.

First Night of Ramadan
Daniel Abdal-Hayy Moore

A single stone is thrown in
and the canyon resounds with the

hallelujahs of angels

A single breath contains the
known and unknown universes

Back behind edgeless
space are motions that

vibrate the heart

Back behind ancient mountains and
historical intricacies

a shadow gives way to Light that has a
door in it to

let us through

We take no step that
doesn't bring us nearer

One sip and the oceans disappear

One glance and the skies
bend closer to hear our

emptiness

One heart-wrench elegant elevation
and we're on a

plateau tossing a stone in the dark
that never stops echoing

Paradise
Vedad Grozdanic

How many memories have been made?
How many musings of gentle hearts?
Few are the ones, in our minds, that stayed.
A whole disintegrates into parts.

How many feelings have we captured?
How many benign people have cried?
Youth is a precious time, enraptured;
we did not preserve it, though we tried.

O, my people: death is approaching.
Let us contemplate what lies ahead.
O, my people: death is encroaching.
The Hereafter will be in its stead.

The realm of pain is a certainty;
the realm of bliss will remain for 'aye.
We can dissipate uncertainty:
our spirits can, toward Paradise, fly.

Prayer of the Wayfarer
Abdus Salaam

يَا مَن اسْمُهُ دَوَاءٌ وَذِكْرُه شِفَاءٌ
(*Oh You whose Name is medicine and its mention healing*)

Empty my Heart,
To embrace all forms
Both vices and virtues
So I may turn and say

اللّهُـمَّ بِاسْمِكَ
(*Oh Allah in Your Name...*)

150

At Thy threshold, I stand
With the yearning of a Moses
And a mountain of sins
Show Thy countenance once more
So I may turn and say

أَلَا بِذِكْرِ ٱللَّهِ تَطْمَئِنُّ ٱلْقُلُوبُ

(Verily in the remembrance of Allah do hearts find rest)

Take *my* prayers
and acts of worship
Through which I adorn my soul,
So I may turn and say

أَنتُمُ ٱلْفُقَرَاءُ إِلَى ٱللَّهِ وَٱللَّهُ هُوَ ٱلْغَنِيُّ ٱلْحَمِيدُ

(it is you who stand in need of God - God is the Rich and is worthy of all praise)

Neither in the silence of the monk's retreat,
Nor the pilgrim's way do I seek
Unveil Your particular Face
So I may turn and say

فَأَيْنَمَا تُوَلُّوا۟ فَثَمَّ وَجْهُ ٱللَّهِ

(So wherever you turn, there is the Face of Allah)

Calamity finds its way to me
Patience has gone astray
Bestow a Khidr on this path of Yours
So I may turn and say

لَّا مَلْجَأَ مِنَ ٱللَّهِ إِلَّا إِلَيْهِ - فَفِرُّوٓا۟ إِلَى ٱللَّهِ

(There is no refuge from Allah except Him - flee to Allah)

Prayer is beloved to me
My servanthood I shall not abandon
Remove any trace of Lordship I have
So I may turn and say

151

وَلَذِكْرُ ٱللَّهِ أَكْبَرُ

(and the remembrance of Allah is greater)

Give another drop or two
Of the wine which intoxicates
before the creation of its vine
So I may turn and say

إِنَّا لِلَّهِ وَإِنَّا إِلَيْهِ رَاجِعُون

(from Allah we come and to Him we return)

Water takes on the colour
Of the vessel
Fall prey to my opinion-net
So I may turn and say

صِبْغَةَ ٱللَّهِ وَمَنْ أَحْسَنُ مِنَ ٱللَّهِ صِبْغَةً

(take) colour from Allah, and who is better than Allah at colouring

Who has eyes to see Layla
Save the one You accompany
Deliver me from the night of the soul,
So I may turn and say

سُبْحَٰنَ ٱلَّذِىٓ أَسْرَىٰ بِعَبْدِهِ لَيْلاً

(Glorified be He Who carried His servant by night)

To cover became compulsory in the sea of Love
Who shall cross save the deaf dumb and blind?
Uncover then the shoreless in this drop
So I may turn and say

هُوَ ٱلْأَوَّلُ وَٱلْآخِرُ وَٱلظَّاهِرُ وَٱلْبَاطِنُ

(He is the First and the Last, and the Outward and the Inward)

O Wayfarer! Kiss thy prayer beads and adorn thy Self
For at the centre of this journey,
there is none but Him!
With each bead, turn and say

شَهِدَ ٱللَّهُ أَنَّهُ لَآ إِلَٰهَ إِلَّا هُوَ

(Allah bears witness- there is no god save Him)

Ramadan
Yahia Lababidi

month of quiet strength
and loud weaknesses

when our stubborn habits
and discarded resolutions

are re-examined under the regard
and rigorous slowness of fasting

testing our appetite
for transfiguration

month of waiting and wading
through the shallows to the Deep.

Prayer
Tazmin H. Uddin

I didn't
raise my hands
My palms,
didn't kiss the sky
With no words
and all heart,
my soul sought.
Hu answered.

An Honest Poem
Ray Lacina

Sometimes rock bottom
is a false bottom
you fall through
into the long deep void
and falling feels like a held breath
someone else is holding
and you can't let it go
and you fall.

And sometimes the room goes dim
and outside you imagine twilight
or the slanting gold of right before
but where you are
breathing in
breathing out
is dim.

And sometimes the wind hits the trees just right
and you feel them inside you
the wind the trees their meeting and the rustle of it

feel it all
inside you
all through you
everywhere.

Sometimes you sit on your folded feet,
hands cupped in your lap
in front of your chest
under your chin
and the ceiling is for a flicker paper thin
the walls, the floor, for a minute, a stretch of minutes
an hour
is a smudge on a window
and beyond
above the room all around you
is something.

Thrumming in the heart of you
answers
something.

A Blink of an Eye
Toneya Sarwar

Posing in front of long mirrors
With high heels too big, that
I stumble and fall.
Now in the reflection I see
Another face like mine, but not
As my daughter pretends to be me

A teenager's bedroom walls
Plastered in timelines and formulae,
I'm rehearsing, practicing, anticipating the worst…
The same exams but a different time as
my son painfully prepares for his first.
A cake and balloons to celebrate
A decade plus eight
When I said; I do and I will
After all these years,
Of highs and lows
these words ring true still
I close my eyes and wonder
Where has the time gone?
Was it stolen or did it get lost?
Or is it that life has a way of moving on.

One thing I know to be true
I'm not alone as I ponder and wonder
As I ask Him with a prayer and a sigh
"Do not leave me to myself
For even a blink of an eye…"

Keeping Watch
Khadijah Lacina

with before dawn silence
coyote slips between
fogbathed branches
the moon leafed across
greybrown fur i feel her
turn watch me musky
scent my head filled
with forest i stand
alone at the open
door knowing one
morning the fog will
lift and i will follow
her call deep
into the night
home

Love Letter to Sudan
Mariam Akhtar

I found Orion's belt
every night I looked for you
we sat in the back
of pickup trucks
on our way to the Nile
our feet became
some kind of dusty red
from soft steps
in your warm earth
your women
are so beautiful
your men
are beautiful
and your children
are beauty personified
every handshake
and every smile
has glowed with sincerity
each cup of *shai*
and all the sweets
I've been fed
and fed again
sit sweetly in my stomach
I'm sure your smoky scent
will race around in every
capillary of my lungs
once I'm back home
you've lent me your shoulders
in nights full of celebration
I ran down your sandy dunes
and laughed with my loves
as we rolled down
your essence of blood glass
in the heat of your sun
our skin browner
and brighter than when we arrived

the rise in melanin
a testimony to our growth
the stars grew with us
multiplying as our hearts exploded
into the sky
spread across the earth
reflected in the dark of night
Barry White played
in the back of white 4x4s
as I looked out of windows mesmerised
convinced we were in space
somewhere beyond the life
we'd left behind
Sweet Dreams really are made of this
euphoria in experiences
mingle with oud and dust
in the ancient pyramids
of memories I hope to preserve
like those preserved
in the chambers of their tombs
for eternity
I'm convinced if I die here
it'll be because
I am from your soil
and I am yours
just the way the constellations intended
I'll be buried beneath your sky
settling with the sun
and rising with the moon
under your glorious canvas
my black hinna'd fingertips
trace your marks
left on my sleepy skin
ice cold lemon and mint
lingers on my tongue
as I fall into a hazy jet lagged stupor
I must sleep now
but until next time
so long land of sun, sand, sweetness and sincerity

Sorry
Muneera Pilgrim

I thought sorry would change the whole world
I thought sorry would spin the planet back on to its correct axis
I though sorry would make the flowers grow in winter as well as in
spring
I thought sorry would make the birds sing
I thought this one word would convince the sun to rise in the west if
only for this one day
I thought sorry would have the ability to make the sun shine after
Maghrib or a waxing moon glow after dawn
I thought sorry would be enough to end wars, to dry tears, reincarnate
the dead
Lazarus is with us
I thought it would unwidow the widow, unorphan the orphan
I thought it would unite nations and tribes
Your sorry was meant to pull that thorn out of my side
I guess I thought the whole world would celebrate because you said
this one word
sorry
So now I'm sorry, coz I thought that sorry would be enough
I thought it would be enough to feed the famished and clothe the
needy
House the homeless and enrich the poor
What's more I thought this lone word could emancipate corrupted
systems, topple despotic regimes
I put so much worth in these five letters but it's just a word or so it
would seem
I thought your sorry would provide medical aid for countries in need
I thought your sorry would show non believers how to pray
I thought your sorry could paint rainbows and make doves fly away
I thought your sorry would give a heart back to his abuser and her
abuser and their abuser and wipe their memory clean
I thought sorry would reenter his cold body become unbloody and
travel back up the shaft of the gun
Sorry was supposed to be Yvonne Ruddock toasting herself on her
50th birthday "Dear God I give thanks for all of my friends I've
known since school.

Like alchemy I thought your sorry could turn water into wine
Or at least I thought your sorry would heal faster than time
I thought sorry would kiss me on my neck, and travel down my spine
I thought these words would hold my hand and lead me through the
dark
I thought your sorry would be like new life leaving you and finding a
new home lighting up my womb or a comforting glow in the corner of
my room
I thought sorry would be enough to sway me
to woo me
to fool me
I put so much weight on to this one word
I truly truly thought sorry would be so much
But it's not and it doesn't so I'm sorry but sorry is not enough

For You Mother

Aasifa Usmani

Tomorrow is the fortieth day of her passing
Tomorrow is the fiftieth day of lockdown,
I write drafts and unfinished lines
they forced and ordered locking Dastageer Sahab Sufi shrine:
mother that must have deeply afflicted your soul...
you exist, like sufi shrine, like warmth of your shawls, like milk to
sustain, like forehead prostrating on the prayer mat.

I read your obituary without your name mentioned
my relief: your name Khalida, means - everlasting,
so many things, occurrences and objects have your presence
embedded
my first memory of everything, suckling and surrendering.
Your hands were like the crown of a swan
Mother for me is the first immortal memory,
no curfew and no silence can ever snuff out the resistance,
this bold resonance amid lockdowns,
Here I kiss your scars.

Medina Baye is Calling
Sukina Pilgrim

Here we lay
Our prayer rugs
On the ground
Like a picnic blanket
And feast on worship.
We swallow *salawat*
Like grapes -
The sweet juice
Trickles
Down
Our
Throats.
Here we sit
Swaying gently
As His names
Wash over our bodies.
Heaven is our canopy
The *Maghrib* sky
Is transforming into *Isha*
And there is something
So magical
In witnessing
The first stars
Arrive.
Here
The villagers
And travellers alike
Gather to recite
Utterances so light
They sail to heaven
Under angelic wings.
Our voices weave
Into a golden tapestry -
The breath of the faithful
And of the grateful
Make marks

On our hearts
That will never leave.
Here
Our guides glide
Through the streets
Like clouds in the sky
And rain beauty
And piety
Upon us -
Our palms are open
As are our hearts
Fertile
And fragile
And we never leave empty handed.
Here I dress
Like a woman from the Sahara
Where the veil is thin
Between this life
And the hereafter
Here.

Realm of The Believers

Jessica Daqamsseh

the making of souls
an elusive entanglement of spirits
winding through ether
penetrating realms
of unfathomable wonder
whispering softly
immersed in divine connection
whispering wishes diverted down byways
lying dormant for eons as souls meander
in search of their golden map--
a ticket to salvation
a restorative redemption
a circling back home
the realm of the believers
where our souls first were born

Enlightenment from Nature
Flamur Vehapi

The world is full of lessons,
Everywhere you look
You see a teacher,
And everything you hear
Speaks a message,
And whatever you touch
Shares its secret.

Nature imparts wisdom
To those who listen.

Right now,
As the stream flows
And the rocks roll
Through the pure water
There is a calming sound
That teaches peace
Within our hearts.

Speakers Corner Ramadan 2017
Asma Khan

Coming from a friend on his way to a station no one knows until they meet it
Fearing only that he will be there too soon
Clever complicated man aware of his hisness ending - not safe with *Al Qadr* not entrusted to *Ya Wali*
he has lost his way, anxious and stumbling, for logic and wit cannot keep him here nor explain anything anymore.
I pass by souls still in that place he used to be - where words flow easily, passionately, louder than the Tower of Babel and just as incoherent
Bemused by their lack of comprehensiveness I stare,
Briefly turn away and see the *huu* of grass and trees, a realm above and beyond this confusion
Such continuous jackdaw noise reaches this fasting, silent listener held enthralled by her inner state *Ya Batin*
In the latter bubbles a silent laugh shared with another passer-by, look at us endearing humans striving to put the puzzle of *Alast*[12] together,
Living in this upside down world where we wake as Ali said when we die
Until then feeling our way in shadowy darkness, waiting for that flash of lightning by which we glimpse the whole then rush to explain it to each other
Why not just let the guide *Ya Hadi* do his work from the start
Why don't we wait in silence for the next Breath to reveal itself witness along with *Al Shahid* the dreams, the visions of our True connectedness?
Why not always walk hand in hand with one who is Light and our secure protecting, loving friend - *Ya Hafeez, Ya Nur*
Why not have a lifetime of awake flying dreams and reach the stars with eyes wide open and see the signs of *Haqq* everywhere
Why not? Asma, why not?

---

[12] *Alastu birabbikum* Am I not your Lord? (Qur'an 7:172) the primordial covenant.

Ramadan is Listening
Medina Tenour Whiteman

Ramadan is listening
by which I mean we learn to attend
leaving tongues curled against palates
reluctant to come unstuck
and clutter silence.

It cups its hand around an ear
knows hollow and resounding
like the back of its ample hand
which, palm up, brings feasts
only mouths that stay closed
can taste.

This month is an aunt
that bustles into your house
compliments you on the rugs then
rolls up her sleeves and does the dishes
before you can tell her to stop.

She pours nitric acid down your drains
the ones you've coated with cooking oil
pulls out books from your shelves to dust
with an "Ooh, that looks interesting,"
the ones that have bookmarks left
halfway in from six years ago
and now you pick them up where you left off
or give them away.

This matriarch gives your kids a rocket
for leaving their wet towels on the floor
and though she frays your nerves
you're thankful someone has the pluck
to say so and still be missed
when she leaves.

Ramadan is listening,

gathering stories to go away with,
keeping them 'til next year
in her voluminous
coat pockets,

more spacious

than the distance

from here

to forever.

Attention Please

Yacoob Manjoo

Hey guys!
I wrote a new post this morning,
and it's literally the most important thing in my world today.
Won't you like it?
Share it?
Comment?
You don't need to say anything meaningful.
Heck, you don't even have to *read* it…
Just acknowledge my effort.
(Ding! Ding! Ding!)
Thank you!

I put a new video up!
Take a look.
Ain't it cool?
Tell all your friends.
And don't forget to subscribe!
(Click… Click)
Awesome!
You're the best!

The most profound thought crossed my mind.
I just **had** to tweet it.
Didn't you see it?
Seriously…you need to follow me.
This thing is about to go viral!
(… Click…)
Great stuff, man!

Just posted a new picture.
This one's really arty…
Gonna get a lot of attention soon.
Hop on before everyone else!
Won't you give it a heart?
.
.
.

.
No?
OK. Not this time, I guess.

This new status I wrote is amazing!
Hold on. Lemme put it up.
Can't wait to see my contacts pushing up the views.
.

.

.

5 minutes and no views?
Is the WiFi working?
Maybe they're all busy.
Yeah.. that's it.
Just bad timing.
They'll come around.
Just in case though, let me send it directly.
(Tap...tap...tap)
There. Done.
.

.

.

Seriously?!
Where the heck is everyone?

OK...OK. I know.
This one is going to wake you guys up for sure.
You'll love it!
(Click)
.

.

.

Huh?
Still nothing?
I don't get it.
I tagged all the influencers. Used all the right hashtags.
But still nobody says a word!
Am I invisible?!
Might as well be...

But why?
I liked them.
Followed them.
Commented when I didn't really have anything useful to say.
And what do I get in return?
Nothing.
Zilch.
NADA!
Why do I even bother?
Do I need to put up a damn billboard to get your attention?!
What will it take to reach you?
Am I not important enough for 5 seconds of your time?!
Come on!
You need to see this....You need to see **me**!

.

.

.

Just a little star. A Like. A share.
Something, dammit!

.

.

.

Fine!
I'll just leave.
I don't need you anyway.

And with that, (s)he stopped caring about others' attention, and turned the focus inward. And lived happily ever after.

Letter to my self

Nura Tarmann

I don't like western definitions, cold, dead, meaningless labels
Schizophrenia, we call it opening
Bi-polar, we say expansion and contraction
Autistic, we say blessed
We say love, they say chemical reactions
We say remembrance, they say obsessive, compulsive mumblings
They say anxiety and fear, we say God forgive us
Tell me was Rimbaud insane or attracted?
Is love temporary insanity or is it a permanent state?
Drugs open doors, what are you letting in?
In the shadows demons lurk
Angels protect children and the insane
Little Faris spoke to me and said I am two
A good one and a bad one and I don't know what to do
I took his hand and walked with him and said you know a lot
Don't worry baby, we are all in the same pot

perfection

Idris Mears

just as plants need the right
soil and water and light
and the right testing
of frost and drought
the age of the perfectly nurtured
body in the perfect garden
is thirty-three
when the glow of youth
meets settled maturity
and until we reach the age of forty
we don't have the fortitude to be
perfectly at ease with ourselves
and white hairs at sixty give us
dignity without airs
and if not perfectly stupid
we start to be a little bit wise
and at eighty all that is forgivable is forgiven
and the age of the perfected soul
is whatever time it takes
to face death with no regrets

The Night of Salvation

Nimah Ismail Nawwab

The long sleep has dissipated
the sick heart has begun to throb
with each verse, *tasbeeh*, opening

The long sleep is banished
as the heart begins its new phase
with each phase of the moon
with each new month and its advent
with the new pages on the tablet of the soul

The long sleep has been annihilated
as the thrumming of the awakened heart
soars with the spirit ever upward
to The Beloved
on a heavenly journey of blessings
with every *niyyah*[13], every prayer, every vision of beauty

The long sleep is fully cured
of all barricades, impediments, veils
on the Night of Salvation[14]
the cured heart, cured soul takes off
journeying encompassed with ultimate *Mahabbah*

The long sleep is routed out
as new beginnings beckon
and the Night of All Cures calls out
and the invigorated heart unfurls
its awakened state heralding the dawn of secrets
beyond the known spheres to the unknown
       as the veils are unveiled.

---

[13] intention
[14] The Night of Salvation – Mid Sha'ban also known as the Night of al-Bara'ah

Eid's Gift

Yasmine Ahmed-Lea

I wish I could capture my grief
in an amber amulet
tie it around my neck
as a guide
to remind me
that in every step of my loss
you have gained an eternity

Unsung Hero
Abdalhamid Evans

I was climbing through the jungle
    On the day I heard the news
        It was Layla calling, said our hero has fallen
    And I can't believe it's true

Our old companion's gone ahead
      My heart wept in my eyes
      He came down in a lonely town
    From a corner of the skies

And I knew I had to be there
    With my pockets worn and bare
      And I tore my way through the closing gates
    And took off through the air

And we came from every corner
    And the mercy fell like rain
      And our hearts were filled with sweetness
    From the sadness and the pain

And the people gathered round him
    Like the leaves around the tree
      We filled that wasteland up with light
    For the Mighty One to see

And one by one we greeted him
    As he lay there wrapped in white
      With his beard and turban shining
    Like a beacon in the night

And we carried him to the graveside
    Doing dhikr along the way
      Past the trees in the autumn breeze
        On that green and orange day

And we prayed there by the graveside

And we laid him in the ground
    And we cried Ya Sin as we filled it in
And we passed the shovel round

And you know how much we loved him
    You can still see it in our eyes
        He just wore out in Your service, Lord
Oh Lord, we testify!

Oh my my, my companion
    Oh Lord, rest his soul

What is this thing you call death?
Rabea Benhalim

Can you still feel
My love
Now that you've gone
My longing
Projected out into the cosmos

Dead or alive
I carry your presence with me
In the kiss
Of the sun
Against my cheek
In the wind
Running its fingers
Through my hair

To say I miss you
Would be wrong.
For it isn't often that you leave me.
But I greedily desire
The safety of your arms.

In a Liminal (Hinterland)
Fatima's Hand

The moon in me
said, sleep!
It dreamt me into
secret gardens
of nights sublime
and peach scented
earlobes
I abandoned
the gardens
intermittently,
and the desert crept in
throwing out hinterlands
around a vortex.
I burrowed to discover
colours on the horizon
and subsumed by earthly loves
I became Alice, then
I was Rupi,
when I was tired,
I hid in the verses
of Hildegard and
the utterances
of Rabia,
on a mat
in a sad suburb of Damascus
where no jasmines grow
and still you waited,
Sidi Muhiyiddin
in the dream
pulling me through the
wormhole,
back to the desert, through the hinterlands
until I arrived again at the secret garden
in wretched pain
eyes still closed in sleep,
but all ears for the

elevated voices pushing
into my liver for a seat.
And with them, arrived
exquisite symphonies,
'between the click of a light and the start of a dream'
swirling deep as oceans,
and light as fairy clocks -
dispersed by a child's breath
on a midsummer's gloaming

Identity
Barbara Flaherty

*I became a slave at His portal; then, duality disappeared; I was absorbed
in Him.*

- Khwaja Abdullah Ansari

Love opened the bars of my cell,
silenced every counterfeit voice.
I begged to be cracked open,
pleaded to be a poured out jar,
a space remembering only Him.
Love broke me, made my every voice
a hollow ring, a thing uninhabited.
Love prowls in the hidden haunts.
His voice is not tame, wolf howl,
coyote, tiger roar, jaguar.
When love came it penetrated
the cave of my will, the vulva
of my heart, the secret parts.
One of us must die, it said.
Love kissed my face, my whole life's
basket unraveled in the wind.

Light Upon Light
Mohja Kahf

I shelter through winter

in a little niche my heart

behind gelid glass

the glass cupping a wick

the wick soaked in oil

the oil from a tree

holding the universe

together roots in earth

tips in highest sky

where a planet blinks

in a long deep night

light answering light

Desert Revisited
Yahia Lababidi

under a whirling skirt of sky
streaming light and stars
groping for that tremendous hem
gingerly over quicksand

as though steadied
beneath some tongue and dissolving
not the absence of sound
but the presence of silence

or, as if transfixed
by a gaze, stern-serene
surveying a dream
foreign-familiar

incorruptible starting point
inviolable horizon
where eye and mind are free
to meditate perfection

there, begin to uncover
buried in dust and disinterest
the immutable letter
(first of the Arabic alphabet) *Alif*

under the ever watchful eye:
fearsome sun, forgiving moon
bless the magnificent hand
all else is blasphemy, a lie

experience quietude
the maturity of ecstasy
longing to utter
the unutterable name

only striving supreme or pure
can ever hope to endure
the absolute face
the awesome embrace.

Tauba
Ray Lacina

You wait for your eyes to roll up in your head
You wait for the light to fall on you,
To dribble from your fingers like milk
Filling the cup in your lap

You wait for the superhero moment:
You can fly
You can stop a speeding bullet
You can turn all to fire, all to light

You wait for the lightning

And all the while behind you
a gentle hand rests on your shoulder
a gentle voice whispers
in your ear:

"Turn
though you screw it up
every time,
return,
though you never get it right,
though you just can't shake the feeling
that you'll never get it right,
turn, just turn
to Me."

University of Al Quaraouiyine - *26 Ramadan 1440*
Saraiya Bah

Innocence.
Is it age restricted?
Does it run deep?
Is the one who remains
unaware asleep?
Or is it a form of
protection from
deep disappointment.
We try to purify ourselves
in fountains of knowledge.
The more we wade into its waters,
the more we drown with
the amount of work we have to do.
Oh Quaraouiyine with
your tiles of green.
Your roof hosts
a hub where human beings
can proclaim their love for
their Rabb.
Where medleys of tongues
can profess their love
and gratitude.
Alhamdulillah.
Merci mon Dieu.
Thank you God.
Where the young
and old can congregate.
Be at peace and love one
another.
Through this show
of solidarity and love,
we're *ibadah* personified.
Alhamdulillah.
Merci mon Dieu.
Thank you God.

Woken by Absence

Arthur Skip Maselli

When drunk with wine,
upon soft pillows of golden thread,
I, in darkness, slept,
whilst sultans' dreams filled my head,
I am woken by Your absence,
that of a restless lover in my bed.

So, we lie awake, You and I,
in silent prayer instead
and offer *subha* in a thunderstorm,
all this over tea and *tesbih*
and sweetened sheermal bread.

Wake me, Darling, from this hide and seek,
for there is no sweeter presence
than the absence of the Beloved
of Whom the silent speak.

Malamiyya
Matthew Bain

taking the blame
to hide truth,
brothers and sisters playing the game
to hide *Ruh*
locked by our fears behind bars
but not outlaws.
Majnun, scorched by the flame
to hide truth,
brother played by the game
to hide *Ruh*
lost in the desert in search of his love
but not insane.
"Scant knowledge have you been given"
to hide truth,
gaming the play
to hide *Ruh*
the book half-lit by the moon,
but not displayed

For "S"
Cherif Al-Islam Abou El Fadl

There was a man standing at a cliff's edge,
before an enduring chasm.

He stared into depths that lead minds adrift,
down damned and hollowed bastions.

The man was faced with fate's insistence
he scale the insurmountable fathoms.

And so he fell through darkness' kiss,
and as hope seemed to blacken…

he began to climb a falling ascension,
he came to face his phantoms.

And he faced them with compassion.

Through life and journey and death and degradation
we face our darkness,
we face our hurting,
and finally we embrace them.

And through the wounds and scars from trials and tribulations
enters the light
turning fall to flight,
making diamonds from desolation.

Faith turns sinkholes into the Himalayas

There was a man standing at a cliff's edge
before an enduring chasm.

He bravely dove into an abysmal unknown
bringing light where it was absent

Unwelcome Guest
Sukina Pilgrim

When pain knocks
We hide behind the sofa
Hoping she won't hear us
breathing.
Maybe she'll leave
And visit someone else.
We don't offer her tea
In our special occasions cups
We don't offer her a seat
We offer her our silence
Our backs turned
Our faces soured
Tear stained and turned away.
We hide under the duvet
Wishing the earth
Would swallow us whole
And disintegrate the pain
'Why don't you just leave!'
We scream, In between
Prayers and 'why me's
What a way to treat a guest
Who comes bearing treasure
Of truth and authenticity -
Blessings packaged in darkness.
Stop running for a second
Look pain in the eye
Take hold of her hand
Surrender
And jump into the abyss together.
Yes, you'll hit the bottom
But eventually you'll rise
Towards a star-filled sky
I promise.
Sit with your pain
She has so many lessons
To gift us
If only we'd listen.

Breathe[15]

Toneya Sarwar

Invisible hands
With long bony fingers
Squeeze my ribcage
Until the tightness overtakes-
Inhale, exhale, inhale, exhale
A rhythmic melody plays on
I hear the whisper of my breath
A tune so familiar I can almost hold it-
Each breath a gift
bringing us back to pure form
Make it count
Make your song the best it can be

---

[15] I was born with asthma and unlike most children who grow out of the illness, I sadly didn't. The shortness of breath, the fear and dread of not being able to catch your breath is terrifying. But the gift in return for the struggle is to truly value each breath and to make sure that each one counts.

Listening
Joel Hayward

Allah is the great silence
the unconquerable quietness

inside and beyond a universe that creaks
moans and shrieks

Emptiness obeyed a single word, "be"
and became an impenetrable fullness

Time began ticking
babies began crying
soldiers calling
for their mothers
when death embraces
them

He owns the East and West
and you will see His face
everywhere you turn

He watches, listens
and is silent

Some say He is the
shout of nature
the volcano
the tornado
the earthquake
the tsunami
the blizzard

He is not
They have
their own voices
His gift

Listen to Him in your soul
Be still
be empty
become the void
drawn near to
death
and listen

and there you might hear Him

Galata Tower
H I Cosar

Outside

I wander
I wonder
If we put all these lonely people together in the tower
(The ones selling – stale nuts, brewed bitter tea, Indian stickers,
themselves,
The ones buying - locals, tourists, those in between)
Would they be as many as the lights of this crazy city

Inside

I wonder
if the smoke from
the cherry shisha has found you
I think of your lips
as I inhale
sour yet sweet

I wonder
If I set out
Onto the open sea
Will I be free
Or just a dinghy
Caught in the hopeless hope

Of temperamental waves

Maybe you prefer the maidens
Who have not been damaged by clay
But I wonder
If I ask you to
Promise me your hand in heaven
Can we shake hands on earth

Outside

I wonder
How many young women have lost their dreams
In these alleys
How many old men have lost their ability to dream
I wonder
I wander

Adab
Hanan Issa

The rug matches the vase on the shelf.
Women fit thickly like trees in a forest.
'Make sure your socks are matching.'

Invasive floral perfume, pendulating
earrings clock the minutes you have to stay.
'Just say, *Alhamdulillah*, you are fine.'

Your chai-pouring skills, into delicate
gold-rimmed glass, are observed with mock
indifference. 'Always take a biscuit.'

Looking over the rim of their cups,
they appraise the servility in your teeth,
the forgiveness in your hips

A Nubian Love Affair
Mariam Akhtar

I finally gave in to sanity
and washed away your scent
from all of my clothes
erased you from the scarves
I'd wrapped around my hair
made you invisible
underneath all the skirts
that had draped over my legs
stripped you from the blouses
that had covered me
and scraped your prints
from the soles of my shoes
anything and everything
to remove you
from me
I'd mourned for four whole days
and remained silent
for four hole nights
sleeping during the sun
comatose in the moon
waxing and waning
silently wailing
until there was nothing left
but to awake
arise and be regarded as present
in the present
so present
because all there always is
is the presence
of here and now
continuously evolving in moments
of momentary moments
til the moment arrives
when I can kiss your face with my eyes
again

and lie on your sand
in the heat of the day
whilst your breath strokes
every atom of my being
but until then
I've given in to sanity
and washed away your scent
from all of my clothes

Future Nightingales
Medina Tenour Whiteman

There is no justice in generosity
no coins left by the guest
on the telephone table or
count made of spoonfuls
of barberry rice

Feet leap to bring bowls of
unnecessary oranges
apples, kiwis, pistachios
tea is made over and over
no one cares to know
how often the boxes are bought
in case counting cuts off the
kindness

A deliberate amnesia falls
to veil *eidi* money lavished
as long as the room is full
and no one is forlorn
apologising for taking up
valuable carpet space
while the plates keep being emptied
dishes returned smudged with

parsley, coriander, dill
it's as though they return to the kitchen
loaded with doubloons

Some declare with a certain
bravura they aren't religious
only so by name but
this unfair advantage
they keep giving me
feels too much like faith
certainty that what the hand grasps
must fly away or wither
—a crust of bread clutched
in a motionless hand—
knowledge that giving
is planting seeds
that will bear fruit
provide shade, be home to
future nightingales
and that nothing is ours
in the first place to hoard—
that is no superstition:
it is thanking the Giver
for letting them be the palm
the gift crosses

Justification
Nargis Latif

What clothes can I wear to entice your love?
What charms can I use to get your attention?
What cleverness can I display
To earn a shred of your affection?

I am at a loss for words as they are only yours
My limbs move only to your rhythm
My senses only see what you awaken
My sins only take me to the path you have forgiven.

My laughter is only your humour
A smile streaming through my shattered face
My wit is only your inspiration
Gliding through my soul's empty space.

My arms are only your embracing tools
Comforting through me to me.
Your names are my lofty aspirations
Helping my teary blinded eyes to see.

My dreams are only love letters sent from you
With words of joy and hope and peace
My future is only your hand
Leading me through fields of life's increase

My wisdom is only your sublime intellect
Teaching sense to those who seek
My kindness is only your Gracious Benevolence
Reaching through me to the meek.

My voice is only your instrument
Playing notes you pluck from chords
My love is only your shining essence
Lighting through this darkness as reward

So how can I impress in all of this?

When only You exist?
How can I feign any intellect?
when perception is at your behest?

Make Your Move
Asiya Sian Davidson

I don't know anything about love
unless you can call this paralysis
this desperation to do the right thing
without knowing what it is
love

this totally giving up
I have no idea and will never know again
love

not knowing
has taken me by the ears
there's no conceivable way
to figure anything out
or to label any emotion
or dissect any situation

in this state, what is choosing?
the means and availability
the tools of appraisal
are gone

was there ever a time in which
I knew something?

this is no numbness
or pretentious gesturing at emptiness
it's not avoiding accountability
or misconstruing qadr

I close my eyes

and a deep sea stirs
in the ebb and flow of wind
outside my window
there are no answers

even if a posse of grandfathers
stepped by now to take me by the hand
I couldn't muster a question
or gesture for direction

I'm a spent force
what can I tell you of love
when I know nothing
about anything at all

except
make your move
take me
I'm Yours

Midwinter
Rabia Saida

Here in the land of 4pm twilight
The hush of dusk resounds in the wind's hollow bluster
Bellowing my ears
As I rush wide eyed through the darkling light of this
Midwinter park

Pattered by rain
Gulping twilight flavoured air
I power my bike
Judging the rate of deceleration
Of the half remaining brake
Well in advance of unwitting strangers
Rain stained in a colour drained canvas
Where

There's no need to distinguish one hue from another
Relieved for a while of appearance's chimera.

The playground is a riot of languages and cultures
Cheerful jewelled headscarfs, niqabs and berets
Gather together as the night draws in
To collect our offspring and take them home again
The chatter and quarrel of children rises
Hanging in the air like condensation
With mist kissed mouths and bike lights
Bright like the mist gathered round drizzle drenched park lamps

The fluorescent glare of the foyer,
Greeting neighbours
Out relationships defined
By lift conversations
About weather
The age of toddlers and dogs
The recent loss of relatives
Old boys who are still lads
And those who are gentlemen
The frail lady smiling through the scowl life etched on her
Through age's blank stare.

Rolling up sleeves
Patting dough into cookware
I indulge in kitchen alchemy
textures, smells and flavours
A feast for the senses
Like a child with play dough
Experimenting with new potions
Bubbling herbs into stews.

Turning out overhead lights
when the evening's bustle
Has worn thin
The dimmest lamp is enough
In the quiet
As the day rolls to an end

Sway
Wajiha Khalil

When you are my Master
I am a tulip at zenith
when you are my companion
I am a rose folded in your fragrance
when you are my neighbor
I am a dandelion
wishing for the wind to blow
when you bloom magnolias
I bask in your glow
Oh sun remain in your orbit
I will lean to your light
absorb greenery
and sway in delight
Garden variation
Lilies & carnations
Cosmic rotation
spiritual levitation
Jamal & Jalal alteration
Even if I am your nothing
to be nothing is to be something
or anything to you
It's all the same to me
because I know you are True
In this Divine storyline

it's not about me, it's all about you ﷺ

Khamsah
Rashida James-Saadiya

You spend your days
collecting the heaviness of this world

unfolding and stitching
every ache into the tapestry of your prayer mat

In *sujood*, you wonder
if your heart can be mended
cleansed of fear, reshaped into certainty

For darkness is a part of this life
and sometimes you forget
that *Ihsan* waters the seeds
and the soul shall reap the harvest

And too often you forget
That your holy book is a map

If not now, when?

When will you let God till the soil
plant a garden in every place you've stored pain

When will you accept
that there is no need to fear tomorrow
for there is nowhere God is not

Faith can not simply dwell in the heart
it must exist in hands that pray and serve all of humanity
look closely, there is a cure in the act of giving

If not now, when?

There is no shortage of compassion or joy
no shortage of food, land or water
If you want to make this world a better place

Let love be your currency and give it all away

For you are an instrument of grace, a reflection of light

Depart from the darkness of this world
remove its weight from your spine
fast from anguish, recite the names of God
cleanse your heart, cover this earth with prayer

Follow the map of infinite hope
For all things are bound together, and all things share the same breath

Go slow if you must, but go
become something as sacred as a seed
plant yourself inside God's soil
grow into the possibility of each breath

Become a testament, a structure of Heaven and Earth
a living mosque crafted to serve and remember God

For you are standing in between two worlds
the one that spins and the one that awaits

Open your hands, let God guide you

a prayer
Idris Mears

in the garden today
i was working for a robin
digging up his lunch of worms
a busy version of the lazing hippopotamus
whose body heat draws insects for his attendant bird
but usually i am just working
in my wasteful human way
for the rats
and in the long run
for the worms
- so much for my industry and utility

but i pray i found
in the stillness and joy
of my work-honed reflection
a moment of sanity
between the madness of losing meaning
and the madness of imposing it

Oh Death!

Abdalhamid Evans

Oh Death! You came riding in
    Never saw you coming
  Never saw you coming
Oh Death! You told us not to be hiding
    We were busy running
  We were busy running

Oh tears! You came pouring down
    Didn't see you coming
  Didn't see you coming
Oh tears! You came roaring round
    Now you got me running
  Now you got me running

  Memories, you come calling on me
    Like bubbles rising up from the deep
  Memories, you keep falling on me
    Make me smile, make me weep

Children, won't you gather round
    The time was near
  Now the time is here
Children, bring your children round
    Hold them near
  Have no fear

Lover, won't you hold me now
    My heart is aching
  My heart is aching
Lover, let me hold you now
    Our hearts are breaking
  Our hearts are breaking

  Time, you keep reminding us
    Our day is surely coming round
  The Angel soon will be finding us
    And our companions will put us

in the ground

Memories, you come flying at me
    Like an arrow
  Like an arrow
Memories, rising deep in me
    From my marrow
  From my marrow

Sisters, wash the body down
    Let the water flow
  So clean and cold
Sisters, wrap the perfumed shroud
    Fold by fold
  White as snow

    O Life! You keep testing us
      Testing us with hope and fear
    O Life! We know you promised us
      It's never more than we can bear

People, join the march through town
    Come down the road
  Down the road
Brothers, lift the body down,
    Take your load,
  Take the load.

People, come and stand in line
    Lay the body down
  Lay the body down
People, take your place in time
    Let it come around
  Let it come around

    Oh Life! You keep testing us
      Testing us with hope and fear
    Oh Life! We know you promised us
      It's never more than we can bear

Prayer at the Ka'ba

Daniel Abdal-Hayy Moore
from the poetry collection Sparrow on the Prophet's Tomb

Oh Lord, the orange cat lying asleep on the
shoe rack outside the Ka'ba
looked tranquil, lean from
living wild in Mecca, but still
cat-like and sweet-faced –
surely some of this peacefulness
could come to me?

Oh Lord, You raise up giant roof-beams in the
world and
hurl great foundations
as deep as the seas –
I am only your creation of
flesh and bone,
but surely some of those
depths and heights
could be mine?

Oh Allah, I sit here facing Your House on
earth, beseeching Your Grace,
seeking Your Face,
my own not good enough in
this life,
my own face a combination of
lusty panther and
awkward ostrich
in this life,
yet I'm grateful for its
miraculous properties in
facing the world,

especially the eyes – close them
and light spreads,
open them and
miracles appear –

especially Your stark square of black cloth rising
endlessly up into the night in front of me now
but Your Face, Lord,
could I catch a
glimpse of it at least?

A white owl flies in the night somewhere,
its impassive face and saucer eyes
fleeing through the air.

Is this my face, Lord,

searching everywhere?

Way to Win
I.AM.SHAHEED

The result is in perfection
The actual is in imperfection
Imperfection is where we are
If we are there we cannot be perfect
We cannot be perfect
If we were perfect
We would never be in need
We would be like The One God
We cannot be perfect
However, we can most definitely be better
To be better we must do good
Doing takes us further away from
Imperfection
And that my friends is a Result.

The Fabric of Creation
Jessica Daqamsseh

The fabric of creation
Brushes all sensations.
It weaves through our being
As elements maneuver into their spaces.
Each intricate design,
Unduplicated.
Divine.

Stillness holds time
In her loving embrace.
Beckoning those of understanding
To not waste her fleeting gift.

Canyon
Asma Khan

How dull witted I become in this heat
unlike sages and tribes of desert prophets
Left only with my stills and screensavers
of Hockney poolside paintings
and O Keefe canvases
Wit and words bleached to rocky whiteness
Yet tears speak, waterfall like unsourced
in the repeating sublime cavernous beauty
and some listening stillness beneath
echoes heartbeat from canyon depths
and the vastness calls out its Word
that no thought mote could ever encompass
falling soundlessly into infinite space
like the glorious soaring of condor
and yearning reach of sequoia
and whispering change of colours in moving grass
and planets eternally casting their circling shadows
soul speech of those friends who know this
the Unseen

lament for seven songbirds
Bushra Mustafa-Dunne

We are seven souls in one vessel:
Selma, Ibrahim, Aiman,
And four nameless
– slipping in through Mama's tears

Tiny fingers clutching black حرير [16]
nestled Selma's روح [17] in their palms

---

[16] Silk; pronounced *ḥarīr* in Arabic
[17] Spirit/soul; pronounced *rūḥ* in Arabic

(I ought to give birth to them soon)

You, I miscarried.
You shaped my insides, I held
Your motherlessness
Your flushed smiles

became you,
You outgrew:
Cracked open.

I'm growing a womb again:
soft pomegranate husk,
fig flesh
from between the نهرين [18]you had dried up.

I am heedless of the first womb – she who gifted me seven songbirds.

(I am still six
with tiny hands curled on her chest, inhaling souls that could fit
between my fingers)

Yet more heedless of the رحم [19]He who said to the songbirds 'Be'
and they were

ascended to a shade that never wanes
from fruit trees ever-bearing womb-fruit
over rivers of milk and wine and honey.

---

[18] Two rivers (the Tigris and the Euphrates), alluding to the 'land between the two rivers' - present day Iraq; pronounced *nahrayn.*
[19] Literally meaning womb, but here specifically alluding to the root word for God's names of Mercy and Compassion; pronounced *raḥam*

Yusuf and Omar
Miroku Nemeth

At fifteen, Yusuf wore a Palestinian kefiyyah around his neck
The day he buried his beloved older brother Omar.
At the masjid, he helped me carry the funeral bier,
Placing his brother in front of the congregation
For the Janazah we never expected to pray.

Yusuf, sweet Yusuf, named after the beautiful prophet,
Born on 'Eid while I was on Hajj, on 2/22/02,
Beautiful son, beautiful brother of a beautiful brother,
After the Salat, you left immediately to comfort your mother,
Overwhelmed as any mother would be, losing the firstborn
She carried, gave birth to, nursed, nurtured, taught, loved,
Worried over, and cared for for nineteen and a half years
In this world. Yusuf ran to her, held her, comforted her,
As women wailed around them, praying, mourning as mothers
Should be allowed to mourn, for who gives more to the world
Than mothers?

At fifteen, Yusuf, the fighter, saw his older brother die,
Tried to save him while the rich boys stood by,
Only later to lie. Yusuf fought to keep him alive, believed him alive,
All the way on the drive to the hospital two miles away,
The rich boys wouldn't drive him to. That night when we went
To the frat house crime scene, after the coroners had driven off with
Omar,
The towering homicide detectives pointed and yelled at him,
Trying to blame him, trying to accuse him of being complicit,
And he knew as a brown boy, as a brown man, what that game was.
Called them on it. Stepped back. Yelled:
"Stop harassing me!"
My son.
Ready to fight anyone who would do him a true injustice.
Hours after his brother died. Hours after anyone with a heart would
know
How deeply he would be traumatized.
But he knows,

Ain't no mercy for brown boys on these streets,
But sure enough excuses for frat boys.
But an older brother the police painted as a criminal had the love to
calm him.

So, Yusuf, on a Sunday, the day we buried my son day,
Rode holding his mother through these fields to the cemetery,
Stepping out of the car to again
Be a man. To once again carry the bier with me.
This time, to carry his brother with me to his grave.
My father hands and his brother hands under the body of the one
We loved and hoped in most, whose smile was our life's rejuvenation,
Whose poetry and art were of the being of all three of us together,
Whose ideas and vision of bringing love and knowledge to the world
We believe believed belive in
We carried him
How does the lion mourn the loss of the cub?
How does the young cub mourn his adored warrior brother?
We carried him with firm Eskrimador hands, wanting to feel all of his
weight,
Take all of his weight with us forever,
We carried him lovingly, never wanting to let his body go,
We carried the sleeping lion next to his grave,
And I climbed six feet in.

Yusuf, kefiyyeh around his neck, helped hand his brother
Down to me, and when Omar's beloved body was in my arms,
The weight fell upon me,
I held him under his back with my right hand
And under his legs with my left,
Cradling his manweight like when he was my baby.
We lowered him into the gravedirt fully,
And in fatherlove and the solemnity of the Muslim burial,
In the midst of prayers and supplications,
I could only repeat, "I love you, Omar." "I love you, Laughing Lion."
He was wrapped as is the Muslim funerary tradition in a shroud of
white.
We turned his face and body to face the sacred city of Mecca Al-
Mukarammah,

I packed the dirt with two believers behind the head and body of my
son, each
Handful of dirt with a prayer and hope that he would be safe and arise
among the blessed
And be among the blessed until that day of resurrection, for he always
Spoke lovingly and unequivocally of being a Muslim.
Yusuf, in his kefiyyeh, looked down upon me, and out of the
multitude,
My son's is the only face I remember looking down upon me,
His eyes shining like two moons in two dark heavens.
As the two other living men left the grave, I stayed, went to Omar's
Enshrouded head, and kissed him and kissed him softly and gently,
As I did in life, and told him, "I love you, Omar." "I love you".

I don't know when I rose out of the grave.
I know only that Yusuf was next to me.
I know that we began scooping handfuls of soil
Into our brother's grave
Into our son's grave.

11am coffee break

Yasmine Ahmed-Lea

Something familiar in that green emerald ring
he twists around his finger
He watches forward as he holds onto his walking stick
Nothing too grand
Just oak, carved with something
who knows
Where he descends from
Not I certainly
He wipes milky coffee
From his beard whiskers
Something comforting in the whites
Of his eyes
So hazy
and I am afraid
Of catching his gaze
But that is exactly what I do
This isn't some grand place
no artisan coffee here
no makeshift atmosphere
provided by furnishings and
inspirational quotes
Just a greasy spoon
On the corner
Of nowhere
But he knows
Something about
What I am thinking right now
And he walks over to me
Slowly
Maybe takes him 5 minutes or more
To travel such a short distance
His brown wrinkled skin
Gleaming from the reflection
Of a dusty orange brown turban
Tying up all the loose ends
Of his thoughts

Slowly smiling and half
Making his way out
Of the door
He hush hush speaks
Not directly to anyone
But also side glancing my way
'no one really leaves, you know'
I look down
Not knowing
That
Exchanging secrets
In brief moments
like this
Is what I live for now

Embracing, We Let Go
Yahia Lababidi

Perhaps, we are negotiating
not just with one, but always two
(who share the same soil, it is true)
one who lives, another who expires

A shift in balance begins to take place
once a love of silence is confessed
its roots run deep, its shade a world
and her fruits impossible to forget

From the first, we surrender something
and, gradually, consent to be emptied
transfixed by so much soundless music
drunk and sated through lipless mouths

What use to name this silent master
preparing us for dying or the Divine
- I'm not sure there is a difference -
but know, in embracing, we let go.

The strangest journey

Joel Hayward

I found a door shaped like my mother
I pressed against it and fell
into a room full of sunlight
cushions and songs

I stayed a while before
curiosity seduced me
like a cat seeing any twitching thing

The door shaped like my father
wouldn't open when I pushed

I searched for the key and found it in a bottle
The room was messy and a light bulb flickered
but great leather books covered the walls. I read
until my mind hurt like a belly full of steak

I peered through a window shaped like me
into a gloomy, empty room. Wait, a small boy
with the face of a philosopher frowned
in the corner. I'll come back for you
I shouted

The little door shaped like my darling
opened like Aladdin's cave

Her perfume pulled me inside
with a rip current. I swam in warm music
and kisses vowing never to leave

There's another door
I'll take her hand. Maybe she'll lead
It has no shape just a welcoming call

We are Weavers
Sukina Pilgrim

We are weavers
We are dreamers
Wearers of hearts on our sleeves
We weave song and blood
Veins and poems
Until we arrive at some knowing
Some ancient
Some fragrant
Some certainty
From a part within
That does not end
Nor does it begin
We weave
Quietly in corners
Or coffee shops
Under the oak tree
In the garden
In the wombs
Of our rooms
On napkins in the restaurant
When the words are so urgent
Any container will do.
We use the meanings
That sit in the stomach
Of words, to remind ourselves
That we are not the first
Nor will we be the last
We are not as different
As we might think we are.
Our stories hold us
To their breast
An all knowing truth
And we rest
For a while
Knowing
We are ancient
But in each moment
Brand new.

Although, Despite and When..
Novid Shaid

Although I turn my back to You
You're still with me
Although I leave You far behind
You're still with me
Although I shun Your existence
You're still with me
Although I treat You like a fool
When I know You're close at hand
All's good with me
When I see You through all the mist
All's good with me
When I'm through You and You're through me
All's good with me
When I see all my strengths are Yours
All's good with me
When I seek You in weaknesses
All's good with me
Show me Your Truth for evermore
Be still with me
And prayers and peace for evermore
Incessantly
Upon the sage and all his kin
Abundantly

I could tell you about a place
Medina Tenour Whiteman

Sit down, darling, and tell me:
Do you want me to make you
feel better?

I could shower you with corny memes
about the awesomeness of your true nature
which you may or not believe

But I'd much rather tell you about a place
you drive to in lashing rain
and darkness and gales
on serpentine mountain roads
with no street lights

Feet puddling across patios
where the bougainvillea is moonlessly dark
though you know it's really magenta
and you enter a room
full of wool-wrapped folk
sitting on orange Moroccan rugs
intoning prayers
voices rising and falling on the simplest melody stairs
halftone up, halftone down

'*El camino se hace andando*'
'You make the path by walking it'

The women sit with their legs
all under one blanket
which the lady next to you folds over your outstretched feet
in the drowsy heat of a gas burner
strip of blue and orange feathers
dancing as though in the gale outside

There's a bare LED bulb
hanging against a bare window pane

and a blue plastic bucket
catching a drip from the
brown bloom in the ceiling

We stumble over cushions

Someone holds her prayer sheet
upside-down

A boy with an Afro
sits under a desk in one corner
adding masking tape to a
working model of a crocodile's head
and everything is completely fine
(the model is not to scale)

An Uzbek calls the *adhan*
in a Turkish intonation
then a Swede leads the prayer
in Eritrean tones
lilting and sombre
and it seems that surah is a
cousin you never met before
bearing your genes from the
other side of the planet

And you'll be so distracted
maybe you'll have forgotten
why it was you wanted comfort
because you know every line
- even the crocodile head -
of this poem is true
and in one of its folds
maybe you'll find
something to believe in

The Khatm
Ray Lacina

That this meat
and blood
and bone
God-touched
can be the pipe that plays
can hold the heart that contains
can cast into the night those words
those letters
that Speech

is miracle enough.

That this heart is tugged by the tide of *Bismillahi*
and flows out after
is miracle enough.

The Inner Tablet

Nimah Ismail Nawwab

Do you see the writing on the inner tablet of the soul
where knowledge of the intangible resides
where the darkest darkness dissipates
where the cruelty of the friendless world dissolves
as we pass through the nine spheres
entering a nascent threshold
where realities turn and spin
with the turning of the stars
in the sought horizon of Ultimate Unity

Mausolée De Moulay Idriss - *26 Ramadan 1440*
Saraiya Bah

We traverse freely
on this blue earth.
Diligently aimless
in this universe.
Chatter disperses
as the *Adhan* calls
us to pray under
blue skies.
Blue domes.
Home of
The Almighty.
Once our obligation
is fulfilled, our chatter
amplifies.
But we remain in
a state of wonder.
Remain traversing in
courtyards that once
held a collective hush.
And though we chatter,
our hearts gush at
the remembrance of Allah.
Dhikr flows from our tongue
like a fountain.
Overflowing in benediction.
A plethora of diction:
La ilaha illallah
Muhammadun rasulullah.

Someday
Sukina Pilgrim

I
It's ok to welcome the darkness
Let her walk beside you
Sleep at the end of your bed
Be the scarf upon your head.
It's ok to be silent as she speaks
I get that you fear her
But I need you to hear her
Look into her inky eyes
And lean into discomfort -
The itchy reality of uncertainty.
Rest a while.

II
Not every day will gift you
With clear skies and a warming sun
The rains will come, often.
And you will run for cover
Dripping, shivering and wet
Sometimes the sky will cry for you
On the days you don't have strength
To cry for yourself
And when the water has settled
Into newly moistened earth
You will jump into puddles
Just to feel alive.

III
Sometimes loneliness
Will be your companion
Will show up at your door
Unannounced, and walk straight in
Before you have a chance
To welcome her. She knows
You don't really want her there.
But she has work to do.
She has come to undo you.

IV
Sometimes you'll feel spiky
And anti-social
And you'll fight
To see the light
At the end of the tunnel.
It's ok to have off days
Days when you can't bend your back
To make everyone feel comfortable.

V
Sometimes you'll wish the universe
Would be quiet for a second
So you can roll down the windows
Sink into the backseat
And swallow the sunset with your eyes.

VI
Some day you'll learn, it's ok to be exactly
As you are, with no apology or disclaimer
Or second guessing or justifying.

VII
Someday.

We live between the eskimos and butterflies
Suhayla Bewley

We live between the eskimos and butterflies
And in the space where we are and have been
Fluttering by swiftly in moments
So sweetly and so completely
Now

In softness and reliance time flies and floats
With impenetrable love bubbles
Preparing you with imagined wonders
And the comfort of adventure and warmth
Then

Learning, yearning and extending
Breaking. mending and falling
Into these arms so encompassing
Accepting, failing, trying and heading to the
Future

I let go of your hand with my hand and place it in my heart
Forever
Moments etched for
Us

Still
Malika Meddings

Still you, still me
What I come to see
Eventually
Is that you are still you
And I am still me
What you came to see
Has ended its brevity
What we were meant to be
Has happened to you and me
What we were before
We opened earth's door
Is what you have gone to be
And here I, still me,
Still sailing this empty sea
Will join you again some day
For all eternity
And while I can only see
My boat on this empty sea
I know that you can see
All there is to see
You are still you
I am still me

Long Goodbye

Asma Khan

Your truth has been lost in life layers of pain and grief
my love, like a mollusc irritated surrounds its pearl
Heaped dust piles hiding glimpses
Of delicately painted tile
Your splendid generous rainbow heart lies there, translucent, revealing
universes of stars we could have time travelled together
If there had been no accidents or fear or hob nailed boots treading into
soft heart flesh to create scar tissue
That strangled your longing to reveal all your self to me
I wish I had the wisdom to enter those wounds now
Invisible and laser like healing with a word or touch of Love
But my light too is smothered by a thicket of failure
and wounding by its thorns has weakened my power
Buried are the golden rivulets of hope we could have drowned in
Swum reverently along, floating effortlessly in that sea of Love we
discovered once upon a time
Now the path is lost, thorn bushes growing back too fast through lazy
inconsistency and no attention to each other's wounds
And making love is just the rust wearing off a little but not enough
deep desire to find a truly precious gem
And so this falsehood carrying vehicle has finally broken down
The journey can't continue without truth to hold it I suppose
Yet Truth remains sweetly, eternally buried within
Although I never could, I beg you dear to blow sometimes on that tiny
flame and fan the fire that will lead you home

Real Again
Yasmine Ahmed-Lea

Arrived at night
Collapsing in
A sea of arms
Same green jumper
Given to me
Countless times
In heartbreaks
Quitting jobs
Losing loved ones
Still smells of fabric softener
And ginger
Faint traces of cardamom
From long nights staying up
Sipping sugary milky teas
Rims forming mosaics
On kitchen counters
Talking about
How We feel
Too much sometimes

and
When I can't
Breathe anymore
On floors and carpets
Throwing myself into love and despair
Aching for mothers who aren't there
Taking whatever you can
That resembles that love remotely
Though of course
Nothing can ever be the same

Waking up to buttery eggs
And Pakistani talk shows
Flashbacks of Saturdays
Newly returning
To the smell of tea

Over boiling on kitchen hobs
Not able to contain itself

Realising that luck
Chance
Happenstance
Had nothing to do with
Coming back to
Where it all began

Boxes
Rabia Saida

I don't like your categories and boxes
So don't try to
B
u
I   .
l   e
d   m
O n e a r o u n d

Blind conformity sickens me

                   delusion of safety
           outweighs any
The claustrophobia
                       .....
                  tune
            Piper's
         Pied
      the
     to
   dance
  not
will
I

Or.   Lost.   This.   Drum.
  Be.   To.   Crazy.   Beat.

Shushtari's Journey
Fatima's Hand

Love annihilated me
nothing existed save it.
The world imploded
and love engulfed me.
I became lost
rendered a wanderer,
came and went as I pleased
into places unimagined...
At the mountain valley
ascension was difficult,
oxygen finite, hallucinations.
I fell onto the icy mountain lake
and froze there
until the breath of an oryx - Arabian - no less,
thawed me
Had he also wandered too far?
But my questions escaped
when we nuzzled forelocks
intellect resigned when
irises locked,
and I became hooves that circumambulate
and found Salma of the hearts
and everything else became the imagined.
With faltering, drunken steps
I left the world of images
I left the world of forms
but could not keep the secret--
it was manifest
to the intoxicated ones,
standing, swaying, when
I returned to the courtyard.
Love wove the voices of the singers
with the star canopy above
until they faded away and
only a vestige of their illumined faces
remained in the night.

Awakened by the ceremonial tea
of flowers golden,
we sipped, dazed by
the removal of cares,
and hatred,
and separation,
for love had obliterated me,
seeping into my senses
until He was, and nothing else

Sarmad
Shahbano Aliani

they say
the mystic sarmad
fell in love
went mad
tore off his clothes

why, you wonder,
do lovers
roam naked?

it's not for the union
you think they want

it's the union *inside* union
they seek

Real Love calls you all the way in
all the way back

to answer this call
lovers would,
if they could,
tear off not just their clothes
but also their skin

their muscle
their bone

anything that binds
holds them together

because every cell
in their bodies
yearns to answer
the call of Love

is desperate
to be free of solid
separation

so it can experience the
everything! everything! everything!
it is

Love takes you low
Nura Tarmann

Love takes you low, real low
Down into the bowels of perdition
Into the depths of confusion
Into those deep dark mines and
I hope you find some treasures
Because every grave is going to be unearthed
Every fear you ever buried
Every wish you never expressed
Every doubt you ever had
Believe me it's going to surface and
Not only the personally yours
Just when you thought you had those little demons under control
There comes your mama, daddy, great grand daddy
And the whole damn clan rising up against you
You wanna come up for air, you do, you really do but

You are in the bowels of that whole and you ain't getting out the way
you came in
Believe me that
I think of that snake winding its body around the tree of life
Whispering suggestions of eternity
Why this jealousy?
That fear of not being the only one
That fear of having to share the attentions of the Beloved
What is this fearsome lust deliriously devouring the apple of life?
Devoid of all tender discrimination
Increasing with every consummation
Is this love?
I fall to my knees and cry
Trying to rid my body of tenderness
Of weakness, of this yearning burning through me
Now I'm in a sort of fire
But is it not worthy of veneration, holy?

Choices

Marguerite Lake

To hold the world in my hands
And not know which way to go;
To see where life must lead
But not the path to tread;
To sense that all is right
Yet still confront the choices;
To be open to my fullness
Yet stay with all my emptiness;
To follow my creative energy
And know this sometimes hurts;
To go where love will take me
And rest in the eternal One

Word Travel
Wajiha Khalil

Who else can travel the ether
gather eucalyptus, sunsets and memories
drizzle it into ink and transform papyrus
unfold hieroglyphics and claim it's amateur

They are the masters of the dream state
escaping the pendulums and slipping into
the unseen unnoticed in the cafes and gardens

Mystics, healers, wordsmiths
swerve between typical channels
collecting tidbits and serving up alchemy
they are folklore, incarnate

What you hear between the words
is the *barzakh* between life
reincarnation occurs a thousand times in their company
for every birth, *adhan*

Woe to the one who slanders the poet who turns
abstract to logical
thought ingredients to edible
broken concepts to coherent sustainable
Spiritual experience to perceivable
One thought into multiple

Do not enter the circle of the forbidden
objectifying the secret and hidden
Do you forget that you are only carried on the ocean
from the abyss to keep it floating?

Tribe
Ahmad Ikhlas

We made ablution from the fountains
Celebrate His existence
Beat di drum dem from the Mountains
Fi communicate in ah di distance
And it's deeper than speaking in tongues
From the mouth-in-side the Heart
You will find He and Art astounding!
And His light did bright-en Up di dark that's how we found Him
Or did He find us?
Showing signs to remind us
He defined us
Made us tribes
DNA ties
Sacred bloodlines that bind us
Perfectly orchestrated
Contemplate this
Never random
Some part of the Bantu expansion.

Emergency Room
Murtaza Humayun Saeed

They rolled me in
Now repeat after us, they said
I was all ears
Say: I breathe in the truth, I exhale out the falsehood,
I breathe in the light, I exhale out the darkness
What What?
Look please focus, time is short
Ok ok ..
So what are you waiting for?
I am, I am, Ok look, I breeee-athed and ex-haaaaaale-d

Now say: The void I feel is the effect of the abandonment by false
gods,
peace is only possible with saying Allah Allah
Look, umm, an injection or tablet will do fine, I mean, to take away
the pain
We are trying to get to the root cause, don't you see? We want to save
your soul!
Soul? I insisted I have a burden like feeling on my chest
Look, keep repeating, this is the real medicine:
The silence will no longer haunt me, the door will always be open if
I'm listening
The door? I coughed
The door through which there is no fear, no competition, no
blindness, no selfishness
I wouldn't mind that
Then be brave, get up from this bed of laziness
pray in your obligatory prayers for the Mystery of Allah to be revealed
to you
and pray in your *sunnah* prayers for the Mystery of Muhammad, peace
be upon him, to be revealed to you
I took a few deep breaths and sensing some of the weight lift from my
chest,
I got up and walked out of the ER, a changed man.
He is Ar-Rahman, He is Ar-Raheem
He knows that this much I can manage
to remember Him and so be at peace,
but I can't keep from getting ill
serving the false gods of our days.

Until
After Rudyard Kipling
Efemeral

I'm where Mercy wants me to be
despite where I wanted to be,
or maybe -
because of it.
Hager will seek to quench
my thirst:
run –
from Triumph to Disaster,
run –
from Disaster to Triumph,

until I run
from I until I
until I resist
I until I
desist I
until I learn the prayer
that grants settlement
in the Zamzam quenched valley,
between the two mounts
until I
treat those two imposters just the same.

Until then, where I am to be is
where Mercy wants me to be,

and maybe –
that is the valley

just the same.

Beginning the Prayer
Daniel Abdal-Hayy Moore
from the poetry collection *Facing Mecca*

I stand facing Mecca
the house all around me
parallel with everything
hands up to my ears
  the Prayer begins

Hands across chest
  time-space capsule surrounds me
no god but Allah
  all Other forgotten

Here's eternity's signature
  signed through space
with severe strokes

Parallel lines on the prayer mat
  past actions cast behind me
    trees in linear groves
stand straight in the Prayer in
  this world
bend from the waist
    into the Next

There are parallel lines
  to the limits
past the
  edge of the
earth are darknesses
the body stands straight then
  prostrates
what does it bow to but
  Absence

Absence that is a
  Presence

we can't see with our bare
  eyes but know
eyes don't see Allah's Presence
  physically
but are themselves
  proof by
pure seeing

His Absence Alive in the air
we prostrate in parallel lines
we stand straight with
  angels in the prayer line
rows of Mediterranean Cypresses
  tall silhouettes against white sky
favorites of foggy graveyards

We stand with
  arms at our sides
against the
  beating chests of our
    turmoils
clasping left wrist with right hand
eyes half-slitted
  not staring
Gaze made to
  fall on the
inside
last actions done
  cast behind me

Dead while alive
standing still
  concentrated
by praying

From the
Next world we
rise into
This one

Transcendence
Nimah Ismail Nawwab

The world transcends
in a blink of eternity
from level to level, period to period
passages of recorded time
another flicker in eternity
we consider it all in proportion
or is it in proportion?

A second of existence
in the full scheme of half-full lives
spent in devotion or devastation?

Cross the invisible bridge
between the realms
and look forward or back?

Cross the bridge
and enter with surety
the field beyond the mind's eye,
beyond faithless time lines
and resolve the Final Riddle of the Essence
as you step into the Homeland of Certainty

Rachida's Poem
Jamila Fitzgerald

My friend Rachida (may she rest in peace),
Raised five children,
Single-hand
The family would appear
In the Land Rover,
Their Gypsy Wagon,
When we had put on extra meat,
Or on many birthdays unknown,
With their newest baby.

Their clothes she'd sewn by hand;
Embroidered seams, beads worked in,
Bells on the babies her
Husband helped birth at the farm.

"Why don't you use a sewing machine
Just for the things you don't care about?"
"Oh Jamila, there's nothing I don't care about,
I swallow also the last thread."

Rachida, from Germany, where our fathers
Fought (each other) to Morocco where
We live/ lived.
Her kitchen a witchery
Of dark bottles, little
Tea-pots hung on nails,
A red gas stove-top,
Germanic, carved wooden tools
I wish I could hold in my hands right now.
I painted two pictures of it all,
One for the children to keep.

Their father died on Abdullah's eighth
Birthday, getting the cake.
Training for a bicycle hadj
Look south, just after lunch

Into the sleepy sun
There he is...

The little girl showed me an
Empty spot in the garden
"Where the puppies were born."

Rachida raised five children single-hand;
Land Rover rolling over on her right hand.

A sudden black-out across town at midnight
As I face a white page, struggling
To finish her poem.
"Jamila, you so surprised?
You holding me in your heart.
Light a candle like the old days.
I finish it for you."

The waning moon quickly rises,
Her burnished gold and paling
Profile sailing through
The bare winter trees.

in memoriam
Idris Mears

the party has washed up on the shores of dawn
and only we lingerers and early risers
are out at first light
combing for amber on the shining strand
sand hard packed by the weight
of the receded ocean
pebbles gleaming like gems
yet to be dulled
by the march of the day

between the tidelines
a marcher kingdom is revealed
exposed to the night chilled air
and the stabbing beaks of waders and gulls
savants of where to pick the bounty
concealed beneath the surface

in the night on the high tide
two more of our boon companions
the heart-stirrer shanty singer
the spirit-rouser hornpipe dancer
rowed off in a skiff to the holding ship
moored out beyond
the curvature of the earth

now and then we spy on our horizon
the bobbing white flag of its topsail
a noah's ark of ones of a kind
at peace with the sea and themselves
the learned navigator
the diligent log keeper
the resolute bosun
the stalwart mate
the kindly surgeon
the reformed pirate
the dear ship's boy
and the exemplary captain we long to meet.

After Ramadan Comes Thanksgiving

Mohja Kahf
with thanks to Abdal-Hayy Moore for his book, The Ramadan Sonnets

The table spread with split pea soup and corn bread,
the mail-order mejdoul dates and local harvest apples
of Ramadan, red, delicious, over-spill the horn-
by the time the fasting season finishes,
you no longer sprint, ankles unbound,
to the delights of eating. Something diminishes,
the appetite subsides, long enough for thought
to rise a notch above the normal settings, and for worlds
to appear within worlds, seeds hidden in the apple core
There is a space before the broken habits build back up
by next Shaaban, a spiral staircase to another story
There is an opening in Ramadan, vaginal
and slender as the newborn moon, a sliver
of consciousness at the edge of the month,
unseeable at other times, before you slide back
into the sludge and heave of all desire
It is twenty-eight red apples chopped
in buttery wedges softening on the black iron skillet
of the last ten nights, it is cinnamon, it is a sea
of amber grains, it is the grace and spice of God, it is
"shall we iftar on Chinese or Mexican tonight?"
it is awareness of the blessing, ground up
in you like cardamom floating in warm milk,
its fragrance overwhelming, it is the gratitude
that comes back like sensation to the numbed palate,
it is the fine red skin around the moon-
colored inside of the fruit, it is "Indeed, we have tasted
of this before," and we will remember, will remember
as time goes back around, this year, this tender lamb
or turkey ham with split pea soup upon the table spread

248

11th Hour Plea
Yahia Lababidi

One foot here, one foot there
how much longer, weary pilgrim,
lingering at the threshold?

One step forward, two steps back
—still lusting after this world—
what about your old promises?

To die to your *nafs*, to transform
the mud to gold, to give up
distractions and consent to be born?
*

O, you who do not believe
in demons, they court you, nonetheless
See their faces
in your contorted features
Hear their voices
in perverse suggestions

Despite their myriad seductions,
their aim, all ways, is the same
to degrade, defile and desecrate
all that is holy...

Rumi's Line
Abdalhamid Evans

I read a quote from Rumi
    years ago
        close on forty
I cannot find it now
    try as I may

He said that his words

were like fish
pulled alive and quivering
from the water
and die, quivering
on the bank

or like bread
pulled fresh from the evening's oven
night passes over it
and it does not taste the same
come dawn

And yet
and yet…

the heart pulls words
into the mind's ether
and they stumble onto the tongue
or pen
and paper

And sometimes
just sometimes

they hold the note
some sweet sustain
some tearing gain
some loss
some sweet surrender

And reading, listening
we may travel back
and taste the spark
reflected in that pool

Medjool
Rakaya Esime Fetuga

Not Ajwa or Ambar or Safawi
not Khudri, Kholas or Medjool
12 years she wanted to eat a fresh date
so she wouldn't have any at all.
Sayyidah Rabe'a al Adawiyya
from birth a queen amongst women
crowned in her slave-hood
by a lantern floating over her head in prayer
the colour of yellow date flesh
gorgeous bright, fearful awesome
that shined with such authority
her owner rushed to let her
free from his dim house
and into the desert.

God taught her discipline.
Her conviction was a date seed,
firm stone in a world
sticky with self-adoration,
ribbed pit, like stern lips holding
under the foot of ostentation
never flattened, never crushed
the seed would rather be stamped deep
in the dark of the ground
never bothered, never found
turning the Divine love that left her
hungry, thirsty, constricted and alone
into date palms, abundant
stretching out of the earth and
out of herself entirely
until her human needs fell off her
like ripe fruit off a laboured tree.

The world was a festering of wants
of feasting and flaunting and taunting
and men asking futile questions

of egos with greedy suggestions
that never aligned with what
Allah had lain out on the plate
which wasn't a soft, easy life
or a sweet jewelled date
but to rely on no one and nothing,
knowing something in everything
would fail her
that desire was the true cell and jailer
that the true love of her endless spirit
Was greater than the world
and everything in it
sweeter than Khudri, Kholas, Medjool
Ajwa and Ambar and Safawi.
Fasting from all but worship
of Allah, the Enricher, al Mughni
let her drop this crisp fruit of a globe
from her hand
and set her saintly free.

Ruku‘

Ray Lacina

You stand and you bow and you rise and you think this:

"The thing that bends folds on the outside
but curls within."

Like paper turned here, turned there,
bent, creased, bent again and voila:
a crow, a crane, a child, a swan.

But when you bow and rise and fall
on the inside, you think, you curl.
Like the fingers of a cupped hand,
like a child cupping water in her hands, laughing,
amazed that it's there.

That is the folding, there.
This is the curling, here.
The water cupped, ripples
and the wind is the wind that lifts you.

dream-walk in the city of saints
Bushra Mustafa-Dunne

The city swoons
with ripples of your hand on her face.

In the dance is stillness.

I search for the back of your head
but it is only a new moon

in a drunken haze
I push through throngs of men with your name
wetting their tongues

– where is the water?

I see a هلال[20] leading me a new way.
I see the dappled shadow of a Lover
as I am drawn up the path
and she draws
water
and I drink.

We rest in the hand that ripples

the still point

every sip is a veil
and the franticness, its lifting.

---

[20] Crescent moon pronounced *hilāl* in Arabic

254

Magenta
Rabia Saida

The poplars shimmer sunlight again
The ceanothus is a cloud of indigo
While an azalea in my garden
Is more hues of magenta than you can imagine
The sun is gentle these long fasting days
Some an endurance test
They still lend me more discipline than I naturally possess

The orchid cascades alabaster blossoms
Over the windowsill in the kitchen
Pots of basil and coriander
Have been snipped a bit thin
To garnish *harira* and salads
For fast breaking

My son stumbles from bed
To eat *suhur* bleary eyed
I try to pack enough nutrient dense calories in
To support spiritual and physical growth spurts
And pray for our protection and guidance
In this labyrinthine plane of reality

He's better at fasting than me
I am insomniac
wide awake in these short nights
Until *fajr* rolls in
I need to nap
Cat-like in the day

Some manage to pray all night
I just try to survive the ride
Of circadian rhythm disruption
And learn from the alteration
Of feast and famine
Hopeful some of the blessings of the month
Will settle upon me all the same

Part of the miracle
Is the routine breaking
No matter how uncomfortable or inconvenient
Making you view things from a different perspective
creating space for reflection

The brokenness of people and the world assails me some days
There is so much pain and trauma
on the news
woven into the web of relations we are part of
We must be here to alleviate some of this
We must be here as healers
For ourselves and one another

Yet the flowers and trees are perfect
Plane trees unabashed in their majesty
Horse chestnuts resplendent in full candled canopies
Jasmine an explosion of perfumed symmetry
Roses impossibly exquisite
Acers fractal in their colour and delicacy
While clouds tell vast stories across the horizon

The moon is full now, veiled by wispy cloud
Still visible in the coolness of early morning light
In a lull of quiet
before the dawn chorus strikes up
Having measured the days with illumination
It starts to wane again
As days slip away
With the imminent departure
Of our trusted friend
who never fails
to shake us up
And embrace us in blessings

The Pulse of Remembrance
Yasin Chines

As my *sibha* is strewed,
I sheaf the remains
with your velvet string.
On each bead, I,
ink the spine of words
to the palms of seas.

The surface I am on
undulates as I watch
the receding shore,
where you took its clay
and moulded each bead
to the breath of my thumb.

I gaze reflectively
to where I am headed,
as you scatter the
sun's pebbles atop
the rippling sea;
offering me your palm.

You dip me into the sea
then run your fingertips
dearly, over my frozen eyes;
awakening me with a flock of
red, indigo, yellow and green,
leaking over my grey canvas.

Although I cannot send you
palms of my own, I offer
the red of this melting sunset,
or the streak of that yellow moonlight
on the other side of the sea
Still, you exceed their beauty

With the sea's fluency

you thread my beads
Each bead now a tear
that dreams to assemble a stream
fluidly carrying my words to you

Like the moon's face on the sea
you're present even in my absence,
ready to always let me in
as freely as air lets in light

Isa
Ron Geaves

The light glowed on his polished brow
the moon at the last midnight.
White pearls hung their heads
    too delicate for the heels of men.
Each one threaded to a tapestry of green
                yet so gently seen
as he strode the hills.
In solitude the collectors of ills were avoided.
The Pearl of greatest price
one breath that had returned to the source.

She's a Mystic

Abbas Mohamed

A mystic is a poet:
Poetry coursing through her veins till
a mystic walks poetry
breathes, eats, and talks poetry
exudes poetry
one for each and every mood, poetry

That's a mystic:
always a laugh in her cheek,
a smile forever hiding in the corners of her eyes

A believer is the mirror of a believer
A mystic is the mirror of the Divine
in herself

A mystic is a mystery
she is hidden to those
that cannot see her

But once you open the Eyes of your Heart
once you polish the Mirror of your Heart
once you see through the Lens of your Heart

Everywhere you go
you will see another you
I will see another me
you will see a me in you
I will see a you in me

You'll see that all is One
and that One is all we see.
How else could it ever be?

White Trousers Muhammad

Hanan Issa

"Who told you that?"
"Muhammad gave it to me."
"Long hair Muhammad?"
"No."
"Chip shop Muhammad?"
"No."
"Won't speak to women Muhammad?"
"No."
"Chinese Mohammed?"
"No."
"10 Kitkats Muhammad?"
"No."
"Posh Muhammad?"
"No."
"Graffiti Muhammad?"
"No."
"Ripped Mohammad?"
"Hey!"
"I mean Personal Trainer Muhammad?"
"No."
"Well, who then?"
"White trousers Muhammad.

Estaghfirullah

Asma Khan

You promised us forgiveness
For sins as high as the clouds
and now they span the earth
You breathed us
We poisoned Your air
Your oceans watered us
We filled them with plastic
To satisfy thirst of a rare flavoured kind
Your trees raised us in their silent peace
Adorned our existence
reached to shelter and comfort us
We axe their loving hold, serial killers
Let their bark peel with pollution
engineer their fruit to our taste for the new
You gave us cattle humble serving meek
We butcher them and their newborn regardless merciless
You rush to us with Your *aşk*
So we may know Your treasures
We toss them aside for valueless bitcoins
You created planets to show us the way to
Become their whirling from You, by You, of You
We want to own even them
spend money that could feed thousands for an ego that cannot journey
even an inch in You
We prefer our nudity to Your veil of *huzoor*
In our new and improved Garden of Eden
Crass contemporary entertainment for us
not timeless humane witnessing
You promised us redemption no mother could offer to her most
unruly children
self absorbed in their game
We will play it to the bitter end unsatisfied ungrateful
Forgetting to You we belong
And to You we return

Loss[21]

Toneya Sarwar

Did I not love you enough?
Were you a blessing that I missed?
Was I too busy with today
That I forgot to see tomorrow?

You came and left so suddenly
But left an ache that didn't go away
It was too late when I realized
That you were not here to stay

For years and years, I blamed myself
I refused to accept the decree
That somehow my lack of love
Took you far away from me

But in all truths that come to pass
There is a wisdom so profound
That if you surrender to His will
What is lost is always found

---

[21] Only 7 months after the birth of my highly anticipated first son, I became pregnant again. This time was different. I was anxious and worried if I would be able to cope. Such a contrast to the first pregnancy that was full of elation and gratitude. After 6 weeks I miscarried. The guilt of losing the baby was at times too much to bear. In time I learned to accept that all matters are from God and that He is the best of planners.

Guidance
Emny Kadri

When I started down this path, everything was about you.

Everything.

Although, deep inside I knew, Allah was the Initiator, the Caller.

He patiently Echoed inside my soul.
Never once stopping.

Like a Gentle Lover, Caressing His Beloved. He remained. And I witnessed His presence. I witnessed His immeasurable Beauty.

The journey had already begun, with my love for you. Through that love I witnessed the Divine. I witnessed the Whole. I witnessed the One.

Ash-hadu an la ilaha illa Allah.

From deep inside myself, He called out with inspiring words.

He told me this path is His.
That I would join Him...

Never Give up - He reminded me.

All I had to do was forsake the other.
Strangely I held on...

I held on to the memories and the thoughts.

How could I jump out into the Heart of the Beloved when the heart of a human seemed more tangible?

My heart was overwhelmed and overflowing.

I knew from the beginning this Love was a Divine love.

It couldn't be warded off.

Likewise, it needed to be returned to its Creator.

To love another was to proclaim disbelief.

Profanity.

Inna lillah wa inna ilayhi rajioun.
From Him we came and to Him we shall return.

My passing has already begun.

My journey.

I'm coming to life where before I was most certainly dead.

Difference Engine

Matthew Bain

Love cascades like mist
down stepped fields
wetting them with dew.
High and low
is all love needs
to shed tears.

Like wind
blown between isobars,
love needs fluctuations,
heterogenous zones,
to manifest.

No borders between you and me
but ebbs and flows, undulations,
mean we must love to understand
or else put up bars where none exist
and break the flow, for what?

In God there are no fissures, only Names.
God is One.
His universe, this difference engine rolls,
not changing Him but displaying
relationships that mean much more than things.

Count things if you can -
two = enumerate the infinite relationships between things is futile,
it's where love is to be found, requiring multiplicity:
one = love is too profound
zero = ground.

Forever Beggars in the Laughing Lion's Court
Miroku Nemeth

Marissa cut her long beautiful hair
Hair that flowed like dark waterfalls
From the Andes, from the Sierras
Now all waterfalls of our collected tears
She solemnly cut it to mourn the loss
Of my son her step-son Omar as her people do.
She could never be more beautiful to me
Than when I look at her now forever
And see her short hair tucked behind her ears
And Mapuche heart honor.
Together we walk near the precipice path
On the edge of this loss abyss
Falling into the numbing cold blackness, crawling out
With tearflow hand holds or being lifted
By sweet memories of Omar's smile
Like his big strong sturdy hands
Like mine, but bigger and more beautiful,
Or given flight by the warmth of his kindness
Or his fierce Sufi chivalry
How since a boy, he would fight to protect
Anyone hurting
Deadlocked laughing lion
Gentle hearted and wounded
Who put himself always last.
Who died first.
We survive for the
Remembrances of who
He would want us to protect here
And who he would see flourish
So we live still
Cut so deeply
And honoring love
In such tears and love
That words
All words
Are forever
Beggars in the Laughing Lion's court.

Darning
Rabia Saida

So many of us are
Off kilter mixes
Of overindulged deprivation
Like a tapestry in holes
Worn by time and damp, moth eaten
Mended with silver thread and gaudy bits of string.
Even children are this patchwork
Cashmere and acrylic covering ripped seams
Holes in families and communities
Stitched over with cheap yarn from China or just love and stardust
Does anyone still know the art of invisible darning
or do patches always look absurdly out of place?
Perhaps we were always like this
Droughts and death digging hungry crevices in souls
They tried to fill with land grabs and subjecting others to their will
The web of pain spreading needing unending alterations
to mend the damage done
Yet these quilted bodge jobs
Are testimony to beauty
And our unfaltering search for new methods
To fix the latest fabrics damaged in unprecedented ways
Never discarding the seemingly unfixable as beyond repair.

the ant's world

Idris Mears

bowling along the lanes of a landscape sculpted
by generations of human use and neglect
the windscreen of my life and times'
addiction to the auto-mobile
puts the 'screen' between
me and the eye-
smarting sweet reek of the bonfire
the shoulder-hunching bluster of the wind bowling
the bone-dry leaves along

in this remove of movement
eyes extract each detail
that poplar with those storm-weathered pennants in its rigging
that wisp of smoke dark cat on its morning patrol
padding with intent through the overgrowth of the dew-silvered verge
that face of a child pressed like a prisoner
to the window of a car passing
into that exact future

i like a wild-eyed vagrant
stuffing scraps of paper into the pockets and
sleeves of a tattered coat
for later reference
or to pass on to some ragamuffin
who tags alongside for a while
in the companionship of the road
in hope that on one scrunched scrap
there is a glimpse of a secret
name signifying
something

oh to stop
and press brow into cold damp grass
smell the chill of the earth
still the heart and cool the eye
in the ants' and other worlds

What Have We Got
Daniel Abdal-Hayy Moore
from the poetry collection Facing Mecca

At five o'clock in the morning after the
Morning Prayer on the
first day of two weeks' notice of being "let go" from my
job of eight years because they
can't afford to pay me any more, what have I
got? Dear Lord,
You. First.
Foremost. This
earth a
tiny place. The
heart holds all.

Five senses, light-filled near
clock-tick, distant
car-swish, this early. Dark outside.

I've got wife, blue and
starry skies shining
silver behind her when she
embraces me and says she's
with me no matter
what, and she also
her own world's proof and truth.
Our children
guaranteed blessing of provision by their
very souls' existence in our
living domain, their
sustenance
written for them from
before eternity, it comes in material form through
thick and thin, seeking them
out... And

they themselves
stutter forward in

growth-spurts on the
chronological movie, joy in their
surprise consciousness, their
own beings throwing out
unique lights casting
twelve-dimensional shadows in broad daylight
against the air.

And I've been
in and out of the earth, up and
down on it, and
keep arriving
back to this point, actually
landing upright, Lord, Lord, after
any upsets, retrievable
miles unrollable inside of
more highway into dark wilderness, that
ends up in
familiar
territory each
time,

and this love of writing it down,
that maybe its
aroma remind somebody casually passing under my window,

and, my God, my window given at
birth, window
till death, same
window beyond, our
windows, each of us has
to see through, reach
through, breathe steam on the
glass pane to write out Your
Infinite Name.

Memory lapse

Yasmine Ahmed-Lea

I sit on the wall outside of my house
Humid summer sticking to my eyelids
Making everything hazy, blurring colours
I swing my legs back and forth like I did
When I was ten
And you were
Always there
Squinting now, I create you
Looking far down the road
Walking slowly up the street
Your scarf wrapped, falling slightly from your head
Your slow sway in that cream cotton
Only saved for days like these
Mumbling words of wisdom to yourself
Or maybe a thousand prayers
To the sky
And as my eyes fill with the reality
That this is but a mirage
You walk past me
And smile, looking at me knowingly
From the corner of your eyes
Marching ever onwards
To your real home

O Love
H I Cosar

When pain feels dense in my chest
And my eyes are a swollen mess
I remind myself
I
Said
Yes
I was simply in awe
I could not say no

Yet when you break a promise
Is this love my heart whispers
Is this love my pride demands
When I feel no shame
As I place my love under your feet

Then I see a wild flower
You placed at my window
A smile on your face
In full bloom, a full moon

I read my name in your eyes
When you call me yours

I become certain
This is as close as I get
To finding the divine

I laugh at myself
For I was not like this before

A proud rock stood
Where I am
Your love turned me into sand
Once a rainforest
I am now ash

Once an oasis
Now just a mirage

I can only sense
Beauty around me
If you are in the frame

I can only taste life
When you give me your lips

O love
Save your money
Keep the jewels
I need nothing from you but
you
I have no desire for sweet words
Just be at the end of each road

O love
With you
I am no longer I
Without you
I am no longer

How Beautiful is the Moon
Muneera Pilgrim

As the day is dusted and done away with
As the sun sets and the orange red sky rolls back to welcome its blue
black counterpart
How beautiful is the Moon?

"Marhaba" says the day greeting the night for how beautiful is the
moon

How comforting is her gaze offering warmth to those who seek solace
in her light
Who seek respite from the toil of the day this moment we call life
An opportunity to catch their breath before they join back the fight
a pause between the wounds
a chance for the blood below the surface of the skin to bruise
How beautiful is the Moon?

This is a song for sweet Sara
Dark Sara
same colour as the shade Sara
granite sapphire Sara
Why couldn't you escape in the shadow Sara
disappear like a mirage in the Sahara

Sara

this is a song for you
a few years shy from your teen softest voice to have ever uttered
most mysterious eyes you've ever seen
who belongs to who
you to the moon? or the moon to you?
the tales of your foremothers are present in your pores
your whole existence is a cause for awe
cool midnight tone
strong chiselled cheeks
cushions for lips
beauty is out of reach

brocaded with sincerity and godly speech
Daughter of the south now in the bustle of the north,
in the bowels of the city
Dear Sara how did you get so far from home?
How is it that you are alone?
How it is that no one greets you even when they pass with their robes
and thobes?
Choosing to ignore you until they need you to iron their clothes,
until they need you to wash their clothes
until they need you to clean the yard,
fetch the water cook the food
your whole being lights up because someone greeted you
with the greeting of Salaam in the way that we all ought to
Ya Sara
sweet Sara
serenade your name Sara
may angels surround you Sara
protect you now and in the *akhirah*
Ya Sara
Please tell me how beautiful is the moon and her light as it reflects on
you.
How Beautiful is the moon and your skin as her light reflects on you.

My Heart is Exhausted
Sukina Pilgrim

My heart is exhausted.
All the times I told her
To calm down
And stay quiet
And not feel so damn much
Is catching up on me.
I kept her in my palm
And clenched fist
Whenever she got carried away.
We don't have the privilege
Of losing control -
It's not safe for coloured girls
To love too loudly
Or feel too deeply
Everything has to stay steady
And just so.
Us women with skin
The colour of the earth
Can not give birth
To the type of rage
That could set the world
On flames
Without being demonised
Or criminalised.
Our emotions
Give birth to passions
Perceived as aggression
Then used as a weapon
Against us.
So we sedate our hearts
Just to manoeuvre
Through life -
Approachable
Non-threatening
Easy-going
Entertaining

Or invisible.
Anything but me.
I'm tired.
Are you

Difference
Sabila Raza

You made up your mind
My headscarf
My skin colour
My gender
All spoke for me
When you were being told about me, did you listen for my voice?
Did you pause, think, search, for the truth?
I did not choose my skin colour
I did not choose my gender
My faith, I believe to be my saviour
To you I am an inferior other, a threat, a criminal
But, I am the one left feeling like a victim
Born into a system where I'm unequal
Burdened by pain, sadness and anger
Because who I truly am holds no value
My externalities make me irrelevant
My voice is silenced
I am already spoken for

Mystic Underground
Wajiha Khalil

The mystic underground
alone we are words, together we are poetry
the berries budding 'tween pine needles in winter solstice
meeting at the mysterious clearing within
the forest that welcomes encampment
and greets the traveler upon every path
salaam

Our pens dance upon tablet
Like oud infects bark, curing
one another with original
God sent hope in folded love notes
Carried in bird's beaks
visit us and stay awhile
there is no rush and plenty of room
ahlen

Earthly disguise cannot prevent us from
one another in the Land of Eternity
or this temporary cabin stay of a day or two
Our cloth was cut long ago
and threads do wish to tie
despite all odds
to reveal the heavenly garment
of poetry

What the Migraine Said
Yahia Lababidi

As I lie, here, half in and out of consciousness
I imagine my migraine as a world migraine
my cluster headache as a cluster of world aches
that we must tip toe around like a sleeping tiger

The sleep of reason produces monsters—
this we know from art and the news:
murder and sham leaders shooting themselves
in one foot and chewing on the other.

But, the sleep of reason produces angels, also
like Love, which is no whimsical thing,
a love like bull, bullfighter and bloody cape,
billowing in the wind, like an open heart

Beckett said this best, truth in paradox:
The mystics I like...their burning illogicality
–the flame...Which consumes all our filthy logic...
Where there are demons there is something precious

Once we know this, the rest is silence.
The master is not permitted
the same mistakes of a novice.

The Seed (shouted)
Yusuf Abdalwadud Adams

The seed was planted
With the best of intentions
On the site of the Tower of Babel
Before any person questioned one single tongue
But yet grew stone by stone
To dare to think it could threaten
The stars

For it is a garden within which
We broke apart
Myriad tongued and multiple
Yet one

Not before raising up a
Single city to pierce realms
Did we come to be scattered
Yet still
The garden ran with us

Humankind
Dwelt on the earth and learned to behave
Like water on a leaf when we desired to so be

What was first planted grew and it was a delight
Dwellings rose and lay or hung among the greener desert slopes
Nothing was then built upon
No land was scraped flat nor river diverted
Until the beauty shone too bright
Art & Science soared

Only then did we pierce the earth
Such screaming beauty was made
With this earth's blood my dear beloved friends,
Digging down to build our great foundations and systems of irrigation
The ease of our prowess in survival became the cyclones of waste
Pouring down

Then to find
Drilling deeper
Divinely finite
Black life blood
For which death is the price
Yet no one knew
Throats ever thirsty while eyes hungered for the completion of
The city's roaring spasm of technical transcendence
So much energy diverted into this single spire
Hewn from aether and fire
While the gifts of the garden lay waiting
Eternally Patient

Answer to Your Cries
Emny Kadri

He watches your face.
Beautifully covered in tears.

You thrash about and kick and scream.

He watches that also.
In all your wildness.
Exquisite.

You are safe in His eternal embrace.
He is your Beloved...

But do you, oh young, young girl, realise that you are His?

It Was the Last Hour
Arthur Skip Maselli

Now is the last hour
of the year's last day.
Here is the cloud mottled midnight sky
diaphanous gun smoke gray
something craving light,
as faint as far away.

Soft moon specter, lucent veil
can you not even seduce a poem?
Can no winter air hold my breath
cradled in this town
of pale, pretty abodes
of emptiness?

These nights, I am a bone dry quill,
aloft in windless restlessness.
The branches bereft of leaves,
tease my chaste silence into
blushing breathlessness,
this empty page, my jealous mistress.

Ten thousand starlings' murmuration
mimic spring and summer songs,
by a lone frenetic peregrine,
their sky is split, and two moments later,
winter's come, then gone, gone,
gone.

Mystic cyphers turn the many spired stars,
while love assembles secrets
in the mirror of those endless silver eyes.
Clues that disclose the senseless demarcation of time.
Hush dear one, there is no hurry
in summing it up in metered rhyme.

Lost and Found?

Nimah Ismail Nawwab

We lost the core
worship diligently
with minute, particular movements
wrapping touted diction
extolling the mundane without spirit
We lost the core

The Beloved's love
The Great One's Mercy
The spiritual bond
are out of the equation
we lost the core

Who savors the fruit

and leaves the heart, core,

Reviving the essence
we embrace peace
and are devotees of Higher Love.

I Think I Heard It Again

Nura Tarmann

I think I heard it again. The sound of a heart breaking.
How many times can a heart break?
The pieces are getting brighter, smaller. Over and over.
I keep asking, no answer comes back, only a deep quiet,
going on into Infinity.
How many times can a heart break?
How many motherless children roaming dark alleys
How many fatherless sons searching for approval
How many lonely women yearning for their men
How many times can a heart break?
Is it something you get better at, like adding sums in your head
or mixing ingredients for a cake?
How many times can a heart break?
The old man sitting with his bottle just laughed at me, after me with
me
and I smiled back.
How many times can a heart break?
Try not to count maybe you'll forget.

Sabr
Aaishah Mayet

"Make *sabr*; make *sabr*"- whispered the sea of cloaked figures
Her throat tightened, her chest heaved, her eyes burned, her ears winced,
HOW HOW HOW?!?!

"Dhikri, here, drink"
Darling? Water? Sugar? Now?!

"*Sabr*"- there came the hissing reminder again
Patience? Really? To keep a good attitude
Good attitude? Now?!

She bit down hard in the early morning numb disbelief
"No, no...it's not her!"
"But my sweetheart, it is..."

Like the prediction of a violent thunderstorm on a clear summer's day

"Pleeasse nooo!" Yet the way of the world is sure:
Live. Love. Lose. Live again

One day her gurgling belly laugh will echo joyfully
Her love for richly hued kaftans will overpower the white shroud,
And the aroma of her freshly-baked cherry madeira will subdue the
camphor so dense in your nostrils today...

"Dhikri"-Yes. Dhikri. Darling. -she called you that...
Thunderstorms have a way of restoring that enraged-elephant-battered
uprooted earth

Water

Asiya Sian Davidson

swaying slightly
we do not see his face
sitting centre *mihrab*
recitation runs through us
a river of gold
we do not see his face

this is the way it is
we climb mountains
searching for rain
returning disappointed
it wasn't like last time

step inside briefly for an *al-Fatiha*
expecting nothing
and the room has become
an ocean

make me host only to this
only to
You

clear out my house
all the disaster
that comes from the wrong kinds of
aloneness

I need a village
like Hajar
I can't find water for my child

make me a water that can extinguish
all the disaster
that comes from the wrong kinds
of initiation
make me host to your river of gold

Khushoo'[22]
Toneya Sarwar

Dear Prayer mat so beautifully designed
What did you hear today?

A three course meal, plus ingredients I need
A meeting I must prepare to lead
A friend's birthday gift I have to buy
A new outfit I want to try
A fleeting thought of how much I've spent
A mental note of when to pay the rent
A plan to fix a broken door
A job is left – the kitchen floor!

So much to do – can't think straight
Was that seven *rakah* or eight?

Assalamu alaikum wa rahmat Allah
Assalamu alaikum wa rahmat Allah

---

[22] *Khushoo'* refers to when the worshipper is able to connect with their Creator with absolute devotion and attention. Often prayer time for me is the only time the world stops for a few minutes. Hence my mind starts to wander. Gaining Khushoo' has gradually improved over the years as I've learned more about my faith and my relationship with it. However, it certainly remains a work in progress.

Love's measure
Tasnim McCormick Benhalim

Love has no calculating in it, if we hold and sing it through.
We can be generous and confess when we are not.
Can soar in our awares - angling toward awkward, uncomfortable truths -
    that when finally met are all breath-taking beauty
Forgive ourselves and all we love and circle back and forgive again.
Reset with grace and the exponential spheres of gratitude.
Pour out our heart in the stillness of night
    gamble everything for love and meet the morning free at first light.
So deeply flawed, so fully human, so right.
Dancing the *barzakh*.

February 2, 2018
Miroku Nemeth

It's one day until tomorrow
The anniversary no one wants
The death of my Omar.
He will forever be nineteen and a half.
And I don't know how I will mourn
What I will do. If it will be like every
Other day. Every other hour.
Every other minute.
Where a memory of his kind grin
Or laughter or the look in his eyes
Or the way he walked out in the yard
Barefoot and graceful and tall
Truly magnificent
Truly beautiful
Or words of insight he spoke
That were all love and listening
Or how his eyes watched who
He listened to
Fully polite
Fully present
With you
Whoever you are
As I raised him
As his mother raised him
But he was always better than me,
And I don't know if one day until
Tomorrow on two days after the
New Year of 2018, one month after
The worst anniversary, if it will be
The hardest for me, like every hour,
Every minute, where a memory
Of Omar, my sweet Omar, makes
All my words fail falling like men losing
Their handholds and plummeting
Into the abyss, all my words becoming
A formless fog from which the heart's

Reality cannot be expressed and all
I have is these overwhelming
Anniversary sobs and more tears.
And on January third, we lost a third of ourselves, all of ourselves, for
Omar
Was more than a half to Yusuf,
More than my whole to me,
(But Yusuf is as well)
And I just don't know if there are anniversaries
Here in temporal hell.
But because he was Omar
Leonine in strength, countenance, loyalty, will
I feel his smile still
I feel the Baraka in his faith he almost
Drunkenly professed to me
Smiling smiling smiling "I'm a Muslim"
A week before his death
Still professing, Inshaa Allah, after
Being washed, enshrouded, buried
By a father's and brother's hands from
A place of light and everlasting safety
With his dreadlocked warrior poet benevolence
But this father begs
His brother begs
His family begs
His loved ones beg
Oh Lord, please rain down Mercy on this anniversary.
Oh Lord, please rain down *Rahmah* on this
anniversary.

Nothing Else Matters
Shahbano Aliani

come, Friend
so i can breathe and live again
without You
my heart is constricted
and my breath
comes painfully

come!
so i can expand like the sky
soar up like the wind
pour out like a cloud

listen:
all day i collect beautiful words
to string into songs for You
when You are away
they wither and turn to dust
come, so these beautiful words
can bloom and grow a garden

come!
so i am swallowed up
by the space
around You

nothing else matters!

Eid al-Adha 2019
Ray Lacina

Pretty much everyone is sick after hajj
as you come home to a house that suddenly feels
like a foreign country
and drop your bags inside the door
you're snuffling maybe, maybe coughing
maybe just getting over a fever
that had you sleeping on the long flight home
that you maybe felt coming on as you packed your bags or made your
final circuit
around the House
maybe you felt the trickle leaving Mina
or during the last few days there
getting used to not wearing the clothes that once
had been so you
to not being in *ihram*
after days in that sacred state
lifted with the cutting of your hair
you likely felt fine at the final stoning
and even if you felt a little trickle, a little
woozy
that final denial of the darkness
would feel like a seal of all that's gone before
just as the first stoning days earlier felt
like the beginning of the end
after the long night on the open plain
where you gathered stones then slept out under the sky
the lights
exhausted but light after the long day's standing
at Arafat
but more so
before your Lord hands lifted or cupped or covering your face
to capture your tears
impossible to believe that just that morning you woke in your tent in
Mina
a galaxy away
where you had readied yourself for just that moment

walking through the sudden city
hearing every language
seeing every color of skin
now wrapped in white
all different
all the same
with no contradiction
at this place you came to walking, or came on the train they'd added
since your last time
leaving Makka after the running between the hills
the first circling of the House
in your freshly wrapped *ihram*
put on just hours before maybe
on the plane or maybe
as you paused at the *miqat*
looked over your shoulder at the parking lot
but not at the parking lot
but rather at the journey that brought you there
from the life you'd put on pause
the days in and days out of it
the long years that all led
to this
the many Eids you'd celebrated hoping
exactly
for this.

The Orphan's Song for The Kaaba - *extract*
Novid Shaid

It's like the Sun heating up all space
And the people, the planets, orbiting with haste
It's like the sky on a darkened night
And the pilgrim stars shining around it so bright
It's like a magnet that our Lord has fixed
And humanity crowds and encircles it
It's like the heart beating silently
And the blood flows around it eternally
It's like mighty Saturn, darkened, flattened into a cube
And the ring of pilgrims beautify the view.
It's the House of God, and He loves His guests,
And He answers all who make sincere requests

Photons
Medina Tenour Whiteman

On the wall
sun is crosshatched by the blind
scrambled by the tree outside
between the snatches of white
the lines are diluted ultramarine

Why should I remember this moment?
There's not much that it's redolent of
only my Zanzibari kanga shirt
the one that reads
"Amenitunza ndiyo maana ninapendeza"
("He, or she, has cared for me:
that is why I am beautiful",
and the beauty of that genderless Carer)
my two year old chanting
"Uppy", or possibly "Happy"
the gnawing emptiness
of the last half hour before Maghrib

breakfast long digested
mouth a faintly off clam
filling time with Jeeves and Wooster
as at any other non-memorable moment

only

I keep looking back at the
evening light strained through the blind
a rhombus of oscillating photons
the dying place of sun fire
that has travelled 100,000 light years
(this only occurs to me later
when water and spaghetti have
returned my ability
to read something into anything)
and wondering how many
non-memorable moments pass
unaccounted for
and if they should be accounted for
if they're not more important than the
gunpowder moments
burned white into retinas
for us to mourn their passing

The Metaphysics of Mercy

Barbara Flaherty

God forbid that I put over my shoulders the garment of religious rectitude
if love fashions a cloak for me out of the sackcloth of blame.
                    - Nūr ad-Dīn 'Abd ar-Rahmān Jāmī

Jāmī, you were the apostate
of every rule that ever made Him small.
You walked the naked blaming streets,
yet the walls of your hidden garden
were written on in love's alphabet.
A wolf at the inner ocean's shore
is howling to the hidden moon.
Where is my lover if not here?
The moons of all the planets
hang in the bowl of one sky.
Each day He strips me of all my fancy clothes.
One day He will strip my skin and bones.
A voice whispers, you were made
for the naked blaming street.
He alone is your cloak, is your identity.
What name could you ever have that is not His?

Perfumed Fountain
Shahbano Aliani

i was eating sawdust
before you let me drink
from your perfumed fountain

what did i know of fragrance
of being thirst
of being quenched
of love and longing
even
of
my
self
before i met you?

it is no small matter:
Love

it marks all its prisoners
for complete annihilation

even if i wanted
where would i go?

it is the entire cosmos
and holds us
enthralled

The Beloved
Paul Abdul Wadud Sutherland

I ask a scarecrow to speak, if it can, about
the Beloved: it turns its straw head and says:

Beyond what pain is un-understandable
no further torture exists, not burning bars
but the Beloved's arms ready to welcome.
Be confused – who's beloved, who's you.
Can't separate; then accept, be bewildered:
a holy state, the blessedness that follows grief.
The Beloved's already approaching to hold
you between sense and nonsense. Be empty
as my straw legs and head, easily on fire.
Give up on reason, don't fantasise
you can out-smart the Eternal One
or keep your individual pursuits.
The Beloved will use you like a rag
to change the world you now despise.
What's beyond indiscernible sorrow, is Love.
Sniff it when you see the blank wall bloom
and try not to name it – rose or jasmine –
just say YOU over and over to the Beloved.

This is the Marriage
Daniel Abdal-Hayy Moore

This is the marriage of a
very small horse and a giant green valley
at the dawn of the world

This is the marriage of sea foam and the
wind that blows it into spray

This is the marriage of a dark cupboard and a
hand that reaches in looking for diamonds

This is the marriage of all our faces to the
soul that makes them smile then makes them weep
then makes them smile again
a turquoise songbird and the emerald
branch it lands on

This is the marriage of sky and stars
light extending by day but going out by night with
a million lanterns to see itself by
self-illumined, eyes ablaze, singing at the top of its voice
like our hearts,

This is the marriage God wanted with us
before the creation of the world
before the Gate of mist and topaz opened
before the gorgeous fires around the edges of things ignited
alive squiggles outlining each lovable entity

This is the marriage of two people in a canyon of glass
under a real sun in a
procession of elephants and gazelle
both bringing the entire biological mystery together
to be delicately tied tendril by tendril into the knot of life
watched over by eagles wheeling the sky
by blind worms deep in their earthly meditations

This is the marriage of a
room and going into it
of a house and entering by the front door
of a country and obtaining a valid passport
of the air and the mockingbird's song that
flows into it
of a river and setting out in a green canoe to explore
new continents and their whispering people
and the extraordinary black orchids that grow there in the dark
in even the worst of circumstances

I call on the colors of the rainbow to bear witness
    sun glint on wave troughs

I call on the very thoughts that pass through our heads
at this instant to bear witness

O God, we are your loving creatures
still dew-sprinkled from the first
    deep ache of creation
trying to stand full height in a strong
wind to call on You.

Fill their youth with the wisdom of the seas
God's navigation by the stars
the sound of waves calling His Ninety-Nine Names
one by one and all together, never asleep

This is the marriage of our feet and the very
earth they stand on

The bodies we stand in
sinew by sinew and the inclinations of our souls

Two bodies a man and a woman
gazing at each other from their
facing towers of parakeets and milk pitchers
nasturtiums and spontaneous song
desire for perfection and deep knowledge of God in the heart

And we bear witness to it
before foam passes over a waterfall
and is gone

Before the flower of our lives becomes married to the
root of our deaths

With a tiny white horse in a green valley
at the dawn of the world

And we ride away into the light

Let it be
Eisha Basit

What if you let the moment be?
Let the rose petal fall silently?
Without catching,
Sweeping it away.

What if you let the moment be?
Let the rain pour thunderously?
Without ducking,
Running away.

Just let the moment be.
Let your voice break tremulously,
The floodgates open merrily
The pain, wax and wane steadily
This stretch of time, a melody,
Its birth and demise, a remedy
Be still...
In this moment, today.

Precious Cargo
Ayesha Ijaz

How many destinies had to collide
for you to traverse
through time and space
to end up here...

Yet, you worry He will forsake you.

How many eyes opened and closed
just so you will get to read this --
in this very moment...

Yet, you worry He will forsake you.

How many storms and celebrations
to get you to
where you're headed...

Yet, you worry He will forsake you.

Tell me, again,
how many days has it been
since the Day of Destinies?

Orkney Trout Saga
Abdalhamid Evans

You think you are going to catch them,
and maybe you are
but if you do, be aware
that the Orkney Trout may also catch you

Catch the part of you
that recognises
the act of hunting and stalking
deceiving one's prey
and feeding mouths afterwards

That primal figure
buried deep inside
reflected in the ripples of the loch
and the rippling sky
and the wind, always there, always present
and never more so than in a flat calm

With the stones under your boots
carefully you step,
stick in hand
among the skerries

Looking for a rise

and sometimes if you are fortunate
you may arrive at that place…
where the wind settles like a friend
behind your left shoulder
giving you that smooth extra loop
taking you that bit further with ease,
like a gift
and the ripple and the light merge
and settle into that rolling almost oily blend of
colours like spirits
undulating

on the top of the water
and in the underside of the air
And what a dance it is!

- and then the tug... ....
Aayyyyesss!
like electricity right down your wire
so alive, wild, darting
shaking his head
telling you his size
leaping in a quiver
diving down hard
and sometimes even running
for the horizon

Until he comes in, on his side, to the net
Last rites in the name of God
and the final quiver
whoooohh... and all that aliveness escapes
back into the loch and the sky...

and then the golden belly,
the black spots with a few red ones
and the silvery gold of the flank
are just there with you
in the boat
or on the bank

And you are caught...
hook, fly and floater.

Caught for life, most probably.

So, take a couple for the pot
and a few for friends on a special day
like the one we had on Boardhouse
that blessed day with three generations of us
afloat and reflecting

Time on the water
and on the stones
spent together, spent alone
spent in search of Orkney Trout

Heirloom
Rashida James-Saadiya

Somewhere there are tears and bombs
rupturing the beauty of sacred land
Somewhere there are boats
filled with people carrying nothing
except the gift of breath
Somewhere there are fathers using every inch of their bodies
to pull their children across borders,
for the comfort of safety
Somewhere the sun has left its place
And there is only my Grandmother
For when the sky is full of darkness and the world is asleep
She sits alone and prays

"Ya Allah, surely you're the best of weavers. Weave a song among us.
A joyous song of love upon our lips, so that we may leave the sorrows
of this world, for the mercy of your wisdom. By the setting of the
stars, my soul is a wanderer in search of the true purpose of my feet.
Please show us the way. Help us to walk with certainty despite the
spread of darkness.
Verily it is by Your labor and mercy that we exist though the world
may injure our bodies. It is You, who preserves the soul. Remind us.
Help us to turn the soil with our hands, to plant something better. To
mend our bones, to purify our hearts in oceans made of compassion
and infinite love. Ya Allah! Give us more than we deserve."

For somewhere there are broken hearts
waiting for a new song, a joyous song
one that removes sorrow from bones
one that guides our bodies into vessels
capable of healing this world

Voices
Yasmine Ahmed-Lea

What I would give
to hear your honey voice
once again
trickling through my soul
making this bitter bed
a resting place of sweetness
that laughter and melody
telling me to 'eat eat eat'
foreign words never sounded
more like home
what I would give
to hear your phrases
once again
'sadness has no place
inside you'
'eat well
and be merry'
'life is life'
'this is not everything'
'May God and His prophet be ever watchful on you'
'Don't worry, Be happy'
such simple words
hold so much meaning
depending on the voice
that is singing them out

what I would give
for you to tell me
these things
over
and over
and over
again

Nocturne
Fatima's Hand

I dreamt of the cosmos
It came one night
As I dreamt
I was driving
There was music
It expanded in me
It was all the cosmos
It kept me hostage
It dawned in *me*
When I awoke
The cosmos had vanished
It had been obliterated
All I wanted
Was to sleep again
And be awoken
In the dream
Driving
Through that nightscape
Of syncopated
Arpeggios

Discovering God
Murtaza Humayun Saeed

So many say they know the Truth
That they have the right to make everyone comply
Making others victims of close-mindedness
Burning hell they promise no less
If you transgress

I opened my own eyes and saw things afresh
This world as our temporary home
For every breath I felt blessed
Much less a fixed reality
Truth I found is more a Journey
I must strive for Him
Do more than survive!
Together with an adventuresome attitude
And wisdom born of gratitude
I shall find Him again and again
Alas! I shout for Joy with every living breath
I am aware I can stop and pause
And discover God over again!

Be

Cherif Al-Islam Abou El Fadl

Your presence is the solvent of cursed expectations mine
if happiness eclipsed were the price
and perpetual abandonment of flesh's pleasure
and ubiquitous tepid contentment mocked
i would pay it all to be with You

if oxygen took victim to silence
and companionship hung from a void of inexistence--
alone, in nothingness, with no memory of light
so no conception, nor reverence of color's beauty
i would undo and ergo have done myself
for with me i am undone
yet with You, in veritable serenity, I am done

some think i am a fool, others deranged
i am neither for i am not
how could snow covet warmth?
how could flame yearn for drink?
you are stuck in "here" and "there", "there" and "here"
while i have found everything in nothing

Your presence is the solvent of cursed expectations mine
You take my: to be with you
and have left me with: Be

Moss Praise
Fatima's Hand

The green halo'd beloved pours
an ancient wine
and as it falls from heaven
the pines and grasses quaff
and from the gnarly bark and sinews
will come flowers
in pursuit of Layla
and at their roots
mycelium of agarics seek her too
stretching deep
into the praise
into the shared warm breath
of earth's womb
where the sacred *sama'*
never ceases,
and when Layla enters
a deep stirring melody can be heard
from those inner chambers
awakening the mossy lashes of tree roots
from which come forth the murmuration of
a thousand birds

Scent of the rose
Jessica Artemisia Mathieu

I whisper to you of the rose,
her beauty,
her tender red petals
dewy.
Her kiss
and sweet breath
carry you to a garden

beyond death.

I whisper to you of the rose,
but how can you see her red petals
when you are surrounded by a glass dome,
swirling colors of blue and green,
pink, and brown.
Your world, a snowglobe.
Thick like a citadel
glass surrounds

I wish I could be the bell,
the sound that shatters your walls
causes the drawbridge to fall,
and tears the battlements apart,
because how can you know the scent of the rose
without having touched your nose
to her sun-warmed heart
and touched her tender limbs
with your skin?

I can shout, I can scream,
but you won't hear me,
even at the top of my lungs for eternity
or 5 years.
Look! Look at what I've found!
Look at the beauty I've seen!

So, at last, I leave
to find a companion who can share the scent of the rose
with me.

I'm so sorry.

Shikast
Matthew Bain

God put a light in my heart
but He had to break it first —
I had to break it for His sake —
my heart had to be broken for Him.

When I started to break my heart
it was hard and cold like lignite.
I had to chuck it on the grate
where it fissured somewhat.

Smoke started to seep from the cracks -
presumably some impurity —
that had to be smelted off.
It smelled bad.

Then it started to weep a substance,
I don't know what.
A chemical tear
pissed out of the rock.

My chest cavity ached
where my heart had been.
I watch it splutter
from my vacuity.

"Do I have to do this to myself?"
I asked God.
Well, would I rather someone else
tonged my heart with iron?

I whacked it
to see if it would split.
It did.
Funny that.

Could you have broken my heart?

You could have lifted my heart with your touch
and rested it
on some sweet surface —
cushions, ermine,
your lips.

As you tenderly smiled
and caressed it,
my heart would have sighed
and melted.

No such luck

I Ran
Yahia Lababidi

I ran hard and far
to outdistance my pain
But, when I got lost
my pain found me -
caressed me, wordlessly
and carried me Home.

Something like happiness

Yasmine Ahmed-Lea

There come those quiet feelings
Of love and something like
Contentment
Rushing into my heart
So suddenly
You can be raised
But not yet have lived
He said
Feeding her gently
Graciously like alms or
Rights of passage
To be earned
I can't love any more than this
I think
But as beckoning cries stir
The still slow beats of my heart
The cracks burst open a little more
And I find myself
Overflowing again.

For Those Bereft of Dew

Yohosame Cameron

like confetti… swirling within my mind~
your image among the debris.
in silence,
it was not hard to find~ your skin, within, the heart of me.

and i won't forsake you, for i do not mistake you~
dancing on the precipice of now.
and for those bereft of dew,
let them have a drink of you~
you can't take that to your grave, anyhow.

out on the streets… copping espanola gold~
gathering what's been spilled as i've been told.
one foot in front of the other,
are you somewhere down the river, my brother?
send me line sometime…
if i don't answer, (and i won't answer)

leave a rhyme~

so i don't miss you.
the fact that you exist, soothes~
the restless nature of a heart that's set to roam.
and for those bereft of dew,
those words once sang are true:
"if i knew the way, i'd take you home"~

like confetti… twirling within my mind~
your image among the debris.
in the barzakh, where our stories come to unwind~

ours is still the one i long to see!

so i won't forsake you, for i do not mistake you~
dancing on the precipice of now.
and for those bereft of dew,
let them quench themselves on you~
you can take that to your grave, anyhow.

Untitled

Asma Khan

I always loved the sound of the wind
coming across the great park opposite my house
I sat and watched a lot of sky and clouds pass by
before the era of iPhones and tablets came
That wind, the air taking my breath away
and the feel of stones and walls and mud
rough stone I remember
scraping my back as I searched for a lost cricket ball
Behind the garage
I never minded those dark outdoor places
Fingers in crevasses, picking up worms and spiders
And always that wind at night, my lullaby
One night it took me back to a time
I couldn't place, before me, before even it
and anything or anyone I knew
And the sheer vast joy of it all felt safe
Tonight the wind down here sounds just the same
And I know no more than I knew then

Love

Yusuf Abdalwadud Adams
(spoken or sung or spray painted in fragments on walls)

Love is loving and never spent though we unwind and break and bend and shatter and grow and glisten and know and smile and shiver in our embraces.

Love reaches towards unity in all instances without thought or pause for It is Its own cause... and we may fail to comprehend or be gentle or be bold or be quick-clear or patient-slow but the heart knows while being also flesh and blood.

Love reflects the spectrum of light, sometimes dark and sometimes too bright to behold, too subtle to be told, it will never deceive though lovers shake and grieve in their mourning... Sweet deaths and hot tears or bright laughter and well kissed tales to transmogrify the years into a taste upon the tongue that results in vision.

Love reveals and makes clear, despite the delirium encountered there and then where desires exacerbate the drum beat of the veins, the usurpation of the brain... What remains of fear when love is here?

May your lovers be kind for there is no other form of loving than loving kindness, no ecstasy but in what is given freely, no demands will be satisfied, forget the lie we were sold to fear by, we are not the paid up prince or princess, remember that all the empires are a fraudulent bloody mess.

Real myth speaks of that which is real, validate it in the bones of what you feel, in your sacred gut and your sacred groin and the sacred crown upon your head... A truth to taste now and take with when dead and gone full grown and unfolded into grace.

The one full and empty face of love smiles with your smile, your lips, your love.

Become a cultivator of roses, plant flowers for the bees, and forget everything else.

Tide of Pain
Shahbano Aliani

the tide of pain
rises
pulled
to the moon
of Your Remembrance

wave after wave
lifting
from the ocean bed
of my heart

searching, seeking, failing
falling
soaked up
at the shore
of Your absence

just when i think:
i can't endure it!
that without You,
the next breath is impossible
the pain retreats;
i am distracted
by the sun
the day and what it brings

duties beckon
and shopkeepers ask:
how much of this
will you need today?

for a while
i forget heartache
i become of this world
i count the change,
laugh at a joke

fold sheets neatly,
place them in cupboards

until somewhere
a window opens
soundlessly
the breeze steals in
sweet and heady
with Your fragrance

and i am struck again.

hard!

right in the middle
of my chest

each time
the blow is as new
as if you parted
in that instant

left the whole world a void
where nothing but
my ache for You
stares back at me

Fisabilillah

Saraiya Bah

La ilaha illallah
is the message that *Rasulullah*
sallallahu alayhi wa sallam
conveyed to man from heaven.
An affirmation that should aid
the manifestation of my heart.
To change the parts of my existence
that is the Devil's playground
I struggle to exist in.
In my mind, my deeds are
only for Him
Indeed.
Yet, without fail I always succeed
to allow my flaws to supersede
my actions of good intent.
My deeds, indeed
Will follow me to the day of recompense.
And it makes me wonder how seriously
I make measures to repent.
Am I really letting go of ego to truly worship Allah?
Or am I simply clocking in the minimum requirements
Not allowing my actions to be led by my heart.
And I know there'll be gasps
and '*subhanallah*'s
but does this not cross your mind?
In your haste to prostrate
before His merciful grace
have you been miserly
with your time?
I guess I'm offloading my mind
because when I truly
contemplate this *deen*,
it's one of a kind.
Where Allah says if I walk to him,
He'll run to me in double time.
And I still allow my *nafs* to get in the way?

That's a crime.
Which would make me a criminal.
Yet life isn't always that simple.
Because even in imprisonment;
Allah can work miracles
Because confinement brings redemption
and He is oft-forgiving.
So if His mercy takes me from darkness to life,
Then surely that's a worthy reason to live in
Conscious Love.
From above.
That is felt in the heart.
But where do I start?
And the answer begins with the Changer of Hearts.
At first it wasn't apparent to me
difficult for me to perceive
that The Beloved will intercede for me
If only I follow his ways.
That the emulation of his manners;
to live with the fact that no soul
possesses superiority besides those
who radiate goodness and piety.
Oh Changer of Hearts!
Your mercy transcends through
light, space and time
That revolutional love that
feeds the souls and the minds.
That love that metamorphs into a key
that frees me from the fortress of ignorance.
Then shapeshifts to a gentle hand
that brushes the sand from my eyes
which blocks the radiance of Allah in my life.
You may not be here physically
But the intention and goal is
that your character will live on through me.
Insha'Allah.

The Name of God
Daniel Abdal-Hayy Moore
from the poetry collection Chants for the Beauty Feast

1
The Name of God came haunting down the hall
and dazzled all our eyes and ears and
hearts, and made us

swoon into this hard physical life,
and we'll be wakened and called back

and then we'll leave this world as
things departing from shadows
leave their shadows in heaps like
old clothes at the
door

through which we'll all depart to go back to that
chanting school, those corridors of
pure reverberation through

pine woods, mountain cloud, egrets hovering in an
updraft, sunlight on
rock, sun twinkle on

stream gush, that exquisite

Name of God again, repeated by God's own
speech on the tongue of everything.

The Name of God foghorns
out at sea where
blackened darkness deepens within darkness.

The Name of God suspended in amoebas hovering just below
the surface tension of a moonlit lake.

The Name of God in the first movements of an eaglet inside its
high shell on a cliff beaten by
wind, its brother and sister eaglets
starting to stretch inside
their shells at exactly the
same time.
The Name of God in the high wind beating against them.

The Name of God in rigging out at sea
the high wind beats against.
The Name of God in the audible beats that
accompany the wind, in the
silent beats as well as the
ones sounded out, the lapping as well as the
silence as the sea recedes.

Laughter followed by the silence of death.

The Name of God in them both.

Miraculous

Shahbano Aliani

we sit
you and i
under a translucent
grainless tent
of blue described only
by one word:
sky
as far, and farther than,
the eye can see

trees on patient vigil
birds bursting suddenly
into flight or song
ants rushing
to their daily chores
on pebbles and grass
that slowly hand over
to the day
little bits of dark-damp
clinging to the earth
from the night before

an enormous round
slice of lemon
hangs high in the east
raising unseen breaths of air
that kiss a fine,
almost invisible,
curl on your cheek

you breath in
you smile
your eyes light up
words roll off your tongue
liquid, sweet flowers
that i taste deeply

beyond my senses

you breathe out
and the
fragrance of your breath
mingles
with the breath
of silent trees
blue sky, hot sun
birds, ants
pebbles, grass
and all other things
we cannot see

this effortless
simultaneous
connected
being

as miraculous
as surrender
in a single drop of
rain

A Song for Morakinyo
Muneera Pilgrim

We are all supposed to be here
each individual in here is supposed to be here
there are no mistakes or coincidences
no accidents
in this very instance we are fulfilling prophecy
like Moses split the Red Sea, we are fulfilling prophecy
like Jesus returning to Galilee, we are fulfilling prophecy
like Mansa Musa, Rabia al Adawiya, Marcus Mosiah Garvey,
Oumou Sangare, the Saharawi and the tribes of Mali
I swear we are supposed to be here
gathered in a room, to honour you two and the life that came forth
from you
Morakinyo - I am rejoiced on seeing this brave man
I've never borne babies
I've only birthed poems
as they leave my lips they take the form of prayers ripping away at the
layers of my psyche
the lining of my thoughts are peeling away to make room
for this concept that will soon consume my everything for just a short
time
these words of mine are not mine at all
seeds from the beaks of birds
swooping high
extending wings
their feathers knocking on heaven's gate
flirting with grace
these seeds will fall
and inevitably flourish tall as trees
rooted in the centre of the earth
or as seeds rooted in the centre of your womb
preciously placed inside of you
a space outside of space
the cocoon that is your womb
where heaven and earth meet
you are the universe that gave life to your Sun that was inside of you
you are his earth without void and form

you are his let there be light
you are his *kun fayakun*
inside of you there was an almost human
part mortal part soul
part here part other abode
part breath of life part womb of light
never underestimate the creative forces working inside of you
that fertile ground that was sown, that darkness that was once home
We are all living, walking, talking miracles and we just don't know it
the subtleties of this supernatural phenomenon is so familiar that we
don't know
We are the reason that the sun glows
the cause of the grass to grow
we are the reason the sea crashes and beats the shore
and I am sure we are the prayers of ancestors lost at sea
the prayers of our ancestors taken to new lands
the prayers of our ancestors who were never taken but witnessed their
loved ones
stripped away sand in hand
slipping away with no way to stop it
they would return to the same place day after day
hoping that their loved ones will come back to them
and years later, here we are
we are their prayers and their purpose
we are alive and have more than survived
we are thriving
Our beauty
Our intellect
Our not even trying is so genius
The God stitched into the fabric of our skin
Your love and your community
Your trust and your honesty
Your work hard and do your best

Until your best gets better
there are no mistakes or coincidences
no accidents
in this very instance we are fulfilling prophecy
Witnessing and praying for your family.

Spoon Language
Medina Tenour Whiteman

I give up trying to understand
this peculiar language
all '*bozorg*'s and '*qashogh*'s
and instead just sit on this
finely knotted rug
cross-sectioned carnations
on a pomegranate bed
and allow the whirl of Farsi and family
to weave around me
like a wind dancing
around an awkwardly
positioned sapling
disturbing my foreign leaves
insisting on one more plate
(spoon language is universal)
and listening to my father-in-law tell
through my husband's translating tongue
about the Russians landing
on the beach seventy-five years ago
him, a ten year old, bravely
remaining with his brother and sister
while the rest of the town
retreated to the mountains
and the soldiers in their tanks
ruffled the hair of these plucky kids
told off the town patriarch when he returned next day
and even now he can remember the Russian
for 'cigarette', 'matches', 'sugar'

In his whiskery, elated way
he tells me how he
chopped wood in the forest with an axe
fished for weirdly mole-faced sturgeon
looked after horses
became a rice farmer
to support his family of eleven

tells me ten words in Turkish
asks if his son is a good man

At night, he says, he prays
two *rak'ahs* for his
late wife, she who
appeared in dreams
embracing a blond boy
brought by her youngest son
she who nursed nine babies and
those of other mothers, too
housed students from the mountains
brought in beggars to eat lunch
wore her name: 'The Crown of Women'
and those prayers
return them to each other's side
for a few minutes each night
after the dinner guests
have gone home

Prayer
Malika Meddings

my palm open hand up to face
a heart lurch a fond think a moment's displace
I face you some recklessly
a breath with no ruth
and here in an innocence
facing a truth

a night's blessing sends a warming day's rain
a painful forgiveness with no hope of gain
a naked embracement of mountain bare rock
a foot on the earth a death ticking tock

so this game is over and life is begun
in this time I'm easy, forgiven songs sung
and this moment now is this moment now
and then is a never and then was somehow
melted, and going, and leaving and gone
leaves echoes of loving and ok and song

Would You?
Nargis Latif

Would you weave a tapestry with the threads of your soul?
Would you paint the future with your light?
Would you walk through the burning fire of my passion?
Would you cleave through the darkest of my night?
I would.

Would you swim through the bitterest of tears?
Would you caress the folds of my scarred past?
Would you embrace the poisoned shards of my fears?
Would you cover my sinful stains with your gentle glances cast?
I would.

In a heartbeat I would.

Her
Sabila Raza

There was an innocence in her eyes
A passion in her voice
Her smile extended across her entire face
Her touch
Once experienced you didn't want to let go
A calmness surrounded her
Her heart so gentle
I was afraid the slightest thing could break it
She was present yet somewhere else
Her mind questioning
A consuming dissatisfaction
Peace she desired
In chaotic unexpectedness
She never masked how she felt
Emotions always on the surface
Pain, grief, sadness, joy, love, hope
Were a part of her humanness
Never a weakness
There was no one like her
Uniqueness embodied in her essence
Always true to who she was
Completely unapologetic

death wish

Idris Mears

i have a wish

when i take my final breath
may it be a birth
witnessed by children
who hold me
in the same gaze of joy
that spilled over
from the ocean
of my heart
when i first held them

may i do what it takes
to be that man
may they do what it takes
to be those people

Rumi and Shams
Abdalhamid Evans

Where are you now when we need you
   Rumi and Shamsi Tabriz?
All the words you spoke and the rules you broke
   That's the only thing that really can free us.
     We'll follow your light through the tunnel
     That takes us through the dark and the cold
   Follow your light through the wild and windy night
And out into the daylight so bold.

I was way up in the crow's nest, just looking out for land
   Trying my best to shade my eyes, with the back of my hand
Scanning the far horizon for any sign of life
   Keeping myself awake at night with the point of a knife.
     We came in through the big bay, and the mighty city rose
     We drifted through the harbour, so I put on my clothes
       I went down to the market, just to get something to eat
       But nothing took my fancy, so I beat a quick retreat.

So I went into the school room, just to see what I could learn
   And tried to find a topic that best suited my concern
I tried to find a teacher who understood my needs
   Tried to find a writer who could tell me what to read.
I looked around and it seemed to me that the writing was on the wall
   And their high ideals and principles were just about to fall
     They showed me how to play the game, and told me what to say
     But I saw where it was heading, so I simply walked away.

So I headed to the country to see what I could grow
   Followed all the winding lanes and the straight flight of the crow
Found the rolling valleys where the ragged people stayed
   They took me in and let me win, I thought I had it made.
     I planted some potatoes, and learned to milk a cow
   Learned to sew my britches and just be in the here and now
     But the here and now kept shifting till it was only now and then
     I wasn't sure which way was up, so I moved on again.

So I headed up the mountains to where the spring begins to rise
  To a high place where the water seemed to mingle with the skies
And here I met a wise man who looked me in the eyes
    I met his gaze and spent the days learning truth from lies.
    And then he turned and told me things that I already knew
      But I had just forgotten that the truth is really true
      'Go down to the city, and find a place to stay
      Go downtown, look around, and find a place to pray.'

Well, I found them in the corner, on the edges of the park
  They reminded me of Noah when he was building up the ark
They said please come and join us, there's room here in the line
  We've all come down the same road, we're sure you'll fit in fine.
So I washed my face and hands and feet and lined up with the rest
  Turned my face and heart to heaven, my hands across my chest
  Bowed my head in wonder and put my face down on the floor
  And then the place just disappeared and I became no more.

And now we are walking down the highway
  On the contours of this well-trodden way
Following the road and the reality
    With the night folding into the day.
      And you'll find us where the light meets the shadow
        Where the dawn meets the setting sun
      Where the city meets the flowers in the green green meadow
        Where the many all get folded into One.

And here you are, now when we needed you
  Rumi and Shamsi Tabriz!
All the words you spoke and the rules you broke
    It was the only thing that really could free us
      Now we'll carry the light through the tunnel
      That takes us thru the dark and the cold, cold, cold
    Carrying your light through the wild and windy night
Just like you did, back in the days of old.

A Muslim Death

Asma Khan

I want to tell you a story that you may not have heard before.
This is not about swarms or is it hordes of displaced Mohammedans
escaping terrible violence at the hands of their savage countrymen
nor is it about the vengeance and pain of those who cannot make
peace with a corrupt world where thousands die yet are instantly
forgotten
nor of those who seek redress, their misplaced anger at human
imperfection shrouded in the blood stained clothes of yet more dead.
It's not about analysis and half truths and agendas and votes and hand
wringing liberalism.
You see, this story I wish to share
is far too subtle to sell newspapers, too complex to explain why the
ghettoes you malign do in fact thrive
with hidden life, behind red bricks fountains and gardens
it's a carpet of intermingled, ancient dyed wools from many lands that
was woven in such a pattern that no soundbite could describe it, for
this tale is eternal, breathed outside of Time itself.
It is a story of a man dying, having made peace with his life,
surrounded by the prayers of those he loved, of sacred beauty piercing
a prosaic room,
of angelic presence at a bedside and unspoken witnessing,
it is relatives washing the body with dutiful care,
prayers and visits from friends for days
with food cooked for a grieving family
no questions asked
it's about comfort and sweetness in the sharing of dreams of their
loved one
in a sincere quest to remain connected to him as he makes his journey
into an astral sphere… to the land where 'the joy of which no eye has
seen' awaits
of hundreds filing past and blessing a body unknown to most of them
except as human with the same origin and return
of a unity felt with the Universe as auspicious rain fell on his grave
from a cloudless sky
of Love being witnessed by those left behind in all its many forms
until there are no more tears just a sweet surrender, a ripening within

336

It is a story of a grave visited and prayed over after his morning surgery
by a son each Friday because he wishes 'to draw near'
and of other families doing the same and an echoing peace that
radiates from beyond this nameless patch of Yorkshire land.
Their quiet duty to something greater ennobling their day, comforting
them with a sense of being led and connecting them to great souls who
have gone before through a unifying practice
It is a story of a heart expanding, wisdom training, beauty seeking,
secret joy revealing, transforming way of life
You see, it is an honour, this faith of ours, this precious treasure, it's
not a 'fable of the men of old' to be replaced by a New World Order
It is our truth, our first and last love, just Islam

On Parting
Mariam Akhtar

and this is how we lose a generation
on ships and in assimilation
these borders between
my skin and my tongue
the language that tiptoes from my teeth
stuck in my mouth
a personal kind of secret
my very own cave and conclave
the words
they grate and grind
like the slow wearing down of
years of partition
60 years
70 years
somehow it's still named a celebration
when I'm split from my sisters
and dad says our ancestors were from delhi
but when I met the gates at lahore
I wept instead of rejoiced
locked out and shut down
rather than able to greet them

19th Rak'ah

Ray Lacina

Throbs your back,
your muscles a fist
your legs catching the gasp before the cramp
your back
throbs

Opens the *qari'* his lips,
up lifts his tongue
flows out lilacs
flows out lavender
flows out each spark of every fire showering light
to the wide warm dark
sky.

Aging

Yahia Lababidi

I'm being hollowed out, I feel it
in the subtle droop of skin and will,
Like the life stuffing were slowly
being spooned from me

My mind, too, is being emptied
of needless concerns
(such as, who's in charge)
traveling lighter, demanding less

One day, I'll finally slip out this
loosening body bag
Simply sling it over the shoulder
of my sturdy spirit.

Before I Knew

Elizabeth Tasnim McCormick Benhalim

If I had known it was the last time
to sit so casually and feel the breeze together
To watch the day fade into bright pinks and darkness
To speak of trees and the nearness of stars
To sing I See the Moon and the Moon Sees Me and
Shine on Harvest Moon for Me and My Gal
and hear you call my name lilting
and uplifting with your special welcome unlike any other voice
I wish, now only wish…
Would I have lingered over goodbyes and breathed a long, longer sigh
over your heart so well that it could warm you as you rest,
first buried in our green hill cemetery with its single name,
LOVE?[23]

---

[23] My father, Charles Allen McCormick, was a great lover of life, of his wife and family: his 6 children and their spouses, and the 25 grandchildren. He was sometimes stubborn and headstrong – but inevitably for what he thought was for the good. He energetically encouraged those around him – most especially those who society foolishly marked "less" – striving to give a glimpse of the possible: a more courageous, capable, beautiful and successful self. He loved music, laughter, trees, starry nights and myriad other wonderful things. His grave marker says simply: *A Legacy of Love.* As we learned about green cemeteries – and fenced off and set-aside the acres on our family farm that dates back to 1852 – dad said that all we needed to call the new cemetery was *LOVE* – and that's what we did. He was the first buried in our new green cemetery, November 2008.

Love is to Fly Towards a Secret Sky
Sukina Pilgrim

Lovers sit under a secret sky
That only they can see.
The heavens hang low
Like a sacred blanket
Just above their heads.

The stars flicker
Just for their pleasure
Decorating the heavens
With cosmic glory;
The newest chapter
In their unfolding love story.

Yesterday's sunset
Gave them a gift
Of lavender and dusty pink
And they danced
To the song the birds sing
Just before dusk.
But right now -
Their companion is the night.

Her head rests upon his shoulder
His heart rests in her palm
Fingers woven
Like a wicker basket,
Their hearts so close
They need only whisper
To be heard.

Their auras merged
Into a sacred melody
The colours of their spirits
Dancing in unison
Giving birth to tones
That made the rainbow jealous.

These star-crossed lovers
Star-gazed in amazement
At the inky sky,
Waiting for the heavenly bodies
To make their entrance
And delight them
With a light show
Only for their eyes.

One starry-eyed lover
Points out constellations
To the other
And they chuckle
Into each other's necks
As the patterns in the cosmos
Become their companions
For the night.

The vastness of the galaxy
Has become a canvas
For their love tapestry.
And
All the elements are in attendance
Paying reverence
To Love's presence
Tonight.

Please Mind the Gap
Mariam Akhtar

I knew we would remain like this
ever respectful
of these self imposed force fields
the ones that maintained
the space between us
please mind the gap
between our shoulders and thighs
careful not to cross any lines
the ones that were drawn
like curtains and sunsets
silent and slow
as we observe the world around us
all the quiet inflections
loud in infliction
the way he
teased her
a little
how she laughed
a lot
keep your distance
and I'll stay behind mine
fences and tiptoes
this quiet dance of
I saw your eyes
lay fire to my waist and
I heard your mouth
speak something that still burns
what was it you said?
I want you to look like this
all the time

Eviction
H I Cosar

We left with nothing
But ourselves
And our mistakes
From a home
That had everything

Many have forgotten the taste
Yet when I suck on a persimmon
I remember

Many forget the fragrance
Yet when I inhale
April violets
Or wild roses
I remember

When the minstrel sings
A soft love song
I long and pray for that place
That I only know
With spirit

I wish I could remember
More than these fragments

These fleeting moments
Shake my core
I am in a constant war of wanting
to return

Whenever I see a shooting star
Or a photo of my love I lost
Whenever it rains after fires

I close my eyes and breathe

I long to see my true home

For it is tiresome
To run around and around
In life's vicious circles
That lead nowhere
O it is dreary
To dwell in this palace
Of false grace
When you know
It is just a lucid dream

Desire for Freedom
Shahbano Aliani

my desire for you
is not for
conversation
your touch
your love
or your affirmation

my desire for you
is desire for freedom

unlock me
pour me out
empty me

make me forget
everything

where i was born
what mother said
what i learnt to speak
to do, to think

from books and trades
from cousins and friends

make me forget
who i am
names people call me
names i call myself

enslave me totally
every part, every piece
every fiber, every atom
leave nothing of me
for me

take it all
away
make me empty
make me free

Along the Way
Nura Tarmann

People appear along the way
Kind people giving words of advice when needed
Giving people, a hug and smile at just the right moment
One millisecond before you're giving up
A call comes someone asks about your day
God's grace always comes through people
So quick we are to dismiss the messenger
The message received makes us feel self sufficient
But a web of relations covers us continuously
Fine membranes hugging the heart as it beats
I try to empty the feelings each day
Pouring them out of my eyes
Whispering them out of my mouth
Praying them out quietly
Some feelings just cling so tightly
Like a new born monkey baby
They don't want to get off my back
I get up heavyhearted and smile
People all over with their monkey babies on their backs
Passing me along the way
Sometimes we let them jump down and play
So often these babies fight and struggle
Sometimes they recognize their own species and laugh

The Women of my Family

Muneera Pilgrim

The women of my family are graceful, insightful, spiritual, wise,
sensitive independent, intra-dependent and dependable, depending on
what's called for at any given time.
They are giving, compassionate women.
Their words are more soothing than the smoothest of soothsayers
They have maroon crushed lips, rounded hips and a back so straight, it
leads up to heaven's gate.
Mary Magdalene meets Nana the Maroon,
The blue and white Nile eloping in the centre of Khartoum.
Joan of Arc, Sojourner Truth, Rabia Aladawia, Zulaikha, Makeda,
Frida Kahlo, Nikki Giovanni, Phoolan Devi, Hagar min asSudan
wife of a prophet and mother of a nation.
The women of my family contain them all, and more, what's more,
the women who've raised me are so gifted
They are so so gifted, they're almost mythic at minimum they are
mystic.
I wouldn't have believed it, if I didn't see it with my own eyes and
breathed it in like the kiss of life, the existence of fire in ice, the
horizons after the night skies.
They are the thread of white that separates day from night, the specks
of black that are fading from my grandmother's eyes,
that seems to be the *hukum* of becoming wise, the *hukum* of being
precious and prized, the *hukum* of leading a rich life and giving,
giving, giving abundantly like a willow tree with an endless amount of
leaves.
Not even autumn can shake you, like a stake firmly rooted in the
centre of the earth balancing the planet and all of God's children.
I've borne witness to women who make something out of nothing,
sense out of nonsense.

I would tell you I've seen them battle demons, but you would swear
that it's a lie.
But what else is the beating of drums at a kumana under Jamaican,
cool, moon lit indigo skies.
What is women lined up in church sanctuaries, speaking with the
authority of God.

Healing the sick with their prayers, keeping families tided with their prayers, keeping their families alive with their prayers, they keep on praying,
because they know the streets of England are not paved with gold,
and the stories they were told that made them leave their homes were baseless.
But these women, they are the gold that pave the streets, Gracious and Gold.
I've sat in circles with women drenched something between sweat and tears, women of all years.
Calling his name until kingdom come, "thy will be done, on earth here and now, we are not leaving, we desire healing and you are the one who we believe in".
Even though we may call Him by a different name, them showing me, instinctively that they we are all one
Divinity has blessed me with my mum So I say sweet Lord Manifestor of mercy, firstly I thank you for the greatest gift earthly, may you continue to bless the wombs that bore me, walked on water for me, for truly I am blessed.

visions of the same
Idris Mears

do we but live in versions
of the same dreams
so do you too return to a clearing
in clear winter light
and through the tracery of winter trees
see a track up the slope of dead bracken
to the flint wall of the great estate
and know that if you were to set off
there is a small gate with the latch left off
somewhere along its length
and beyond it exquisite and unbounded
an early summer garden endlessly fresh after rain
and in your yearning can you all but smell
the alchemy of its fragrances
all but feel the gentle breeze
all but see the shaken silver of the poplar trees
all but hear the rustle of each leaf
be all but embraced by its utter ease

A Tale Untold
Khadijah Lacina

you with me
the sky blue
unshed tears
the grass soft
beneath our
backs the
world
for a moment
a globe
magically
filled
with snow

Call Out My Name
Shahbano Aliani

i knew who i was
where i was
when i was with You
then you took away all
but a flicker of this knowing
blind folded
and left me out
all alone
in a long, dark night

lost and unconscious
trapped in my self
the knowing that was i
buried deep,
deep somewhere
covered
in layer upon layer of darkness

this flicker
blazed sometimes
when i saw
the face of one i loved
with a love that choked thought
made me forget
everything

this flicker
flared up sometimes
when i stood enchanted
by the quietest of lakes
in the heart of a red-earth mountain
filled with awe
that felt like unspeakable terror
made me tremble
made me shake

this flicker
became a torch, a light
when a verse of poetry
a verse of prayer
squeezed and wrenched
and tore my heart
made me yearn for something
i could not name

the night is still dark
the flicker a flame
dancing ahead
playing hide and seek
with each step that i walk
towards this light
the path behind
closes forever
even if i wanted
there is no way back
and ahead
the night is my path
stretched out
forever

speak to me
give me a sign:
call out my name

please!
call out my name!

Lost Voice
Abdalhamid Evans

I had to go down the valley before I could reach the summit
    I had to lose the map before I could find the way
I had to lose the plot before I could see who done it
    I had to lose my voice before I had something to say

    The place of darkness is the place of light
        The place of wrong is the place of right
    The place of laughter is the place of crying
        The place of living is the place of dying

I had to lose my temper before I could find any patience
    I had to lose my grip before I could really take a hold
I had to jump off the train before I could make it to the station
    I had to pay all the penalties before I could score a goal

    The place of blindness is the place of sight
        The place of weakness is the place of might
    The place of failure is the place of success
        The place of need is the place of excess

I had to lose all the attitude before I could make an impression
    I had to lose my vision before I could really see
I had to hold my tongue before I could make an expression
    I had to shut myself in jail before I could set myself free

You got to change your habits if you really want to kick it
    You got to break your heart before you can fall in love
You got to break a spade if you really want to dig it
    You got to fall on your face if you want to rise above
Well I'm telling you the truth and I ain't no liar
    You're gonna go to the garden or you go to the fire
Better hear the message, the good news and the warning
    If you don't wake up at night
        better wake up, wake up in the morning

A Tiny Window in the Palace of Rahma
Medina Tenour Whiteman

"A mercy to all the worlds":
Can you comprehend that?
The world of rocks, of mushrooms,
winds, seas, whales, mosquitos,
jinn, trees, underground rivers
bacteria, bears and ozone
the dizzying telescopic jump
the human mind can make from
the tiniest imaginable
—and where the imagination
can take you beyond—
to the vastest galaxies
digitally coloured in pink and pistachio
for who knows what colours
we'd see them in up close

All the worlds:
angelic, demonic, uncertain
and solid, theoretical and tangible
the dead, the made and the
still only an idea
the embryo forming unknown
in its private universe
secrets that bud in shy chests
genetic shifts as yet unstudied
the germ of a song
a singer wakes up humming
and whatever cats get up to
when we're not watching
the meaning of a child's
felt pen diagram
the *lutf* that turns grass into milk
and manure into sweet oranges

If we imagine his mercy
was like ours, extending to our hands

the kindness we place in our words
sent on prayers to where they're needed
we take all the worlds
and reduce them to a
kitchen knife
telephone wire
postman's trolley
prone to electricity cuts and
over-long breakfast breaks

You need imagination
to even see through
one tiny window in the palace of *rahma*
and if our imagination is so mean
clinging to the drainpipe of dogma
how can we ever get inside?

Or if not
Jamila Fitzgerald

May we welcome change
Or if not,
be ready for a new phase
Or if not,
accept one...
Or if not,
when it happens, hang on
Or if not,
Survive the Landing,
Or if not,
Beam in God's
Hands with thanks

Ramadan is Burnished Sunlight

Daniel Abdal-Hayy Moore
from the poetry collection Ramadan is Burnished Sunlight

Ramadan is burnished sunlight on the
cheek of the Beloved at the

first dawn of creation

first fruits burst on first green
branches in the first Garden

their ripening a whole
lunar month without being picked

till they burst with the
celestial pleasure of pure being

Ramadan hunkers down in the extreme
depths of heaven and earth

simultaneously

as deep in the earth as the sky
bound together with immaterial

coils in the
knot of our fleshly hunger

It's a luminous door down a long hall in a
yearly wall in space

past rooms of resplendent solitudes and
incantatory gatherings with a

vision at the end of a tall silver stag whose
antlers are flames lighting our

way to inconceivable pastures
where endless bounty abounds

A weighty touch from an emptiness that
strikes sparks in our hearts

a turning from one light to another
even brighter than ocular radiance

Lick the tongue of it with our tongues!

Clear the throat of it with our throats!

Surround the sight of it in a blind blizzard of
overpouringness into our

suddenly increased dimension
as we stand a bit shakily at His

window
praising His Name

Made of Sea
Asiya Sian Davidson

what does it all mean?
I ask you this in the deep heart of the night
the pulsing of stars, the quiet vigilance of
a plum tree
with feet wet on concrete
standing, I catch a glimpse of the moon
peeking above the
old pear

what does it all mean?
this life that has no coherence
and if I try and rid myself of the 'rogues'
or return to a recognisable narrative
God has other ideas
'those aren't the weeds, fool!'
sometimes gently and sometimes not
gently

listen, there's no need for comparisons with
sturdier, more conventional stories
in the still of the night, there is only
praise

shoulders flecked with
scattering mists from lazy night clouds
silver streaked hair receiving
some more
moonlight

what does it all mean?
Life, pressed into small tight spaces
burst forward
carrying with it the collected flotsam of
a tsunami
scattering all over inland villages the rotten debris
of a lifetime
people who didn't see or hear the wave, baffled

and you running down the road, naked
a live wire
that no one wants to touch

take comfort
not the land but made of sea
no storm can break water
shut your eyes and know that it flows
from the inside

beloved by atoms and ants
trees and sandy beaches, each grain
inscribed with praise of him*
this body-longed-for, a
sustained lapping of waves
that soothes the ribs

Love, hiding in the torrent all along
night sky is a soft and warm cloak
it says, 'what concern do you have for drowning
when you are made of sea?'
love body that ripples
from the inside

*sallallahu alaihi wasallam

Dull your Senses
Muneera Pilgrim

Close your eyes
Close your ears
Close your mouth
Cover your nose and stop feeling they say
Stop loving they say
Stop caring
Somehow stop your heart from beating
And stop being..
You
In the midst of all this stopping don't forget to stop breathing
And have I already mentioned stop feeling stop feeling stop feeling
Stop your essence from breathing

You're not from here he said you're from another planet or maybe a
time long ago
Your songs are beautiful and yet I desire to hurt you
Your skin's brown, soft and subtle the type of skin maybe one day I
can make a bed if you survive me
yet I desire to scar you
Your words are cleansing
Give me a moment while I silence you
Cut your tongue out and leave you to bleed
Keep bleeding just stop feeling
Stop loving, stop beating, stop breathing and stop being
You.

I Come Home to Myself
Mariam Akhtar

it's in your mid to late 20s that your life will form
your face will finally begin to fill the shape
it was always intended to take
your concord nose will eventually cease to grow
thank the Lord
so your space dish eyes that you stopped lining
with black cables and whips and lashes
can once again take centre stage
because as irony goes,
the lines and letters of lust and longing
that seem to follow
are really not a cause for celebration
your expression softens from
leave me alone - all the time
to - ok maybe you can come in
sometimes
you're all soft now
it's all just softness
and softly
you could knead a lifetime into those thighs
you could bear a dozen children from those hips
you could paint a map with the vitiligo on your back
a game of dot to dot from borders and breaks in skin
constellations and all the countries you lay in
each one marked between your shoulder blades

Don't Let the Darkness Eat You Up
Rabea Benhalim

I feel the Fear
Rising
like vomit
in my throat
or tears held back.

Something is wrong.
There is madness
An evil
And we are just
Denying
Apologizing

We aren't
responsible.
But we are being
held accountable.

A shift is happening
And if we don't act
with swift, exact care,
Tragedy upon tragedy
will continue.

Carefully executed
precision is called for.
It is time to get out
of the kiddie pool.
Whether we know
how to swim,
we have been thrown
in the Deep End
and the sharks are circling.

Ten Men
Hanan Issa

We say *timman* for rice, not *ruz* like other Arabs.
I heard a rumour that the word came from the British
When Iraqi farmers refused to feed the colonisers
shipments of Ten Men rice arrived from India
Heaved onto the backs of men, stubborn as *hakaka*
with sweat on their faces and revolution in their hearts

'You are next,' the bags of rice teased. Like the Ten Men
my great-grandmother came to Iraq on a boat
An Indian bride for a soldier whose eyes turned further east
Although my great-grandmother's skin mimicked belonging
the faces around her used letters she couldn't pronounce
she ate bitter *noomi Basra*, craving the fiery comfort of home

She gifted her daughter with Indian features
and the knowledge of *biryani* that burns your tongue
My family were taught to turn their eyes westwards
settling on my mother – a lighter bride for the bloodline
They try to bury the story of a woman who sang Hindi songs
Triumphant, they nickname my palest sister 'Snow White'

How to Think of Cancer
Iljas Baker

Not as a battle
but as a question that slowly emerged from the distant past
telling of the future

Not as a battle
but as a precious lesson in threefold surrender.

Say:

This the forge
of the faith maker.

I Saw a Saint Today
Wajiha Khalil

I saw a saint today
my heart fragmented
in a hundred directions
all pointing to God

Each path particular
but none contradicting
the other

Green Gate
Asiya Sian Davidson

to be a sparrow that drinks
at his pool
Grandfather of the golden axe
I choose the green gate

Beloved, your face in flames,
cinder my eyes
bloom of mountains streaked with
sunset, rose and violet
pastel blush
hush my heart and hush
my dust

cherry blossom, branches bare
soft climactic effloresce
fructify this longing
make my every answer 'yes'!

recitation from a hidden room
in this hive of love and incense, hash
Grandfather, in one full out breath
take my longing into ash

Some Fasts
Ray Lacina

Some fasts are like a clenched fist,
some tremble like a lover just before

Some fasts barrel down the highway
thick as cement, plunging

Some lift, thin, porous
to the wind
porous
to the rain

all fasts are a soft breath blown
on the ashes of the heart
all fasts might, just might
stir the light.

A Message from Our Conscience
Randa Hamwi Duwaji

I see you today, Humanity, astray..
In semblance of safety
humbled and hushed.
Sequestered in fear
for dear Life,
all else fading to dust
as indeed it must.

There has never been
a time such as this:
Binding, bonding
world population,
when far beneath
initial doubt,
truths untold
and evidence buried
lie heavier
more profound worries:

What is my purpose?
Why my hurry?

I, Me,
My ever-craving greed
for things I should own
for what I don't need...
In timeless wisdom
new trends do not keep;
so-called luxuries
gone cheap
as indeed they must.

'Goods'
with little good in them,
have no rightful place
in God's Kingdom.

Stand apart, Humanity,
stand apart.
In what shall come to pass
you have little say.
You, who were blind to all that you hurt!
You, who were deaf to the beat of their hearts!
Stay away!

Stay away within your borders
and Nature shall regain her order,
as indeed, she must:
In God we trust.

Humanity,
take your rightful station
within Creation.
Don't live to regret
where you stood today!

Was it with the best,
the better, or just the good?
Or with those who
should've realized
and should've understood?

Stand down, Humanity,
give up the scepter.
You do not want this crown!
Stand down,
and look around..

See Life's motion in devotion:
Watch Earth breathing her own...
Watch wildlife roam
Watch fish swim free in their ocean
Watch bees keep their nectar
Watch birds tend their young
When you know your place;

When you feel your place:
Humankind
without color or race...
It had to take a disaster
to reveal your best
To prove you never were master.

I see you today, Humanity, aware
of what you'd taken for granted:
Real joy, true wealth
in peace, kindness, love, health...
Most precious, most dependable
while all else is expendable.

Reach out, Humanity, reach out!
You've learnt what it's all about
having lived its explanation!
It is entirely your obligation
to maintain rightful balance:
Yours should be
a most noble existence
in God's kingdom!

When your moment of silence ends...
When you rejoin loved ones and friends
enjoy, and guard
what in solitude you found:
Your innermost beings, humble
as your spirits rise and tremble
in a symphony of beating hearts:
Rejoicing!
Rejoicing in being but one choice part
of a magnificent whole.
Honored, and privileged...
Fulfilling your role.

Just Another Pilgrim
Flamur Vehapi

Waking up in the morning
Realizing that I am alive,
I gratefully start the day
Like a bee from its hive.

Jumping flower to flower
In search of truth and light
Meekly seeking knowledge
Morning, noon and night.

Hoping to live this life
As humbly as I can
Knowing that in this world
Nothing but a pilgrim I am.

Tethered
Rabia Saida

My child
Prayer
Is a form of self-care
Bringing yourself always back to God
No matter where you've been
Or what you've been up to
Honouring the sanctity of your soul
Here I am
Here I am
You are always here.

Ever Compassionate and Forgiving
You're never unworthy
Of standing again before Him
Who are you to limit His mercy
to your human judgement of your worth?
You with your Adamic nature
Can choose to be above the angels or lowest of the low
And have been granted sacred signposts
To secure each day by
Anchor your days with sacredness
Just turn
and turn
and turn again
I give you what has helped me

The Prophet was prescribed prayer
In the seventh heaven
At the distance of two bow-lengths
When he was closest to the Divine Presence
Let every prayer be an *isrā' wal mi'rāj*
Stop what you are doing
ascend through the heavens
And remember that meeting

Scholar's Psalm

Cherif Al-Islam Abou El Fadl

Caught within the agony of an abused and bound body.
The scholar bleeds coils of thorn and vine through ink
Constrictions of mortality transmuted into pages laden with light
as envelopes of suffering unfold the veils of sanity's brink
The responsibility therein, for most imposes too high a price.
Fragmented over fragmentations through delusional disillusion
And the weeping cherubs perch unseen
telling psalms in torrents of song.
Gushing from between the clenched fibrous fingers,
which shield weeping eyes;
a river of beneficent regret at the will of his Lord.

Illness has made the body the nemesis of intellect
A twisted parody of cannibals and the heritage of a renaissance
Alone, preserved in the scholar's memory to haunt
    atop a column made of feather
within dreams made of glass.

Hiding away from mankind embodying their own satire
Abandoned by time to timeless struggles and pursuits
    for fleeting and bounded understanding
    life for a glimpse of a glimpse
    of the light upon light

Whirling Hearts
Murtaza Humayun Saeed

Is it fair to insist that God bring to life that same rose that you are
clutching
When He brings to life roses all year around
Is it fair to doubt that there will be ever-lasting life
When every day the hearts spin in a longing to behold Him
Just as the physical earth shows us how.
Is it fair to insist that God prove a point by bringing back yesterday
When the sun rises with every new day
The abyss of nothingness that we worship
Makes us slaves of ourselves
Is it fair to insist that you yourself are god
When you can't bring back a fly on the wall

Songs of Nature
Zakriya Riaz

Do you remember my beloved?
The way you flared up our never ending cerulean sky.
Your blazing inferno gave me elation and a sense of hope.
It is curious that one like you could ever be bashful.
Maybe you played coy. But you, even you, hid behind the clouds
when it rained.
While at night, you became a luminous spectre
howling in the wind.

feat of clay
Idris Mears

i broke my back today
shovelling a trench in clay
and now i know what clods
we sons of adam are

lumpy and cloying
as common as muck
stuck in the mud sods
resisting the workman's spade,
weighed down with the elemental
rain that won't drain away,
clinging to the soles
with a dead hand

needing artisan hands
to knead us on the slab
shape us on the wheel
anoint us with glaze
fire us in the kiln
make us useful
maybe even
beautiful

Coffee Prayers
Efemeral

The alarm rings before the Alarm rings
I'm up
I'm up
I'm not up.

I lie
in the liminal land escape
between the cover
ups and downs and half-explained half-truths
I lie until I can lie no longer.

Feet touch cool floor
every moment-movement on the Path
an old floorboard – squeaking
giving me and my position away.

I debate my position
Toss and turn,
Set trial dates for my position,
weep and yearn
cop, judge and jury
death row
record my position on my position as a summary execution!
No mercy in the decision that was not mine to make
to begin with.

To begin with
the alarm rings before the Alarm rings
is a Mercy.
As I lie in the liminal land escape between the covers and half-filled
cups of coffee:
All praise is to the One
Who gives me life after giving me death
And to the Merciful One is my return.

Never meant to be
Emny Kadri

He needed to scold you.

You needed to be told when to stop.

Do you understand, this world was never meant to be yours?

Now fall.

Fall all the way down.

And when you finally reach your beginnings, start afresh.

And He will be waiting there for you to rise again.

He will take your hand and raise you up.

If you reject everything other than He, He will walk you all the way to paradise by His side.

Dawn

Asma Khan

Do you know this pain?
That creeps through cracks in a seemingly ordinary day
Molten lava that no longer explodes just oozes
To tearducts and tingling limbs unopposed
What use resistance when this sweet heart wrenching is more precious
than life as you know it
More than even those who plead for your love
Need you now in this moment
When this old pain arrives they are
Felt far far less, why?
Tonight it returned again
Alone without tangible loss or memories as aides
So familiar
but now a sea of rootless desire mingling with sweet surrender washes
me clean and cool
Like Muhammad's tears for his lost child
Like the music of soul friends and their knowing
Is it loving test or punishment?
I know this much
It is at least Truth - causing no anger or complaint just earnest longing
to remain
Intimate Present
At dawn, separation will come until
like a rug worn by the footsteps of a returning guest
My heart wall spots
rubbed away to silk will tear
and I will die, leaving only this Love

Good Intentions

Nura Tarmann

I wish I could sort my feelings
Like stacking shirts in the closet
Or sorting the wash
Coloureds go with coloureds
Whites and blacks separated neatly
But there has been a pink tint to my clothes for a long time
And white lint on the black trousers and my whites have turned a little
grey
Ah I wish it were so easy
Clear demarcations between people and things
I still have trouble matching my wardrobe
Oh how I would like to be so perfectly put together
Matching bag and shoes, perhaps my coat a suitable shade to match
the ensemble
But my life was never so neat or so well thought out
It was just full of good intentions
Intentions that all seemed to get muddled at some point and
overlapped in strange places
Like some punk rock outfit that's made to shock and repel
But somehow draws our attention and gives a little jolt in the right
direction
Speaks to the rebel in us all.
How often we fall short of our ideal of perfection
But then I slip on a warm sweater on a cold day and realize
Life is not meant to be perfect and as it is it, is not bad at all

Light
Khadijah Lacina

sun dapple
past day
slips away
a coyote
a dream
for more
a walk
through
water
holding
my head
above
a
breath
of light
welcome
in the
soothing
sound
of dark

Desert
Rakaya Esime Fetuga

Sometimes this city can look like a desert
concrete dunes that stretch endless
further than the London eye can see,
parched travellers riding the nine to five like camels –
fatigued, legs beginning to falter – buckling under the weight
of expectation, the weight of finding happiness in
a title, or in
a bank balance,
in a notification,
or in tiny pixel idols that
our flesh will never become.

London can look like a desert when water
is a glimpse of God's signs
and our hearts are blind
sandstorms of self-indulgence swirling up under our eyelids
grains wedged between our teeth
can't speak – some lose belief
that there is another way.

But many
will grip the truth even tighter
knowing
there is water when you know where to look
there are floods, guided by the one
who had water flow from his hands
streaming a straight path through
the sand, there is goodness over
flowing
people who quench dry throats
with Blessed Names
looking past themselves
to see everyone is a vessel – topped up
with water, knowing
serving people is the work of
hydrologists

to be with Allah we only need
to look at the world
at each other
pour a little of ourselves, find that
we are *dhikr*
and let the monsoon dissolve
what's left of us.

The city can look like an endless
desert
but they swear it is a shore-less
sea.

Du'a
Saraiya Bah

my palms bear the weight of my sins
though they vary in extremities
they leave the same taint
translucent
almost as if they are not there
but I know how heavy
they weigh on my palms.
in my heart.
constant on my mind.
playing with my brain
making me feel that
my prayers aren't enough
to cleanse my palms of this filth

The Visitor
Paul Abdul Wadud Sutherland

At his impulsive arrival,
hunting for the lit path
to a Sufi master's house,
he stooped under curves
of an unopened jasmine.
A wadi sounded, running
to a calm roar, in its valley
mountain water searched
for its ocean and diverted
fed cloud-shaped orchards.
Sweet fragrance, held him.
A hung moon altered steps
into apparitions on stone.
He rounded a bend to see
an old wall straying under
a lean-to roof; hurt, plaster
steps crept up to a wicker-
railed porch. Half turning
he panned shadowless sky.
Assembled white iris, under
a date palm's serrated fonts,
spoke galaxies. A worn lamp
blued a breach in a doorway.
His greeting *a salaam alaykum*
carried away in midnight air
the visitor was called inside.

In The Beginning
Rashida James-Saadiya

What was once heavy, now fits in our hands
so we throw it away

scattering broken pieces
across a midnight sky
We pray for rain and wait

If water can purify the soul
perhaps it can flood the past
scab over festering wounds
help us to build
new homes from our breath
make love
not memory
our first language

Damascus
Rabia Saida

We slept on a roof in Damascus
For a week
Twenty years ago
When it was a city
With centuries of history
That had not been torn apart by war.
We dozed between trellised jasmine
And the stars

The memories come back tonight
With no ceiling or cloth as a barrier between us and infinity
It must have been desert dwellers or sea farers
Who first saw the sky as a map
The pattern of illumination above them as greater signposts
Than featureless sand or waves.
Now we are so myopic in our busy, messy lives

And have wrapped ourselves in so much air and light pollution
We don't even notice the birth and death of stars
And the movement of celestial bodies
Right above our heads

On that roof in Damascus
Our generous hosts, who put our whole family up
And entertained us for a week
Although we were only the friends of friends
Served us homemade ice-cream
In the evening after supper
Then at dawn we woke to *adhans* from every direction
Because there were so many mosques nearby

A Crushing Loneliness
Yasmine Ahmed-Lea

A crushing loneliness
That not even
a cool breeze
Can lift and break
An ancestral past
I want to claim
Yet know nothing about
Forever not belonging
Is getting exhausting
I get drunk on melancholy
Exhausted by my own solitude
I never was one
To work hard on relationships
Now people come and go
And I smile knowing
I don't want to try
Mirror work on beautiful cloth
Reminds me of you
Pricking my finger gently
On broken antiques
Never to be fixed again

Sieges in Kashmir
Aasifa Usmani

Kashmir must be the only paradise on earth-
Even in her shattering deaths,
Kashmir is reborn
festered in the colonial inexistences
Kashmir voices her existence

Pieces
Nura Tarmann

Walking carefully surrounded by fine threads holding people together
I step over broken eggs that try to tell me something
I don't really understand the language
Some likeness to the delicate nature of women and children
They were thrown so carelessly by the angry young
I scrub the sticky, yellow mess off windows tarnished by rage
At love which was not strong enough to cover and protect
Wrath growing out of broken homes and bones
A bottle that promised deliverance broken for its lies
Covers the pavement in front of me
I hear of a country where innocence is bombed
As if there were not enough broken pieces to go around
Somewhere people pick up the pieces
and start laying them together again
A mosaic is forming slowly of mismatched ideologies
That have a common vision of beauty, peace and children
Safe and laughing.

Liminal Spaces
Abbas Mohamed

I exist in liminal spaces
Carved deeply
Pushed to the edges

Between this
And that

Neither this
Nor that

Belonging both
to this
And to that

1.
Pushed to the edges
Of my own self too

Carving there
Two
layers deep
Not deep enough

2.
I exist to ask why
but not to answer it
just to stick around
for what does come
next

3.
I exist to serve spaces
Until they become spaces
Of self determination
That push me away

To the edges
again

To the liminal
Where I carve
again

I exist in liminal spaces
To erase traces
Of time wasted

I exist
to summon graces
to go places

I sit still
only within

the carved spaces
of myself

but in every other moment
I am pushed to the edge
Where I continue to exist
In the liminal spaces

I exist
In liminal spaces
Carved deeply

Renaissance Man
Mohammad Durrani

It is said,
"Die before you die"
so that you may live
this life, in its entirety.

What does this mean?

Let go of all books,
knowledge, and your degree.
Set a fire to your inner library.

The Sufi sits on sheepskin,
signifying the annihilation,
death of the inner animal.

Don't rush to define yourself!
You spring from the Divine Ocean
You are the cosmic big bang!
Give yourself time.

Drunkards at the tavern
sing songs of aged wine
Let yourself age, then, in
the Divine cask of Time.

Then, even the angels
will sing heavenly hymns,
marching in unison, for you,
line after line.

Word Forensics

Medina Tenour Whiteman

Does it take violence to enliven,
laceration to thrill

Do you delight in disgust
oyster grit, poison krill

Must I eviscerate you
grate your nerves with snapped taboos

Do you need smoke burning your windpipe
to make breathing seem new

Are you so congealed inside
you beg for fever, embers, brands

Medicine that kills the ills in you
stings you to understand

Am I insulting you enough now
or do you need a deep harpoon

To prick your wax, pull out your wick
and light your midnight moon

I am tired of word autopsies
fingers stained green-grey and red

If you need to be cut open
find a tougher tool instead.

Bargaining with Whom?
Yahia Lababidi

The price we pay
for exquisite secrets
is exorbitant

In private rooms,
we are fleeced.

Far from the madding crowd
at the bazaar, there we are,
sheepish and sly

Seeking to strike a deal
but with... *Whom*?

A diamond truth
is up for auction
for those with diamond hearts

To kiss a mystery,
a miracle to hoard

Naturally, is well beyond
what we ever dreamed
we could afford

We give our lives for such
shuddering intimacies

And hope and pray
our lives will be enough,
the balance cancelled

The guardian of the riddle
must only speak in riddles.

Lost in my dreams

Jessica Artemisia Mathieu

hello?
is anyone there?
can you hear me?
i'm lost! please send help!
i went searching for my dreams
and i got lost inside.
i'm stumbling around, blind,
not knowing which way is up
which way is out.
a forest of mirrors
and all i see
are my faces
everywhere
my desires
my dreams.
i'm on my knees.
please help me.
i'm lost in my dreams.
please,
set me free.

Taken
Nura Tarmann

You've taken God out of the Universe and left us with the demons
You've taken belief from our hearts and left us with cold reason
You've taken love out of life and left us with sexual attraction
You've taken mysticism away and left us with mental illness
You've taken meaning out of existence and now there is only death
You've taken systems of order and turned them into chaos
You've taken religious principles and claim them as your own
You've taken saints and turned them into madmen
You've taken women and turned them into whores
You've taken respect and turned it into fear
You've taken our natural high and left us with drugs
You've taken our natural state and turned it upside down
You've taken our children and claim them as your own
You've taken and killed, raped and tortured
Stolen and confiscated, used and manipulated
Knocked down humanity, humiliated..........
But we will rise again! Till then my friends keep dreaming
of that Deep Beauty and Goodness that lies within

Freedom
Sabila Raza

Your values
Respect
Liberty
Only a PR campaign
No substance
Over time you carefully constructed your superiority
You'll never see me as your equal
So, how could you afford me the same opportunities?
Towering over me that's what you prefer
Anything you can use, you will, to put me in my place
Is it still considered freedom when you're constantly watching my
community?
My hijab, was always a threat
Odd, baffling
You couldn't understand
You didn't want to understand
Questioning it
Ridiculing it
Belittling it
Just as you publicly, institutionally
Try to devalue my faith
Essentially, trying to shame, break, who I am
I am not oppressed, subdued
Illiterate or uninformed
I have a voice
A critical mind of my own
What always helps, the never-ending source of my strength
Is the One you want to take away from me
Which I will never leave

Fate or defeat
Yasmine Ahmed-Lea

Too many days now
I think
I don't belong here
This place was never
Meant for me
They're always telling us
To go back anyway
Maybe I will
I silently think
Walking under grey sky
On grey ground
Heart thumping to sounds
Of trainers made in China
And wrapped up against the rain
In jackets tailored
In India
And made up of all the hands
That wove me and kept me safe
How I owe them my life
How this makes me cringe
And be grateful
At the same time
Yet I want to run away
Sucked into the abyss
Of capitalism and gain
Of stress and pain
Of consumerism and
To keep myself sane
I fake that this is
A promise of a full life
All the while knowing
It's work eat run
Get a man get a wife
Work eat bit of sun
Read about that holiday
To New Zealand

That you'll never take
Too scared you'll be turned away
At the border because
Your melanin flows too much
Feet thumping faster now
In the grey on the ground
Trying to remember why
This is the place I love
And hate
The most

Entanglement
Suhayla Bewley

In the living past,
I am the sea that wages
and the soul that rages
I am the ache that burns
And the voice that learns
To silence itself numbly.

I am your voice stifled
and your great hopes trifled
I am all the doors closing
And the world closing
To all but the listening.

But you,
You are my knots untangled

Have Mercy on Me
Abdalhamid Evans

Have mercy on me I am bewildered by the decree
Have mercy on me I am amazed by what I see
Oh how our lives unfold
Oh and what stories are told
And the things that we do to each other
Have mercy on us all as we try to hang on
Hang on to the rope

Have mercy on me I am a leaf that is falling
Have mercy on me I am a voice that is calling
Oh how our lives have been spun
Oh oh what deeds have we done
And the Patterns that we leave behind us
Have mercy on us all as we try to walk
Along that narrow blade

Have mercy on me I am a bird that is singing
Have mercy on me I am a bell that is ringing
Oh how our lives take these turns
And what we forget and what we learn
As we ride along this winding highway
Have mercy on us all as we dive
Into this ocean

Have mercy on me I am a blind man tapping my way through
Have mercy on me I am so helpless calling out to You
Oh how our lives unfold
Oh and what story we told
As we tap tap tap through our days
Have mercy on us all as we reach
Reach out for You

Bright Spark
Malika Meddings

My finger taps onto a lake its motion
Bracken Water drinks in emotion
and layers - pristine smiles - a token
of doll red lips hide the broken
Open heart tastes -other- to the core
I see inside behind and under
and no layer around me-asunder
Stings from glances sent in kindness
or clumsy, or cruel
or curious vicarious excitement
all reach my centre in a nettle-dance

This will always echo, distant memory can
gallops over time and shows its messy head
and re-tastes in new and unexpected ways
The slap that is today can reach through
bowels of time and the sting it leaves
as it prints its hand upon a face
seeks to redefine features and re-colour the world

In the dark at break of day
a window open
weeps my heart newly broke-awoken
Slumber slept in pleasant dream
then unfolds the open-now
Staring at the broken day
each moment in-breath
a cold new
of smoke cleared vision
an echo inside speaks in a monotone
what now? and now? and now?

I raise my palm
I say for each breaking day
I'm breathing
Slow gossamer weave

descends rose scent
lays gently and patient
unexpected unimagined
little love pockets
lie in wait
in the dark on the window sill
of the breaking day
wait quiet and patient
'bright sparks of Elysium'
molecules of heaven
float down the in-breath
into the chasm
and sing your heart's song
with each breath -
I am here - go on

Untitled
Asma Khan

The cacophony of clamouring needs that overwhelm me daily
The grey clouds and driving cold rain
The ego desires that bury my pure aspirations
The witnessing of injustice and despair
The weariness at the cruelty of my species
Yes even my own defilement of your noble gift
All this can be borne
As long as there is that line of beauty, that buried stream of light, that
spark of Will, that golden hidden treasure, that silken loving caress
Within

The Last Prayer
Nabila Jameel

After the warning is signalled
by the horn, the earth and sky will shatter.

If my book of good is heavier on the scales
and I cross the bridge of fine thread,
I will ascend to the gates of the first heaven.

When they offer me fruit in pairs
and garments of green silk, or ask me to taste
from the canals of honey and milk,

     I will refuse,

and wait patiently, barefoot, on the soil of saffron
and pebbles of pearls and rubies – just there,

     by the gate, for you.

Three Fishes
Rakaya Esime Fetuga

At the bus stop outside Three Fishes Pub
maghrib is descending on the atmosphere
as petals
sink through water. Nine o four
and I am trying to sink into the pub wall
lest the owner of one burley voice
spilling from the window
should look out to see me there
like a reverse reflection
like a dart board.

Nothing will happen.

Ayat ul kursi visits my tongue
soundless, lips barely moving
though my heart grips it like the arms
of its beloved, safety
that embraces all that whisper its secret.
Nothing will happen.

Just like at the station
when the fans surged through
the tunnels, voices like one roar
from every direction, singing
about the direction the ball went
catching sight of us, eyes laughing
up and down
meeting us, leering at the
carriage doors to say
YOU DON'T WANT THIS TRAIN, LOVE.
Nothing happened.
When they ask how I've been
subject to violence
I haven't.
Not a violence I was taught to explain
but like dark at sunset
it hangs in the air
I watch it in my mind's eye
like a petal slowly sinking
through water
never sure if its soft
will touch the glass.

space and time
Idris Mears

one Moroccan afternoon
in the cool of the saint's tomb
i took tea with my companions
among them the holy fool

i was eager to drink in
the light of his face
and watched him closely
beyond what decorum permits
as he was absorbed in the elsewhere

a shaft of sunlight caught his glass
and the amber liquid in it
as he lifted it to his lips
and he kept the glass there
poised at the tipping point
playing with the radiant drop

he is playing with space and time
it is not correct to watch
his drunkenness will overwhelm me
i will be the fly in the amber
i told myself and lowered my eyes
for a humbled moment
before curiosity overpowered
my good sense and manners
and looking up he was gone
sitting twenty impossible feet away
up close to the tomb

the question is
whose moment was expanded
mine or his?

The Revered Word
Nimah Ismail Nawwab

We reside in the land of words and letters
where letters burst forth with every drop of water
poured forth with floods of rain
where letters were birthed with the birthing of humanity
as every word became an island to live on
every word became a wave racing along the coasts
a haven in the scorching heat
a balm under shielding palm trees

As uncharted history unfolded its pages
in reams of forgotten ages
and the world of words rose, amassed, coalesced
through poems and celebrated songs
perfuming the very air
with revered resonance

As the blade of the mighty magnificent pen
sliced through to conquered reason
carrying forth the message, the *amanah*[24],
the Trusted Messenger bore forth
the ultimate of ultimates
in words beyond the ken,
unsurpassed eloquence,
mighty wisdom
in savored, solid passages for mankind
                                    to live by and be lived.

---

[24] *Amanah* – trust

Make America Great Again
Rabea Benhalim

I think we have
a fundamental misunderstanding
of Greatness.
An inversion of sorts.

The desire for the
Greatness of bullies.
Brute strength.
Superiority.
Dominance.

No room
for nuance,
elegance,
graciousness,
gratitude
or generosity.
Much less
egalitarian ideals.

This is a rather
small,
narrow
greatness
you speak of.

Greatness sprung
forth from
insecurity.

Greatness born
from insufficiency.
A gut belief that
there isn't enough.

That the raising up

of the poor
and oppressed
Means a deprivation,
a loss.

A greatness that
fails to see,
fails to dream
of a land
that has
Enough for All.

Enough liberty.
Enough wealth.
Enough opportunity.

A Greatness
limited to
wall lined borders.

A Greatness
of isolation.

A Greatness
of homogeneity.

Greatness in
the known.

Greed

Nile Mystic

Greed
Greed

Ego riding the wheel
again
and
again

Mothers bleeding their last eggs
And Mother Earth taking her last breath

Children abandoned by the desires of their fathers

Greed
Gluttony

Wrath
Lust

Envy
Pride

Sloth

When did the pale horse become our medicine man?

Isn't it enough he took
Our lands
our native beliefs
And made us slaves for his godless empire

Greed
Greed

Every man's seed

Oh children
Let us heal
Let us water our native seeds
Let's give
Let's forgive
Let's be true
Let kindness run like rivers in
Every vein
Every artery

Let the brown fields shine green again

The Hellish Train to Tunbridge Wells and the Mozlamic Infidels
Novid Shaid

Once, upon a hellish train
That my memory will never expel
I travelled down to Tunbridge Wells
With the Mozlamic infidels!

I walked along the corridors
Searching for an empty carriage
Each one was packed none could relax
Three more were along the passage
I went into the first one,
And was about to take a seat
When I glanced upon the passenger
And my skin began to creep.
His eyes were cold and dark like graves
His beard was wild and wavy
He wore a t-shirt with a quote
'Come to ISIS baby!'
He looked at me right up and down

And was seething with outrage
But before I could exit the place
He roared a great tirade:

"Look at you! Look at you!
You Muslim Uncle Tom!
You're worse than *kuffar*, you really are!
I can kill you with a bomb
You sold your soul you big a-hole!
You kiss the arse of *kuffar*
Instead of making war on them
You vote in their referenda!
Look at you! Look at you!
Don't even say a word
If you stay here any longer
I'll beat you like a goat herd!"

The shock of his frenzied comments
Made me flushed and rather dizzy
So I left and tried the next carriage
It also seemed quite empty
I was just about to take a rest
And gather up my senses
When I noticed the other passenger
And his look made me defensive
His eyes were dry like the sands of Dubai
And his smirk was condescending
The Sun and Daily Mail, he held
He spoke, twisted and menacing:

"Look at you! Look at you!
You filthy little Muslim!
Taqiyya foaming out of your mouth!
Go jump on a pile of pigskin!
Go back to the slums from where you come
You don't deserve to be here
You made our country stink of curry!
And now you want Sharia!
Look at you! Look at you!

With all your false outrage!
We can't trust your filthy words
Get lost, just go away!"

So I moved off from this loon
Feeling a rising flurry
At this point I was in desperate need
Of a plate of chicken curry!
His outbursts made me stumble out
Into the corridor
Inadvertently I walked into
The next available door
Before I could steady my breaths
I noticed this cool dude
He sat there with designer beard
And a pompous attitude

"Look at you! Look at you!
You barbaric Islamist
You take Quran so literally
And prayer you can't resist
Why are you so damn obsessed
With God and holy seasons?
Just follow what makes sense to you
There's no god but reason
You're giving us a real bad name
We're the laughing stock of the English
When in Rome be as Romans are
Assimilate or be extinguished
Look at you! Look at you!
Your faith needs to reform
Soon your sort will all die out
Science will be our norm"

I stepped aside and wandered on
On this relentless, charging train
Only one carriage was left
I had to take the strain.
I stepped into the compartment

Shuddering at who might be there
And the two men that I saw sitting
Made me gasp in sheer despair!
On the right sat a Muslim guy,
A white turban crowning his head
Black beard longer than a baguette
And his ruck sack filled me with dread
On the left there sat this man
Who wore a three-piece rainbow suit,
He looked as gay as Dorian Gray
So I stood there perfectly mute
Then the gay man spoke so clear
Pointing at the Muslim
Humour sparkling in his eyes
Proclaiming with a wide grin

"Look at him! Look at him!
This Mozlamic infidel!
He looks like old Bin Laden
And he thinks I'm going to hell
He believes all these fairy tales
About Prophets and flying horses
I think that all he needs to do

Is take some Science courses
Look at him! Look at him!
He's probably got 4 wives
The only thing he eats is curry
He lives an uncultured life
But if all that is what he believes
Well that's entirely up to him
I can sit in the same space
In equilibrium."

The Muslim then looked up at me
Observing my shock and horror
He pointed at the rainbow man
And spoke like a proper Gora:

"Look at him, Look at him
He is so bloody gay!
I've told him that I disagree
But he doesn't care for what I say

Look at him! Look at him!

This rainbow infidel!

He's wearing so many colours

They're giving me dizzy spells!
Although I don't really approve
It's his choice what he does
I don't accept his actions

But he's human just like us
I follow what I deem is true
I aim to do my best
I hope Allah is pleased with me
As life is a profound test
You may think I am a mad mullah
Who can't move with the times
At least I don't change with the winds
So life's for me sublime
If this man here thinks he's right
Well that's entirely up to him
I can sit in the same space
In equilibrium"

I stood and smiled just for a while
Remembering the others
The ISIS man the Nazi man
And the narcissistic brother.
So I weighed up all the choices
In which carriage would I dwell
I'd sit with the Mozlamic preacher
And the Gay man from Tunbridge Wells.

411

This new 'Jihad'
Joel Hayward

Wickedness dances like a Chinese dragon
held high on poles by the grinning

It curls its tail and snakes around the minds
of admirers who see beauty in its gaping jaws

Flaccid and incapable, this billowing beast
intoxicates and seduces the frustrated and resentful

It dances in Karachi, hoodwinks in Bradford,
and slips into the dark places in distracted minds

— this infernal idea more bilious and mephitic than a komodo's bite

It dances wildly in the confused thoughts of lost boys
who haven't noticed its cunning wink

They sway and rock — utterly taken
far more mistaken — until stilled by the slap of death

Waging Peace on Terrorism - *extract*
Rabia Saida

After 9/11
Things changed a lot for me - for Muslims generally
I was teacher training in a primary school in England
While elementary school children near the Twin Towers
Had to run from rubble falling round their ears,
Thinking people they saw fall from windows were birds
And in the days after we saw the images of those buildings collapse
The head teacher of the school I was working at
Had the children sing a song in assembly that went
"Shalom, my friend, Shalom my friend, Shalom, Shalom.
God's peace be with you, God's peace be with you
Shalom, Shalom"
I went and spoke to her, almost in tears,
I said I was Muslim
And asked her if we could sing the same song again using the words
Salaam Salaam
Because all the Muslim children at the school
Would be feeling really confused
Just like me.
So she agreed.
And we sang "Salaam, my friend, salaam my friend, salaam, salaam
God's peace be with you, God's peace be with you
Salaam, Salaam."
But 9/11 is emblazoned in our collective memory
The damage done was far more profound than singing shalom and
salaam
Could ever begin to heal.
Thousands died
Millions were traumatised
Someone hijacked the religion of more than a fifth of the world…

It was as if they took my heart
And the hearts of those closest to me
Which I knew to be good
And full of love
And paraded them on every newspaper cover and TV station

Branded with ugly words of hate and treason
I couldn't believe a coreligionist of mine could have done this
They said moderate Muslims were not like this
That Islam was a religion of peace
But we were all tarnished
As if the blood of every innocent stained our hands
As if we couldn't wash it off however hard we tried.
We spent our time apologising
And trying to explain how we were not like those terrorists
Pointing out that the etymology of Islam
Is salaam
And that salaam means peace…

Now our every misdemeanour is laid bare for worldwide scrutiny
As proof of our further culpability
Every story served up
Under sensationalist headlines
And sprinkled with aspersions
Like some kind of seasoning
Because
Everybody knows that
Muslim goes with misogyny and extremism
In the same way lamb goes with garlic and rosemary
The recipe is foolproof…

But the thing is I'm tired of this bunker mentality
Because I know my religion as something of beauty
Of compassion, of sacredness
Of solace, of wonder, of mercy
Of gratitude, humility and awe
To me Islam is my dialogue with God
My mother-tongue for divine communication
Muslim is the language of my heart
The language of intimacy
A binary code for reading existence
I feel peace when I pray
And peace when I fast
Life without this
Would be tinsel and bling

And pain and tragedy with no meaning
So I reclaim my identity
I say unapologetically
Proudly
That I am Muslim
And my religion is a religion of peace
This is my spiritual heritage
Because whatever the rhetoric is
doesn't change reality.
This is peace for me
Salaam
Whoever you may be
Peace be upon you
Assalaamu alaikum

In light of recent events
Rabea Benhalim

I might become a quiet person.
Someone with presence,
who can easily slip away.
I will master the art of only being seen
when I choose.
A disappearing act of sorts.
I'll become a hoarder of words.
So that when they fall from my lips
you will feel
the breaking of silence.

Infused with Beauty

Yohosame Cameron

_*_

infused with
beauty
your words
remind and reveal
the shimmering shade of
an illuminated melody
i'm left humming...
a tone that takes care of its own:
reverberating
echo & ambrosia
a full spectrum river
that graced your lips
and fingertips
as you made wudu
from the living waters
born from tears not salty but sweet
in the suffering.. necessity to return
full center forehead on the ground
sound waves crashing around
me...
in Your Calm within all storms

Journeying still

Asma Khan

They say I am awareness Itself
yet only tantalising reaches come to me
of Truth
The scent of the woods and something so Pure there
I had to stop my mindless steps today
like I do in that daily trudge across the Bridge
Smiling at the juggler and hunched against the cold
when in a moment Light sparkles on the Thames
and I hear the gulls calling me to stare
at their wild wheeling brazen freedom
Or Joy calls in the giggle of my child
my astral reminding visitor in me and from me
whose eyes sparkle with a light from That realm
whose touch is angelic other worldly Love
or in that pause before sunset when *arsh* descends to remind me of its
overwhelming Knowing Beauty
I want to dwell in That Being of certain absolute *huuuuu* radiance for
ever
step through the door
and return here no more

Come Hither, My Sweet

Ayesha Ijaz

Oh tired and depraved soul
come closer
relax
rest your eyes
for just this moment
forget his hurt
forget yourself
be still
for just this moment
rest your heart
erase your story
lean back into yourself
breathe
then fall
fall all the way
back into the arms
of the One
who loves
who loves you more than
you love Him
relax
come closer still
breathe
stay a while
wipe your tears
or cry some more
Listen,
you have the rest of your life
to weave your tale of woe;
but for one moment
just this moment
you have to let God love you.

Laylatul-Qadr
Ray Lacina

That night we hope
the dust storm stops at the edge of town,
roils back into itself,
rolls up into rain clouds

that night we hope
hands cupped
caulked with tears of shattered joy
caulked with tears of a joy that shatters

that night we hope all the stars shine through
clouds bright with rain
we hope
hearts cupped
to catch it all
the freight train roar of silence
the star filled rain
we hope to catch it all.

Hell
- Sidd

Suddenly the dark seems to get darker,
And the light seems to have diminished,
The sun is a black circle in the sky,
And my life seems to have finished.
The atmosphere is gruesome and my body begins to seethe,
The air, heavy and thick, and I can't seem to breathe,
I realise as I stand before a pit of fire so deep,
That I've awoken elsewhere from where I chose to sleep.

My ears consumed by screams of agony and despair,
My eyes witnessing an ocean of nightmares,
And I finally speak, "I don't deserve this, it's unfair"
But the Angel behind me responds, "it was your sins that brought you here"
Despite all the signs we sent down for you to be aware,
You defied them and the verses of the book so clear,
Didn't care about the afterlife, only worldly affairs,
So don't you dare declare for your well-being and welfare.

My body shivers in fear,
I can't keep my hands steady, if I wasn't dead my heart would've exploded already,
You see, I muster up the remainder of courage and turn around swiftly,
As I speak to The Angel of Punishment directly,
And I say,
"But I thought I would wake up to gardens, rich with verdancy,
roses the colour of burgundy,
with the feeling of fervency,
so please do me the courtesy
and explain this absurdity,
I don't wanna abide by this fire for all eternity."

And the Angel responds in a most deafening tone,
His voice capable of shattering every single bone,
He says,

420

"O Son of Adam,
You were given opportunities,
but your actions reflected lunacy,
You committed mutiny,
And then you walked the earth imprudently,
As if you acquired immunity
From the fire, presumably,
But didn't realise your truancy."

And I begin to wail at the top of my lungs,
"Please, explain to me exactly what it is I have done?!
Why has my reckoning begun,
Under this black Sun,
When I believed in The Being that created everyone?!"

And the Angel responds with a most threatening roar,
Very fearsome and powerful, just like before,
He says,
"O Son of Adam,
You were given wealth but never gave to charity,
Given speech but polluted it with profanity,
Given love disrespected your family,
And spewed hypocrisies and pathetic fallacies,
You were told to show kindness to one another,
Yet, you never even smiled at your fellow brother,
You question why you were cast into this eternal blaze,
But when you felt lust, did you ever even lower your gaze?
You abused the fact that we gave you eyes,
your tongue was tainted with nothing but lies,
And your ears were deaf to the sound of cries,
All over the world, you didn't even sympathise!
And when conflict arose and it all got intense,
You let it get worse, and sat on the fence,
You were sent down with faith to be humanity's defence,
Yet, you stood silent, and watched the oppression commence,
Oh and, did we not assign you with 5 appointments a day?
You called yourself a Muslim, but did you even pray?
The prayers which were there to keep you from going astray,
But now you sit here for eternity, with this fire as your stay."

Now at this point, every cell in my body begins panicking like never before,
Yet, I'm paralysed like a mannequin stuck to the floor,
I'm tryna escape this place, I can't take anymore,
But the darkness shrouds any windows and doors,
Why did I treat my religion like it was a chore,
Something I abhorred, instead it was sin that I adored,
I chose God as an enemy in this unwinnable war,
And it led me here, to hear this pit of fire roar,

But still, I attempt a plea,
"It was Satan, the one who tempted me,
You see, I tried to follow the rules attentively,
But he misled me deceptively,
So why has My Lord then not exempted me?"

Now, the Angel casts a most disapproving look,
He stops reading out my sins as he shuts his book,
As he turns to put the book back on the shelf,
A voice from the distance says, "oh but Mr Angel, I can speak for myself…"

Now every syllable slithers out of Satan's mouth like a snake,
As he says, "why do you blame me for your mistakesss?
Yes, I promised you truth but my truth was distorted,
If you had only followed your Lord then my plans would've been thwarted,
But every time I called you to sin, you allowed it to begin,
You allowed my essence to get under your skin,
Every single one of my whispers were indeed replied to,
You see you allowed this evil to seep inside you,
It's funny coz you were sent the verses of The Book to guide you,
Yet now you sit here to burn, with me beside you."

Now at this point, I realise I have no evidence against the devil,
I am completely cheated,
I have no strength left to argue, I am utterly defeated,
I have to take one last look at the Sun that emits no light,

I see the angels around me sharpening their scythes,
I see Satan smile as he succeeded with his schemes as it seems,
I'm about to join this choir of painful screams!

But wait -
Wake up and it's all a dream,
I run to the window to see the Sun glisten and gleam,
Screams of terror replaced with children running for ice cream,
And I seem to snatch this moment at first glance,
I'm free from death's dance,
I've been given a second chance,
To enhance my status in the next world and advance,
So I'm here to fight evil with a defiant stance,

See I don't care if I fail in this life as long as I'm a success in the next,
I'll say it with my chest,
I'm here to aggress the devil with a holy vest,
Stay blessed,
As I cause Shaytaan stress,
And leave evil under me, like an armrest,
But I confess, when I address the people,
That I'm scattered just like the rest,
You see, I know this life is the absolute test,
I'm not sinless my brothers, I'm just tryna sin less.

I'm just tryna prepare for the day that He expands the grand plan,
He who created man,
Khalaqal insaan,
When He rolls up the lands,
In His hands and causes every single woman and man,
To stand with every strand and gland,
That they had from birth -
You leave the Dunya but your deeds follow you from earth,
Your wealth in this world doesn't determine your worth,
Only the sins that you've committed,
But those that submitted will be acquitted,
Because they benefitted from what He permitted,
So please go into prayer and have your sins admitted.

I'm not trying to say 'don't enjoy yourselves' but we consume this life
with too much fun,
I've got brothers revising for exams but their tests have begun,
You can't run from The One that created The Sun,
Trying to fight Allah is like trying to shoot the Moon down, with a
toy gun,

So all I ask is that we make amends,
And prepare well before the end,
And I intend to find my way there and ascend
And, In Sha Allah, I see you there too my friends.

The Eternal Song
Jessica Daqamsseh

Through echo chambers of despair
to the Majesty of Your Throne.
A chorus of highs and lows
beseech Your Grace.
A melody of timeless existence,
awaiting submission to the Divine Artist
in their eternal home.

Ahad
Tasnim McCormick Benhalim

And the yellow leaves on blue-purple sky
Can break your heart in just such a way
That what you knew for certain is suddenly unsure
And what you can imagine is infinite.

Strange Love
Wajiha Khalil

I transgressed my soul
like pliers ripping barb wire
looked under rocks for help
like any polytheist
I complain to You

You created me
a treasure then
I stole the valuables
and left the chest
like scraps for You
I complain to You

I witnessed
then hid while
ignoring You
my Friend,
I complain to You

I looked in dirty mirrors
rummaged junk yards
drank from the polluted chalice
Forgiving One,
I complain to You

When I took shelter
in homes other than Yours
I was kicked out by
Your Mercy
to return to You
I complain to You

I am shallow and weak
You are all Knowing
and Strong
I've sinned my Lord,

I complain to you

My servant
come closer
complain to Me

My servant,
I taught you
with love and I Am
All Loving
Complain to Me

Cry to Me your sorrows
let Me bandage your wounds
I will heal you
Complain to Me

Stay awake
don't sleep
be with Me
Complain to Me

Your pleas
are My gift to you
open these heavenly presents
dear one,
complain to Me

The River
Asiya Sian Davidson

I can say the word 'God' now
but sometimes I get tired
and I want to run back to
the river

sometimes that word pins me down
into a heavy, weary caricature
of a believer
I was able to come to religion sideways
because Allah was not God
but another Word

some words open like a lotus under
every foot
but other words are stones that
have no step

Allah escaped my post-modernity
Allah was Beyond me in entirety
Until I became a Muslim

Stepping into the mosque
Allah became 'God'
and I wanted to run
back to the river

the river that soothes
things into their
right places

the path to the waterhole
is not here
in these simulated forms
and misappropriated costumes

undress me back to the moment

of my first remembering
beyond the images
we built of self
and other

I'm breathing my way back to country
and the scent of the eucalyptus
after the rain
and delicate pink heath
flowering
in the imprint
of the horse's hoof

and late nights
spent drawing by candlelight
Sidi Ali Sidi Harazem
words in a bottle
water from the river of the saints

there are snakes on the streets again
collecting wives for play
and I'm running back to country
weary of beards and blame

take me home to country
to pristine territory before naming
to virgin birth
and relief from shaming

have you ever seen a soul at home
in a dead body?

breathe me back to my river
where the guilt of mothers
is restored into silence
and where the bloodlines
give way to the water

Sisterhood

Asma Khan

Last night we sat and unpicked the stories of our lives
As we have done before and will, I hope, again
Five women, decreed to hold this tapestry between them
Crosslegged in a prayer of sorts, asking always
what their weaving hides
Trying to interpret the illusions from reality
Straining in this world for a tangible beauty
not knowing what the Unseen could ask

Fear has infected all our dreams
We were taught the pain of the little mermaid
She, caught by temptation that came
In its glimpsing shining beckoning across the bay
entrancing her with its kaleidoscope
until it shattered and she limped home on broken glass
We knew stories of wounds oozing that can send princesses back to
sleep
Or held imprisoned in circular pondering for all time
unaware of the breath that can end their entrapment
and return them to light and clarity eternally

So we reminded each other of all this as women do with heart and
voice and soul combined
And the sharing brought joy to what will after all, pass
We left those sweet companions
With gifted patches sewn to our trailing cloaks adding to their beauty
Revelling in our new found selves
Pining sculptures no more
released by laughter from our knotted woes
untied by Love

Wudhu
Saraiya Bah

I had a dream that I
plunged into pools.
Clear blue.
To purge myself of
the taint.
Remnants of hate.
Residue that oozes
into the stratosphere
& precipitates into
the atmosphere.
I don't want to be here.

Life bears the complexity
of Rubik's broken down to Tetris.
The line between dream
and reality grows ever lucid
& the thread of clarity
remains elusive.
So fluid the transition:
bliss of fantasy to
harrowing reality.

I tried to dhikr the
pain away.
I tried to pray the
pain away.
No matter what I do,
it will always remain
this way.
I'll always have
Jannah on my brain.
I don't want to be
here.

The Homecoming of My Old Friend
Novid Shaid

One day, a painful memory shook my heart,
My old friend had served me since my birth,
And I had cast him out onto the street,
Denying his undying faithfulness.
For my old friend was becoming wearisome,
Especially now I'd made new, trendy friends,
In these progressing times he seemed passé,
My friends would snigger at my companion.
So, I barged him out onto the lonely street
I slammed the door as he began reasoning,
I convinced myself he was an inconvenience,
I assured my friends I had forsaken him.
Many days and weeks passed gradually,
I felt the world vibrating at my feet,
His knocking had halted some time ago,
But still I knew he lingered there, outside.
So I threw off all my guilt and held my breath,
Then leapt into the mires of my desires.
I plunged in hordes of feigned relationships,
I hosted great, extravagant soirees,
Fleeting ecstasies were my preoccupations,
My house bulged with gatecrashers gushing in,
My heart sagged with intruders surging in.
Until one day, as I jigged around my room,
Encircled by my artificial friends,
They closed in on me, stifling my breast,
They pressured me to offer them my heart,
When a slow knock rocked against my door
Its reverberation left a thunderous roar,
My body trembled like a shaken leaf
From deep within arose familiarity,
I staggered to and fro, shielding my ears,
But still the knocks resounded, thundering.
And then the realisation struck me down,
My abandoned friend was waiting in the cold.
And as this certainty aroused my heart,

Tears of shame ran, searing my desires,
Each drop fell, and my heart was up in flames,
The intruders fled, shrieking in agony.
I moved towards the knocking on my door
The tense smiles of my friends stood in the way,
Attempting to divert my attention,
They promised untold pleasure if I stayed,
But when they realised I was intent
They grabbed my legs and fought to drag me back
They wailed and cried revealing their dismay,
And I just kicked them off with bitterness.
And so I stood there, facing my front door
I turned and saw my friends gaping in horror,
I turned the handle with my quivering hand
My heart lamented as the door opened,
I dreaded facing him after so long,
I planned I'd throw myself before his feet,
When suddenly every single thing vanished
My house, my friends, myself and nothing else remained.
And then I found myself not in my room
But on the lonely street, there, shivering
Before me stood a great, glistening door
It opened and my old friend emerged,
He covered me with warm, comforting robes
He wrapped me in His unifying glow,
He sheltered me from sorrow and the cold,
And I had been a homeless, wretched soul,
And by His love I'd finally returned home.

Forms

Nura Tarmann

They send me plastic cards to withdraw paper from a metal machine
But I don't want to put money in a bank with unknown interests
That tricks people with a magic trick called credit
Giving nothing in return
They want me to tick all the right boxes
But I don't feel white today
I feel dark and heavy
I may feel Romanian or Jewish tomorrow
Indian or Asian in a minute or two
Sai Baba looks like my father
My brother the Buddha
And Jesus my son
I don't feel like filling out form after form asking where do I live
I don't live there, it's only a temporary abode
Where were you in the last ten years?
I forgot to remember to take notes
How many jobs have you had and describe them in order
Let me see Is sitting quietly a job description?
Is killing the ego an occupation?
Is the art of living truthfully and with feeling not a consuming task?
Give us references.
My references are unlettered, they don't operate by these laws.
Give us days, months, years
But my days moved as the waves of the sea
Does one count them?
Such a thing is absurd!
I remember the man in the Jobcenter
Being robbed of the last vestiges of his pride
Screaming I need help filling out this form (with what is formless)
Give me a damn broom and I will clean!!

I am not a business man
Abdalhamid Evans

I am not a business man.
I am not in business.
I offer some of what I have of experience, time, skill, knowledge and
vision
in exchange for a negotiable recompense.

I am not an employee - I am unemployable.
I am a Collaborator.

I am the sum of all of my life experience, all of it...all of it.
The contractions and expansions of time have moulded me,
Shaped me,
Given me form and meaning.

The past does not control me.
The future does not intimidate me.
I am free.
Now...

I am a servant of Reality,
compelled towards my destiny,
guided by my inner vision,
my hearing, my sight, my senses, my intellect...my yearning
        watered by the wisdom of others
who have gone ahead.

I have no choice but freedom,
the freedom of no-choice,
for I can only step into the footsteps of my destiny.
There is nowhere else to go.

There is a change of consciousness taking place.
You can feel it in the air.
We are all in it, and of it.
We are it.

You can choose to ignore it, but it is happening anyway.
Or you can embrace it, and ride this wave,
follow the surging curve of the long now.
Now, this continuous moment of presence,
curling through timespace,
endlessly transforming us all.

So make peace with your past.
Take courage for the future.
Be present in the moment.

Life continues to be in the present tense.

Zaki

Fatima's Hand

Joy is my boy child's curls
Ablaze and luminescent in sunlight
While he runs with a daisy
For his Mama
And as tenderly as a small child's fingers can,
Weaves it into her hair
She revels in this -
Before his attention belongs to the world
Before his heart is lost in another
When her joy will become
Discovering old joys
Transient moments
Dancing in the sands of time

Seems to me

Asma Khan

Seems to me
Humanity never had a clue
Seems to me
No idea I mean
just kids with blindfolds
Playing find the treasure
Chase the heart piñata
Which we then smash with glee
For sweets that make us fat and stupid
Seems to me
we don't wait
we don't seek
we are not hungry
Just happy
with our boxed phrased annotated shelved version of games we played
Roaring twenties
Killing forties
Swinging sixties
Stoned seventies
Greedy eighties
On and on. Til clueless we arrive at our present state of
deaf dumb
blind numb
Seems to me
We need to lie quietly like starfishes under the sky and Be Us Now
feel the grass growing around us and not move until we get it
Do as we were told
Sod the rest

In Rumi's Tomb in Konya

Daniel Abdal-Hayy Moore
5/7/2002, from The Flame of Transformation Turns to Light
(written at Rumi's tekke in Konya)

A sky shaped like a face – *no it can't be that*
A winged horse on fire in the middle of the air – *no it can't be that*

A sound of bells that burns from the feet to the heart
A whisper of hidden words falling from the top of the tree – *no it can't
be that*

A look across the centuries that today is enshrouded in the world
The touch of a child's hand who already knows the secret – *no it can't
be that*

A bridge of light in all the usual places
A bird that expands to embrace every living heart – *no it can't be that*

An eye that beholds the cave where the Prophet became Messenger
A sing-song voice speaking perfect rhyming sentences – *no it can't be
that*

Hello before you arrive and Hello again before you get up to go
A kiss across green water that reflects both sun and moon – *no it can't
be that*

A call from within Rumi's shirt so old its threads look like rain
A light that slides up a corner of the tomb and fills the body – *no it
can't be that*

What is it then? Is there any answer?
Is it possible to say? – *no it can't be that*

Ameen was gone for a moment but something remained
There's only a trace left in the air from all of us – *no it can't be that*

Mevlana – we certainly had a magnificent celebration
Does it need to end? – no – please – it can't be that

Last Minute Rush

Paul Abdul Wadud Sutherland

In the King St. Take-A-Way, in a windowless room
we plunge to *sajda* on fresh waves of cardboard

he puts me right, once more, that young blackshirted
worker, born into the faith, who calls me brother.

Saturday midnight, last punters hug their fast food.
At times we forget everything and still are blessed.

He knows the Qu'ran, inside out, and among a hot
sink's last sudsy wash-up, starts to sing its Opening.

I slip-slide through the door, not losing my balance
on best mopped floors, while he envelops the takings.

1.30am, he smokes and speaks the language of Paradise
before gazing out his windscreen, flies towards home.

I wander unguarded between streams of clubbers
the most radiant moon sends down the sweetest rain.

Release...
Yasin Chines

I have stopped looking at shadows
juxtaposed along my crumbling walls
Their ricocheting screams now muffled
to the flickering fury of muzzled wolves.
I offer no more than a vacuous gaze
as my eyes now filled with red wine sauce
gleam of seething satiety.
I am untroubled by the loneliness
of yesterday's hours unfilled with thrills
Like a painter, carefree about sheets left blank,
reducing the artful figure in his bank.
I have stopped gathering rugs to lay on
'my driveway', awaiting a time The Friend has mapped.
I have stopped thinking
about the rightness of my ways
but now let their 'right of way'
flow like paint amalgamating
into a blush matched
by crimson flames of maple woods.
I listen to the whispers within,
rustling like burning crackling wood,
emitting incense smoke that dances...
charming and twirling its way to nothingness.
Transmuted to a vaporous verity,
my heart forms palms that yearn to feel
the texture of the moon's blessed split.
My eyes have stopped leaking icicles.
Like a moth, my chariot heads for the sun,
to smell the aroma of obliteration.
Drifting beyond the fringes of stars,
all I hear now is the rhythm of stanzas
built by love's orchestra that plays
to a loveliness of ladybirds

I am in Transition

Sukina Pilgrim

I am in transition
I am becoming
I am dying
I am arriving
I am S

    I

      N

        K

          I

            N

              G

But not drowning
I am breathing
Underwater
Open your eyes
And witness the miracle
Of life after death
Of life on the edge
Of elevation
Of wings opened
Spanning across the horizon
Blocking out the sun.

I am expanding
My chest ripped apart
Like a pomegranate
My ruby seeds
Dirty the floor
Telling my story
In the colour of blood.
I am love
The type of love
That will remain
After the sun has set
Behind the concrete
And all we are left with

Is darkness.
I am love
Without the light on.

I am entrusting
My entire being
Into the hands of the Divine Fashioner
Who forms majesty out of dust
And water.

I surrender
I surrender
I surrender

Un/opening
Mariam Akhtar

for our ancestors
for languages that slip on our tongues
for letters and words
that escape our teeth
sounding something like insincerity
for secrets that scrape our throats
like grit and gravel against skin
an unholy union
for me being whole
and you being empty
for when I bled from my nose for three days in a row
for everything that's raw inside us

Layla and the Spirit
Medina Tenour Whiteman

Between two shoulders of black rock at dusk
glides a keeling splotch of oil paint
risen up off canvas, shedding its last
traces of livid pink
dying smoke blue

I'm on a sodden track, caged in by tall canes
without a clue of where I'm going
a red sliver on my phone
entranced as night doesn't so much fall
as blossom by degrees

A bat emerges scudding
and for once I don't think of
rubber Halloween witch masks but
a soft blunt brown face
we found one summer, snoozing
in a cleft in a mimosa tree.

It cringed from our curious faces
taut skin between twiggy fingers
held up over its eyes like two fans

I find the bank, recently gouged
by a river that, in flood, decided
to reclaim the track usually taken by
hippie camper vans
sliced a metre off the hillside
obliging walkers to wend new paths
carving new geographies
with her unbankable force

This is what feminine looks like
soft, clandestine
roaring, cool

This is what Layla looked like
the night she put the spirit into Majnun

This is an invitation
to close day eyes, let cat sense bloom

This is the disappearing top step
dream remembered as parallel truth

This is what most prefer to fear:
warted mask, wolf howling at moon

This is half of each sun cycle,
the half that most of them sleep through

This is the deep exhilaration
of releasing all you thought you knew

feeling earth's atmosphere darken
and light years of depth touch you

A bat wing-dances
where the twilight pulls deepest
calls seekers of unseeable knowledge
to shut up and come

Sometimes
Yasmine Ahmed-Lea

Sometimes I get
Bored with myself
So sore with myself
That I pretend to be
That man on the bench
Drinking in lament
Over the wives that he lost
In his fits of rage
Over passion for the drink
Him and me, he and I, so lonely

Sometimes I get so tired of myself
I rewired my whole self
To become that English rose
In full bloom
Posing for the vogue
Click click
Tap tap
On the ocean of sociability
At her fingertips
An oar which I could never
Reach or touch
But inside we both are
bones heavy bones
drowning in our seas

Sometimes I get so lost in myself
The frost in my words
Making it hard to be kind
To this heart that You gave
This head that You made
This soul that You saved
Sometimes
At that time
I want You to be me
I want You
To Be.

Mama said [II]:
Bushra Mustafa-Dunne

Sky me
because home on earth
is rubble

in a place I don't know, a house left with the stove on
door open.

home
is broken pomegranate husk,
red, red, رُمَّان[25]
 under my nails.

White water
home is watermelon:
رَقِّي[26]
green skin suspended in the Tigris,

burning stars I could touch if
I reached out my hand
then found
– closing dreamed-up fingers to catch –
I was one of them.

Home is
a blazing tree
behind my sister

---

[25] Pomegranate, pronounced *rummān* in Arabic
[26] Watermelon, pronounced *reggi* in Iraqi Arabic

445

The Magenta Tablecloth
Aaishah Mayet

They said never to seat you for dinner on Magenta
Lest your appetite ignites like flames to firewood
Lest desire flares
And faculties leave
And food vanishes in the wormhole
Where once you sat

What sorcery is this?
A masculinity so infantile
That femininity is flippant?

Let me teach you how to take me seriously

How did you get to be here?
Answer me

You breathed through me
Took nutrients through my spiral arteries
Learned to fight from the blueprint of my immunity

How dare you disrespect me?

If my placenta denied you,
You would cease to be
Let that sink in,
You would cease to be

Patchwork Playground

Rabia Saida

Where do I fit in?
Between the seams
Between the cracks
I'm not this
I'm not that
Part of the great patchwork
A bit mismatched
Perhaps the wrong colours or pattern

Seagull cries in the crisp morning
Above an east London playground
I almost taste the salt air
As they swoop and glide
Riding chill currents of a December sky
Children play beneath them
From Somalia and Bangladesh, from Morocco and East London

There are the Bangladeshi mums
In their bright sparkly hijabs
So pretty their little girls want to wear them too
there are the enigmatic ladies in their niqabs
The Mauritanian women wrapped in such fabulous colours
I so wish I could pull off that look
There are the East Londoners in their Uggs and pyjamas and the
middle class parents
Who've opted out of the rat race
To run the after-school gardening club and organise the Christmas fair
Where the Somali women have a stall selling their delicious dishes
And the Bangladeshi ladies sell hijabs - three for two
Among lucky dip and hook the duck stalls
While a badly dressed Santa sits in his grotto wondering why no one
comes to see him
The Christmas cakes and biscuits are popular - everyone who baked
them made sure they were halal
There's even a Japanese lady selling her home-made sushi.
We're all a bit mismatched

A quilt made up of left over scraps
Of exotic wraps and pound shop bling, John Lewis cloth and black
abayas.
The Christmas show's a laugh
All the Muslim children take part in the nativity play
Or are dressed up as reindeer
Singing jingle bells
Their parents watch bemused
Videoing it on their smartphones
Their kids speak better English than many of them.

On Eid the Muslim kids take a day off school
My kids too
The other children say they can't be Muslim
Because they're English and don't speak Bengali
So funny
I was told that at primary school too
Then it was because I didn't speak Urdu
Some time in the week there's an Eid party
Children come dressed up in their Eid clothes
They eat crisps and drink sodas laced with preservatives and artificial
colours and play party games in the hall.

This would be a dysfunctional United Nations
But we all get along here somehow
This is where prejudice comes unstitched and true friendships are born
Seagull cries again in the 4pm dusk
I wonder if they're lost
Or somehow like circling above
Children playing football
From Somalia and Bangladesh
Morocco and East London
Perhaps to snatch tasty lunchbox scraps
Reflections of myriad diasporas
Under an overcast sky

How to move on (*Min Bayt al-Kalawi*)
Muneera Pilgrim

First thing first, say *Alhamdulillah* and take a deep breath
In no particular order follow these steps
Drink a glass of water and increase your daily volume
Stare at yourself in the mirror until you see beyond flesh
Tell yourself you're precious and fall in love with every curve of your
body
Every ripple and wrinkle in your skin
Every scar, every cut, every gash, every discolouration
The stretch marks that line you
the shadow above your lips
your eyes without colour your
cheeks without blusher
All of you
everything
Tell yourself you are beauty itself
At first you may not believe it but then Say *Alhamdulillah* Allah made
me beautiful
It's easier to digest this way
By now you may be crying
and it's okay
Don't fight back the tears
See it like a baptism, Yemoja a cleansing ritual
We only drink from moving streams and running river so let your
tears flow
This part may continue for several minutes sometimes even hours
Catch your breath and reach for some *dhikr* beads
Start with a few 500 *astaghfirullahs* and then continue as you please
Take a walk get a breath of fresh air in the cool night air
Smile and greet people as they pass by
Get yourself a bottle of water and find somewhere you can sit and look
up and see the night sky
This may remind you of the things you and him used to do
Appreciate it for what it was remembering good times is cool
Remember also that the Creator wants the best for you
It's getting late now it's time to come home now
Take the scenic route and it's okay to walk slowly

Once home you may feel the need to scream
Do this from the top of your voice for as long as you please
Another glass of water and if you're anything like me
Turn your music up full blast and then dance until you can't breathe
Dance until you fall to your knees
Dance until someone comes knocking at your door asking about the scream
Once they leave you will laugh unstoppably
This is the point you may be inspired to write a little poetry
Min bayt al-kalawi
From the deepest part of you
When you're through
Wash yourself with the cleansing scrub you have been saving for a rainy day
Make *ghusul* and *wudu* and get ready to pray
That *rak'ah* will be the sweetest thing you've ever known
Sweeter than the kiss Lauryn received on her collar bone
Continuously drink water, eat fruit, make *dhikr* and pray
Look in the mirror, see your beauty, learn your lessons, and remember
God made it this way.

Sleeping with Ghosts
Mariam Akhtar

I promised myself
I would stop sleeping with your ghost
months ago
but my body insists
on lying and laying
deceiving others and disappointing me
each month I bleed
and go wild with the moon
full and bloody
fearful and bodied
the sound of your name

leaves a disappointed taste
in the mouths of family and friends
when I mention you
once again
I've yet to find another
your face stays stuck
somewhere between my pupils
and tongue
each cell intent
on celebrating a year
half present
half silent

Mistaken
Emny Kadri

That awful moment when it dawns on you that the other person doesn't feel the same.

Your truest feelings.

Shattered.

Unwanted.

Turned away.

This is how rejection feels.

This is what God wanted to teach you so that you realised that only He was to be resident in your heart.

So that you could realise your own beauty to finally see His.

The Mosque of Seven Companions
Paul Abdul Wadud Sutherland

- built on low rocky seashore -
when Greek Cypriots dominated the area
was reduced to a household residence; now stands
restored to a maqam or sacred site.

Inside Hazrat Ömar Mosque, you -
twenty-five years a covered Muslim
and I - five days from my Shahada -
submit before the tall green alcove
its unfigured hollow topped with
calligraphy you wish you could read.
The Mediterranean's cadences
sound through beats of thought.
Breakers could snarl and hurl
storm-froth on the shelter's roof
yet no weather-mood can perturb
seven green turbaned saints inside.
When, from eight centuries of warring
empires, Ottoman foot soldiers ducked
into a cave and chanced on, laid-out
unaged bodies of seven companions
they appeared no more than children
cuddling for warmth, ready to awake.
The mosque's far-eyed attendant
collects for the abstract-bordered
sajada that we buy. Then, off duty,
discreetly steps out and taking a rod
casts for what he might discover
in rolling turquoise brightness.
In darkness, I see unknown mountains,
enveloped with evergreens, curl
toward seven bare-stone summits
each wrapped in unwarpable
brilliance. You, standing closeby
recite Arabic - *Ya Siin.*
Slow that cosmic prayer moulds
the shore-rocks of our grief and love

A life of crows or drums
Yasin Chines

Hate is the crow
that grows its limbs
and claws in the chest.
And if you won't let it
squeal its way out,
it will gulp and swallow
your blood; without even
chewing on the clots.

The moment
your wound forgives
those who caused it,
you'll feel something in the heart,
stretching new skins on the drum;
rupturing into beat,
like distant hooves getting closer.
A raking of lost notes,
exploding into song.

Fall into Surrender
Shahbano Aliani

stop being ignorant
don't you see
you can't afford it anymore?

there are signs every where

stop.
breathe.
listen.

become all ears
all eyes
everywhere you turn
is an open Book

read this text

i see the circle
of light on your forehead
the mark of one destined
for Love
and obliteration

there is no going back
now
no escape
anywhere

you may once have been a hunter
now:
you are prey

stop running
give up, lean in
allow yourself
to fall
into
surrender

your only chance for living
is this
a kind of death

Give Up
Matthew Bain

"Abandonar
o abandonarse"

"Give up,
or give yourself up".
I follow the path of love,
though sometimes I get stuck.

"Give up"
means stay stuck,
stay dumb
though love has struck.

"Give yourself up"
means get unstuck
but unhinged -
become love's plaything.

To be free is to be
compelled by love
but what about her cruelty
as she unpeels me from me?

Love is the surgeon
and I trust in
her incision
because I must.

What the Sunset Said
Yahia Lababidi

Something happened as the light was dying
it wasn't just post-coital exhalation
where the once-possessed body is used up
and all that remains is bodiless trance

Rather, it seemed they were mirroring
a preternatural stillness,
two spiritual sentinels
transfixed and somehow Other

Science calls it "twilight calibrated magnetic compass"
yet it appeared beyond mere direction-finding
more a kind of existential orientation
consolidating all they knew, and listening

with their entire being, participating
silently, in a universal hymn
until they were pulled, as out of a viscous substance,
by the hungry cry of their nearby young

to become two feral pigeons, again
with this-world considerations
parenting, foraging, keeping alive
and, dazed, they consented to their stations.

Be Still and Know
Marguerite Lake

Be still and know
There is no other way to approach
A sacred destination

What you approach depends on you
Upon your journey, your yearnings
Your soul's impulsive cry
Upon those chance encounters that reflect
Your, as yet, undiscovered being
Whether the mirror be God, man, nature,
Myth, symbol, sound or movement
Only you can know and recognize
The fabric of your soul
In your own way

And what is wholeness, integrity
If not the living stream of divine essence
Passing freely through the sometimes
Painfully carved grooves of body, mind and soul
Trickling, gorging, surging onwards
A great moving spiral, connecting, relating,
Synchronizing, harmonizing with aspects of itself
At all levels of existence
One great knowing meaning, whole and complete
For an eternal moment, triggered at times
By nothing more than the silent
Contemplation of a pebble
On a deserted shore

How to attract that which you know
Is with you at all times, in all places?
How to become who you really are?

Be still and know
It may abhor perfume and fineries
It may deny entry to complacency

It may retreat from noise, rejoice in
Or repel the stench of human sweat
It may require you to be old and gold
In the dead of night or young and silver
In the shimmering dawn; it may require you
To dance a veiled dance, pipe an enchanted tune
Or you may meet it face to face
In the cold light of its blinding truth,
Stripped of your many layered masks
It may join you in simple, selfless service
To the needy, or stand beside you
As you battle alone against life's injustices
In the marketplace; it may even
Only reach you when afraid, alone
Deserted, abandoned, in pain, or in death

Be still and know
And when it comes to join you,
You will 'be still and know' again,
Albeit only in part, for in this one moment
You will know again, this time with certainty
That always and forever you and It are One.

Muftaḥ al-Maṭbakh (Key to the Kitchen)
Efemeral

Poetry is not the point.
Who,
when a rich mouthful of ecstasy
is heaped
onto their awaiting tongue,
ever recalls their grocery list?

The Breaking
Muneera Pilgrim

It feels like He may have made me only to break me....
Then make me, then break me, and then make me, and then break me
again.
But maybe His breaking is the making of me;
Maybe His breaking is the shaping of me.
Sometimes I feel shapeless void and without form, looking in any
direction seeking that warm, seeking solace, seeking light,
Seeking the strength to make it from day to night then night to day
In the moments of being broken I wish I could just wish me away.
Then I hear the *adhan* or see children play.
This is child's play.
Tears stream from my eyes as I cry me a river,
The making is taking place divinely inspired by the life giver,
Sublime orchestrator.
He orchestrates the birds to perform the morning chorus - how
glorious!
He orchestrates seasons to pass and fruits to grow - how glorious!
He orchestrates love to flow from the hearts of the poor and the meek
- how glorious!
He orchestrates the moon to glow, the winds to blow, babies are being
born every second with every heartbeat we are being beckoned to the
beauty of His majesty, His mercy, How glorious!
Every breaking seems worse than the one before, yet every making
makes me want to be broken forevermore if this is what happens after
broken I'm sure
And I'm ever sure if others could bear witness to my life in this
bittersweet Sudan they would only intervene for the Creator has a
master plan
He makes me, breaks me and shapes me
Continuously I stand then fall,
Then he makes me, breaks me and shapes me once more

Tiger
Shahbano Aliani

sleep is the only respite
my longing for You
rises with the sun
gaining strength
on the heat of the day
demanding
that its gnawing hunger be fed

a mighty tiger
behind the bars of my ribcage
that needs the open spaces of
Your Presence
to breathe and be free

i am astounded:
how did it end up here?
did You make me a promise
at some beginning
that i have forgotten
and only
the tiger's insistent hunger remembers?

why else
would Your absence make me suffer like this!

Some things I see women do make me mad
Yasmine Ahmed-Lea

Why so obsessed
With being the tiny woman
Everything about you
Has to be small frail
Slight

Yes you are your voice
No your build is not you
Not my fault I'm 5 7
Not my fault I am not
Fair
Reedy
Waif like
It is my fault if I
Choose to want to
Live this way
In the man's shadow
So proud of my invisibility he
Shouts over me and under me
Is larger than life
Bigger than me in every way
Because I spent my time
Wanting to be small
Cute
Waning
Not my fault that I
Want to be everything
Perfection in sizes
Not voices
Perfection in double zeros
Not thought processes
Perfection in the small
Not in the ones that
Stand tall
Are brave
Are themselves
When everyone else
Looks into
A tiny
A small
A cute
Future

The Thick of Things

Ron Geaves

I am neither flesh nor ghost
yet dance bodiless
In the thick of things

You are not my dreams
that mince scions of solid light
nor unseen leaves
written on like parchment
that blow in the wind

You are not the serpent
that rises to bite its own head
nor the ox which motionless
lows to the plough

You are not quicksilver
that measures the temperature
of all forms
but cannot feel the heat
nor the gilded cage
that keeps ox, serpent, leaves
quicksilver, my dreams
in kaleidoscopes of make-believe

I look at myself
In the mirror
see still flesh
and the ghost moving

I am neither flesh nor ghost
yet dance bodiless
In the thick of things

Night
Joel Hayward

Night crawls like lizards
with tongues of opalescent horror

Sleep is a blanket on someone else's bed

and I jolt and gasp like she had

connected by that plastic tube
to a life finally withdrawn

Sleep is torn from my lungs which choke on fears
that close around me as coal dust

and all I see in the dark are
the worst things she suffered

from cancer's tongues of horror

Then radiance reaches from your woken soul
and you recite Quran over me
like a Southern faith healer

with laying on of hands

They slither away from the light
you've conjured and I sleep oh I sleep

Daylight memories appear as camera flashes

petty poltergeists easily banished

Yet darkness always follows day as an anxious housemaid

Memories slip their skins and crawl
from discarded scales again where they shouldn't

The Wave
Suhayla Bewley

There's a wave coming over
Panicked and enclosing
There's a silence daunting me
Tightening and revolving
There's a spinning sensation
And I am stuck on a wheel
There's a wave coming over
And I cannot breathe

There's steel driving me on
Like a detached motor
There's a panic standing me up
Like a mad insistence
I know I need some air
But the water is all around me
And I cannot breathe

I hold my breath infinitely
Even if my body begins to falter
I cannot let go and inhale
As it will engulf me
The wave that is still coming over me
So I wait wide-eyed
And I cannot breathe

And I hear every noise so loudly
And smell every scent so clearly
As I hold it back - this rising panic
And I hold it in - this sense of failure
And project the familiar image of myself
Whilst I cannot breathe

The project is a projection of a projection
From here under this wave
Whilst the wide eyed child
And the fearless woman are terrified

You cannot see us
Whilst I cannot breathe

Layer upon layer and I hold my breath
For this will pass as all things do
This will subside and there will be release
I hold on and I hold on
Longing to fly above this flood
Whilst I cannot breathe

This is my soul
Drowning in impossible self-expectation
And my battle
With my guilt and my grief
My true ability is to hold my breath and wait
For I know I can do this
Even if I cannot breathe

For I will not fall
And I do not fall
I can withstand this onslaught
I am structured against collapse
And I hold my breath
Because I cannot breathe

This will pass as all things do
The memory living on
This will return as most things do
And I will hold my breath
Under the sea and under myself
Until I can breathe

Acacia tree
Mai Sartawi

the dry desert heat is unapologetic as I
hang on and almost break timber limbs
thirsty for fluid trees' scented molasses
flavors built in instrument's safe cabins

so I stand
      still you
            kindly shade…

swaying thorny branches, green fern and bones
dancing high in sad songs of summer's storms
wordless memories of Caterpillars' breaches
bulldozers' breakage killing kids in masses
       so is mercy
       still woven
             in chastised roots?

Oh Soul
Aasifa Usmani

Oh soul why can't I pray?
Why do I get soaked into trivial waters
Your soul needs nourishing,
so wait,
wait,
in aloneness
wait for gathered dust to rub off -
inside is that radiant ocean.

Seven Heavens
Abdul Kareem Stone

Oh Allah create such vast plain
that the world lies within
like the way he exemplified
with the example of a ring

lost upon a land that's flat
one of the heavens seven
so above and below, like that
proceeds every heaven

Upon this plain let there run
A herd of whitest deer
That numbers more than every sun
In every single sphere

An'each of them upon their routes
As they gallop along their way
Do with their hooves make their salutes
To the Prophet that we obey

and let above a murmuration
of nightingales fly.
So vast that such numeration
even counting angels couldn't try

For every atom create a bird
that flies and sings his song
then a second, then a third
you couldn't imagine such a throng

and the only song they'll ever sing
in their sweet and tender voice
is not the one for their king
but his best-beloved choice

and this rumble is surely felt

and this song is surely heard
by hearts deep in which has dwelt
the love of His preferred

Now with your mind and with your soul
and with your body too
I want you to imagine a shoal
of shining fish swim inside you

in the silence of your ocean,
they shine so brilliantly
a glowing light in motion
such beautiful imagery

and as they swim and as they flow
in beautiful coordination
they're forming words as they go
ones of total adoration

see them moving, see them swim
and they will make you feel so glad
when you see that deep within
they've written Muhammed

Looking to Qiblah
Mohammad Durrani

"He is the Inner and Outer"
The submitter looks towards the Qiblah
This is the outer of looking
There is an inner aspect as well

At the life and example of Abraham (RA),
the who, why and the how,
as well as the House he built

The life and habits of this Friend of God.
How when he sat, and when he laid down

on his side, sat, stood, or while at work,
how he thought of his Creator

Also of interest is how that man of intellect
questioned the universal forces
and came to the conclusion that,
"anything which comes and goes is not my Lord"

So it is Written,
"And God has chosen Abraham as a friend"
"...gentle, kind, penitent" "compassionate"
"steadfast" "stalwart" "a man of truth", and
the "exemplary leader"

"We will ease you into the Easy Way"

There are secrets here for those who use reason
look within for those treasures, that devotion
jump into Abraham's sea
which in turn flows into the Divine Ocean
enjoying simplicity, peace, joy, equilibrium, and serenity.

The sea of the one friend, leads
to the Eternal Oceans of the Divine One
keep this life simple,
and come back to excellence and
the Way of Reality.

Quran 57:3, 11:75, 4:125, 19:41, 16:120, 87:8

doubt and certainty

Idris Mears

on a hard tramp
along the coastal path
i pause to recover my wind
hunkered in the shelter
of a hollow between the dunes
with the autumn sun on my face
and reflect on how this path
tracks a struggle
between land and sea
like the conflicting voices
of the heart

stretches where cliffs fall into the sea
and the bells of lost towns are heard
stretches where dunes succumb
to marram grass and the farmer's grasp

and always the track winds on
relentlessly between
being built up
and being washed away

The Fallen
Novid Shaid

A warm shower of dignified applause
Echoes down the winding road,
As hearses bearing the fallen one,
Glide through, leaving copious tears
And stoic faces in their wake.
Mourners rush forward into the road,
Roses scatter above, gently falling away,
Poor George had his whole life before him
Until an IED sent him instantly
Into the realm of Eternity.
He'd been so keen to serve his country,
Which now stood silently as his body passed by.
High within the Hindu Kush,
Wailing women and screaming children
Shed defiant and agonising tears
As wagons cradling infant souls trot away.
And grizzled elders bury their young,
Who beat them to the grave.
Poor little Hussain did not deliberately linger
When a drone floated above, homed in,
Leaving him a martyred son
And his village burned to a cinder.
He never enlisted for any state or local renegades,
He just happened to emerge in a world
Entangled and suspended in war.
And he will not make any more choices,
For he has quaffed the chalice of Infinity,
Which makes this world seem like a cheap matinee.
Angels innumerable and holy,
Greet him as he haunts their pathways,
And entreats the One who brought him back,
Fallen so suddenly.

Uskudar (sung)

Yusuf Abdalwadud Adams

I'll buy a timber house in Uskudar,
Paint my ceiling blue,
I'll chart out a dome of silver stars to navigate to you.
I'll greet the friends whose very bones make
Lanterns of their resting places,
Lighting the walls.
Hear the air vibrate with bird calls.

I will sit in the gardens of
The happy dead,
With the cats that are
Calm and well fed.
We are illuminated by
The absence of
Doing harm.

I'll be your rock n roll poodle,
Your laissez-faire suffragette,
Divine feminine cave man,
No just a man
Broken cupped and love drunken.

I'll buy a little timber house in Uskudar - Istanbul,
Paint my ceiling blue,
I'll chart out a dome of silver stars to navigate to you.

What If

Jessica Artemisia Mathieu

what if,
in a world that says
"Be Somebody!"
-what if-
i want to pass through life
without making a ripple,
without leaving a wake,
not leaving behind me
successive waves
pounding every life-filled shore
i pass?

what if,
i want to grow up and wither away
without making a sound,
just a simple daisy
in a field of daisies
unfurling from my spindly stem,
leaves unfolding to embrace the rain,
plain face turned toward the Sun,
then slowly fade away
and crumble back into the ground
i came from?

i don't want to be special.
i don't want all eyes on me.
i just want to live quietly,
love quietly,
and then leave this world
without having made a sound.

i think i'm in love with silence.
please,
just let me
be.

Old Age[27]

Toneya Sarwar

The journey begins when
the body betrays the mind
In preparation for the soul to depart from its shell
Between what I want and what I can is an ocean
Memories are crystal clear of what was long ago
Taking me back to the start
Playing, laughing and free
While today is like fog, confusing my mind

Perhaps that's what God wants
To bring me back to what I once was
Childlike, vulnerable, in need.
But rather than call out mama!
We call His name,
Time and time and time again
The cycle of life is thus
We came and shall return
Our eyes reflect time that seems as short
as the flutter of birds' wings

All I am left with is love
All that matters is love
And now I know, that all He wanted was love

---

[27] Recently we had a scare with my dearest dad's health. Spending time with him made me reflect on the cycle of life. How strange it is to swap places with my carer, my protector and my strength.

Reflection
Rabia Saida

Wash me in *Alhamdulillahi washshukrulillah*
Let it verse and flow through me
Merge with the sea.
Make me spin in eddies
Dizzy with glee
Let me dance with light
Celebrating
Reflecting the sky
The moon, the clouds,
Sunrise and sunset
A party to the beauty of ever-now.
Let me praise and hymn
The dawn and dusk
Like a bird or insect singing,
Make music with everything
Be a ripple touching the wind
A symphonic rolling and breaking at rocks
A riot of jumping and drumming in rain
A beautiful echo
An expression of symmetry even when frozen.
Let me evaporate - let me be air,
A prism,
Abstractly painting the sun as an arc
Translating into a smile on reflection

Flow
Asiya Sian Davidson

leave all the doors open tonight
so the breeze can blow through
you will learn that keeping the inside
empty and silent
is the way to assuage it

do not plunge into any thought
let there be no considering
do not ask why

take all the pictures off the walls
when an image arises
wash it like a plate

a newborn baby is not a theist
but who could say they do not know God?

a night lullaby patters lightly on
the pool of your heart, each
drop ripples
salat. dhikr. salawat

this is more a total cleansing than
a cognitive reframing
when it's time
act

you are no more than the first cry after birth
and if you don't find the breast
the breast will find you
in its own time

remember
it was only you who
got in the way

so remember

but as you do
let it float

all you ever have been
is
flow

Silly Rhymes and Sullen Ruins
Mariam Akhtar

I told her I cried again
I cried on my bedroom floor
and I cried in the toilets at work
I cried in the cinema
I cried a little bit here and I cried a lot more
I cried in the corner
and cried by the door
I cried as I looked out the window
and cried as I held on to memories
and vacant thoughts
I burnt my finger on a mug
although the milk was only just warm
I ate jelly beans
and howled at the moon
as my bones went crick crick crack
from the pain in my back
the sullen in my spine
intent on rising in rebellion
I stuck myself to heat and healing
scrubbed my skin with salt
and laced my hair with oil
coconut and argan
green and black
clear and misted
all the while realising
I no longer missed things
people and possessions
all the ghosts of things passed

Hope
Yahia Lababidi

Hope's not quite as it seems,
it's slimmer than you'd think
and less steady on its feet

Sometimes, it's out of breath
can hardly see ahead
and cries itself to sleep

It may not tell you all this
or the times it cheated death
but, if you knew it, you'd know

how Hope can keep a secret.

Don't Even Know
Abdalhamid Evans

Well my knees, they been talking to me
    Saying, man you know you're getting old
I said, knees, you best listen to me
    Better do what you're told
Cos we got hills to climb that you don't even know

Well my eyes, they been talking to me
    Saying, man you know you're going blind
I said, eyes, you just look at me straight
    You must be going out of your mind
Cos I can still see things that you don't even know

Well my teeth, they been talking to me
    Saying, man you know we're droppin' out
I said, teeth, I can hear you plain
    There ain't no reason to shout
But we've got things to chew that you don't even know

Well my hands, they been talking to me
    Saying, man you know you're losing your grip
I said hands, you best get a hold of yourself
    And don't give me none of your lip
Cos we got things to make that you don't even know

Now my kids, then been talking to me
    Saying, Papa tell me what can I do?
I said kids, you best listen to me
    I don't know any better than you
Cos you got things to do that I don't even know

Smile
Nura Tarmann

There it goes again
God smiling at me
      Peace
In your eyes
I saw a reflection of Infinity
      Eternal
Your presence brought a gift
It came unexpected
      Joy
There it comes again
A breeze of mercy
      Sunshine
My heart reflected in your mirror
Bright and I breathe in freshness
      Air
It holds us in an embrace of gentleness
Together and yet apart
      Unity
There is always the One and Only
Sending grace through unknown means
      Mystery
Loving has always had its own magic power
Healing a person from deep within.

revelation
Idris Mears

he is there
just ahead of me
as i follow discreetly
picking a night path
by the light
of the expanding heavens
up through the scree
to the mouth of the cave
and in my standing there
i am aware
within
the echoing word
has been spoken
that subsists
persists
in the held breath
of before before
and after after

Snow

Asma Khan

And it came as promised
Falling like a graceful visitor
From a purer realm
Skirts whirling
Crystalline sacred geometry
Enveloping all the ugliness
of unkempt gardens unkempt lives
Even war zones must be blessed
with its silent whiteness
Jarred unspeakable spiky edges
transformed into soft moulded sinking
Beautifying with the lightest touch
Settling on the eyes and drifting into mind
Soon it will melt away or be so muddied
by our doings it will be unrecognizable
Reflect on the signs urges our Divine
Be with me in these ways so we can know each other again
Mustafa knew when he longed to feel the rain on him
Because he said it had just been with Allah

Habibullah

Yasmine Ahmed-Lea

Funny how we
Be kissing our hands
Touching our eyes
Putting hand to heart
When hearing your name
Never realised before
How sensory your presence is
Every time we send blessings
We want a part of us
To go with it
Our love flying on words
Whispered into the air
Leading to wherever
You are leading us
Every time
Our hands touch our eyes
In case something of your soul
Would drop from them
Every time I hear your name
So automated my hand goes
Straight onto my heart
My finger points to the sky
I know it's because
That is where
I feel your presence
The most
My heart is where
Your home resides

Back

Murtaza Humayun Saeed

I am back
Back from the world of thoughts alone
From the world of picking from multiple perceptions
Back from the prison of mind
From the world of reducing self
And mental mechanisms
I am back
I am whole again
Afresh and aware now
Haunted by vulnerability no more
Nor scornful because of my lack of past experience
For the world awaits me
And lessons yearn to be a part of me
Where real issues will be addressed
I am back again
From the empty well and its darkness
I have found all the wisdom I need
Is found in the core of me, though not from me,
There I am healed and washed
And found again

Dates or Milk

(Ramadan 2017)
Medina Tenour Whiteman

It's not about food or water
dates or milk
we aren't leaning towards breakfast
waiting for the moment when our throats
will lose that rasping texture
dragging ourselves forward
to be reunited with the world

If they ask, say
we're swinging back on our heels
longing for this emptiness to bloom
a season longer
ravished by the flavour of a nothing
that fills without substance
floods without a drop
cleans without scrubbing
illuminates without fuel
nourishes without a single crumb
grace invited in by intention
the cook that delights by turning off the flame
makes it joy to feed others
without needing to share in the gift
because the gift of this presence
beats anything that can fit into
the bowl of a human hand

Depth

Nura Tarmann

There are depths to understanding
Understatements swimming on currents of colour
Did you hear what was said silently by the cat?
As the mouse ran across the kitchen floor?
Did the scuffle of little feet lay out the pattern of a dance?
A dance that's repeated by the old people drumming a beat
The way mother used to kiss me in the morning
Her eyelashes fluttering on my cheek
She called it the butterfly kiss; it was a Morse code of her love
Delicately imprinting itself on my spirit
Like the twitter of birds in the morning
Sitting on branches playing with sparkling sun rays
A language all its own develops
My sister gives me a flower and it sings to me
Of something deeper under the earth
Growing like an ancient tree in unseen soil
A snake stirs in the belly of the earth
It's been charmed into obedience
By the flute of a snake charmer with piercing eyes
Laughter rises covering the manure of pain and tears
Something will rise out of all this muck
I believe it will be beautiful like mixed race children
Holding within their little bodies strands of perfection
The hatred of generations dissolving in their warm blood
Don't ask about my ancestors but rather ask about my connection
To that ancient spirit living in sky and earth
Living in the depths of sea and land
Praised, Praiseworthy, Beloved

The Elusive Door of Enlightenment
Mohammad Durrani

All prophets, teachers, saints,
and gurus are sign posts
showing us all the various
Ways to arrive at the Door
of the Sublime, understanding
of peace, love, and harmony.

Yet, upon arrival, we let the bickering
of the nagging intellect guide us
and instead of adopting silence
which was needed most, we return
home, back to our mental tinkering.

We stared at the door, and went
looking for a 100 guides and found
millions of words of wisdom again
to bring us back to the same handle
the grasp of which eludes, always slipping.

We keep looking for the treasures
on the other side when what we seek
is and always was with us,
in the here and now waiting for
the deepening of our silence,
the evolution of our inner vision
bound by Light in a Holy cohesion.

We must become our own gurus
consulting our inner physicians
about the state of our denials and
our unique sicknesses, trusting our intuitions.
Hence the wise one said,
"Unfold your own myth"
direct experience is the only way
so let us sit in silence, and pray.

All for You Allah
Shahbano Aliani

my silence and my speaking
my blinking and my breathing
my laughing and my weeping
are all for You
Allah!

my madness and obsession
my truth and my confession
my absolute submission
are all for You
Allah!

my service and my care
my worship and my prayer
every moment, everywhere
are all for You
Allah!

my blood, flesh and bone
my scent, song and moan
i have nothing of my own
it's all for You
Allah!

my heartbreak and tears
my courage and my fears
for One nearer than near
are all for You
Allah!

my changing and learning
my loving and yearning
my leaving and returning
are all for You
Allah!

my singing and my sighing
my crawling and my flying
my giving up and trying
are all for You
Allah!

my living and my dying
my living and my dying
my living and my dying
are all for You, Allah!
all for You, Allah!

all
for
You

Allah!

Just a Reminder
Flamur Vehapi

You are here, and alive,
Enjoying life, and all its bounties,
Often, however, without much gratitude,
Or care for the one next door.

But what you are forgetting is that
You have been knocking
On the door of death
Since the day you were born!

And I am thinking:
Isn't that a great enough reminder
To wake up and start changing now?

A Cure for Hay Fever
Paul Abdul Wadud Sutherland

On the warped board you clutch a Cyprus
grapefruit in your hands, rub its cheeks

not yet wanting to taste this blessed
gift from a Shaykh, its tropical scent.

Deep or thin covered, your thumb
stroking its gold-yellow pitted skin

you refuse to plunge inside. Let it
stay a rescued ornament, moon-

bright, surface cratered, a soft Scarface.
You imagine attacks it endured

in a walled, exile's garden, quaking
with others on the same ropey

branches. Hurricane-flailed, it kept
its outward crust, never fell and burst.

You idle, longing to know: whose grip
brought it down before reaching yours?

Dawn of the first spring
Asim the Poet

This is the dawn of the first spring. Mercifully, kissing the horizon of broken hearts of lovers with divine minerals and they are awoken. Grazing its soft lips across the opening. Passionately pouring such illumination across all ill-tongues and entering every crevice of internal umbra caverns. This is a timeless pattern, no matter how tenebrous or hidden, this surpasses all the sons of Adam, all matter, space and time. When such honour was gifted to the *rabi'*[28], surely this brought true element to life.

Reaching us beyond the speed of light, this is the speed of love. As photons brace the extremity of its transition, depicting nothing close to a thousand words, pictures are painted across the fragments of the broken and become endless galleries of mercy and, passion and hope. Each drop of ink trickles across my tender soul, coloured in love that I could spend a thousand years gazing upon.
Or 1400 years or beyond. Because this is heart to heart. My internal candle converts to a roaring flame with just the utterance of his name - that some dare say but with heads lowered and hands held upon chests. As for myself, in my attempts? This type of love holds the poet's tongue captive, choking all the words until I am a blithering mess. Weeping for hours on end. This has become my *jihad*[29] in this task when I write, but forever retracting. Adding and subtracting, my minutes are passing. My Maghribs and Fajars are passing. I have nothing to show. With my life flashing before my eyes but the only time I have ever been alive are these very moments which are more valuable to me than all my poems and odes. Why? Because I am yearning love for you. Hoping for love for you. Wanting and needing this love for you. To then be able to say, I love you.

But this longing has only caused a state of suffering. My lifetime of poetry has been but mutterings. What is the eloquence of a poet when able to speak about him? What is a slave to say about his king? But this is the paradox I am stuck in. Compelled to pad and pen as I drown myself in ink. And still, this thirst has never been quenched.

---

[28] *rabi' al-awwal* – the month of the Prophet's birth which means the first spring in Arabic.
[29] inner spiritual struggle is known as the greater jihad.

491

My heart has never known satiation. Forever in this state of craving. This yearning, burning me, violently cracking me further, grinding my shattered heart into a pile of dust. Whilst others call this madness, I hope to throw myself into the fragrant winds to be swept away and kiss the ground you once walked upon. And even then it cannot ever be enough.

The dawn of that month has taught me that I have NEVER fallen into this love. No. Because we only rise to this ultimate gift. You see this love isn't a ditch, a hole or a grave. The dead do not know love. Lovers are alive, they celebrate, they smile and they exclaim " ALLAHUMMA SALLE WA SALIM WA BARIK ALAY". They cannot constrict, withhold or keep in. Love is apparent, forever expressing in all of their days.
And their nights, as for me? I no longer know the concept of sleep. As I am living that dream. Astral-travelling to those memories, as I'm sat in your courtyard surrounded by parchments and empty pens. Preparing to express but I cannot speak - this is something else. So I am left a scribe. Sonnets, odes, poetry, haikus, what I could do to express my love for you. But I soon realised, your love will always eclipse mine. I mean what is a spark compared to the sun? I was left in awe, lost in your love and then I was taught: I will rightly be found when lengthening my prayers when your name kissed my thoughts. I have always been IN love.

But the dawn of that month. This warm sun. Has been like a yearning mother, embracing her lost child. Compassionately, firmly held, unable to release, with tears profusely cried, lasting a lifetime.

The spring of his love does not last just for today, this week or this month. It is something that flows like **rivers**. It is not taught, this love is divinely **gifted**. Into the frozen hearts, **fissure**. Streaming through every crevice, **zikr**. Across the chest into arms; **fixing** my instrument, this pen into- **scriptures**, of praise equaling: **elixir**. Healing injuries, pains, traumas, **blisters**. And breakages, elevating every known and unknown state, **richer**. More than all of the kings, but **consider**. A slave, bestowed his love, I am **triggered**.

Is this not true love, all of this? All by the first sight of the dawn of the first spring.

Open the Door Here
Shahbano Aliani

there are only shadows
in the distance
God is holding up a clear mirror
right here
you are surrounded
by Love

look! how eyes light up
when you enter
everyone draws close
to be near you,
breathe your perfume,
melt
in the velvet
of your softly uttered words

if you could only see
people pick flowers from their hearts
and strew them at your feet
so you can walk on fragrant silks

this incredible sweet light
is reflected
from you
this
is what fills you up
from the *inside*

stop chasing mirages on the horizon
speaking too many words
thinking too many thoughts
reading too many books

open the door *here*
in side
and meet your self

Death
Malika Meddings

A needle through a cloud
a whisper puff
a stinging sunray
so complete
a whimper grief
a dream in nails
where angels dread
yes I fear to tread
embark on lonely shadow
dust that flies up behind
my sunken step
merge with earth's
meniscus mingle
a moving edge
a blade through soft

Breathing out a winter breath
bright cheeks glowing
in cold's fiery embrace
water came to demonstrate
how moving moves the ice
a vaporous vanishing
bright spark so sharp
it makes the happy wince
the delight shrivel
the laughter echo
mocks mocking makes
the shoulders tremble
the heart quake.

The blade's sharp meets no mate
no master, its art
to draw the final from the heart
to slay hope and her fear.
to forget the tale of golden song
the needle's tip finds her own

and shimmer vision is no more
the burst raindrops fall to ground
and water nourish what will come
and the vision sent to home
the gold transmuted to a light
the song vanished to the wind
and I an empty echo mocked
for every tear, each choke
each heart quake remote
removed in lead, forged to dust
forgotten light hoped for trust
and in the throes of winter's despair
then again I find you there
the golden vision, hidden dream
spring's song inside a gleam
echoing your hopeful tones
calling voice is only light
your gracious friend
is enough
this is my home
fair and well

One
Suhayla Bewley

Seeing through the cracks
with such clarity the view opens up
expanding infinitely
with a single beam of light
the walls crumble.

I can see through the stars
and beyond them
until I see us, all of us
encompassed in this beam
so complete.

With little air
and constructed confines
Created with concepts
I can see out
with that beam of light.

I think it's beautiful.

Happy Place
Abbas Mohamed

Grace
manifests and becomes visible,
a portal to the Indivisible,
Mysterious Source, the only You,
Divine Friend, Unnameable Hu,
protect and provide for all of my crew,
sustain smiles on faces of family too,
Save our souls from ourselves Lord,
deliver us from the smorgasbord
of vices that we fall into daily,
remind me of Your Presence if my memory fails me,
I am truly forgetful, I get lost, I get distracted,
I fail to contemplate how I have acted,
perfect my character in the image of Your beloved,
Sallallahu Alayhi wa Sallam
Bring me closer to the paths he perfected
The Messenger whom You personally selected,
Ya Mustafa, the reason that any of us are here
Is so we can send *Salawat* on the being You hold so dear
So our tongue becomes the means that Muhammad is praised
On the Fateful Day, with his *Ummah*, may we be raised
I sing *Salawat* for my *Rasool*, I hum it when I weep
I give my heart and soul to him, my life is his to keep
Durood before the dawn, *Durood* before I sleep
Durood in every single prayer, and also in between
OH Lord, send your blessings on Muhammad, I beseech
And on his Holy Family, starting with Ya Ali
On Bibi Fatima too and her sons, Hasan and Husayn
Bless their light and bless their love, from which we hope to gain
And bless them for their lives in which they endured so much pain
Oh Allah, bless the *Ahlul Bayt*, no greater family existed
And I pray that through Your love for them, our sins may all be lifted
That through their lives and lessons, our perspectives can get shifted
That we can be grateful for the bounties they have gifted

اللهم صل على محمد وآل محمد

OH Allah bless them
OH Allah bless them
OH Allah bless them, and bless us too
OH Allah bless them
OH Allah bless them
And through them, bring us close to you

اللهم صل على محمد وآل محمد

Ameen

The Loving and The Loved - *extract*
I.AM.SHAHEED

And if perchance you should be stirred
To seek The One
Who embraced the flames of your passion
And if perchance you should be stirred
To seek The One
Who walked barefoot through the plains of your emotions
And if perchance you should be stirred
To seek The One
Who became the gemstone through whose facets love shined
illuminating the treasures of your subconscious
And if perchance you should be stirred
To seek The One
Whose soothing serum healed the farthest reaches of your spiritual
extremities
And discover him gone
Don't fret. Don't be afraid, for He is never too far away!

The Wood for the Trees
Medina Tenour Whiteman

I thought Ramadan was bliss but
Ramadan is death
elders slipping through clefts
warps pulling away from wefts
souls graduating from nests
spit-hardened hearths of chewed earth
bored of counting trees and standing back
to see the whole in multiplicity
instead entering the rings to seek
the eternal central dot
catch the impossible beginning
like trying to say "Now!" and already being
out of date at "ow!"
hearing muffled in search of the
seed of silence
cocking ears to an ever quieter wave
always finding new nuances
until they are certain
they can step off the bridge and trust
that there is no jolt:
the line is a spiral
and the more you tease it out
the deeper it leads you in

Twenty-eight 'not yet's,
Ramadan is ego-drive death
a million momentary deaths
reincarnated with every breath
 'til no more breaths need to be taken
out of fear of no more breath
and there is no doubt left
that the last shudder of chest
is not descent into stillness
or cold, sepulchral rest
but a heart
meeting the wave
where it crests

Dare to Pray Big
Rabia Saida

I read that if you recite *ayat al-Kursi* when you leave the house
70,000 angels will protect you from the left, right, front and back

And I thought, '*how could God spare 70,000 angels to protect me
just for remembering to recite a verse?*'

But I was applying earthly logic to the realm of the Unseen
which is not subject to scarcity
or bound by laws of time and space.

Prayer is the ticket in all of our hands to access this boundlessness
When we are
Powerless to change all that is wrong around us–
All the tyranny and war, hunger, pain and suffering,
Despairing
"*in the face of such huge injustice, what can I possibly do?*"
But somehow we're shy to use our ticket.

Maybe because the power of prayer is beyond all measurement
And it's slightly scary that
One earthly prayer uttered by one weak and powerless soul might

mobilise thousands in another realm, unbound by the physics of this
sphere.

We may be small and powerless
But we can all dare to pray big.

Dust
Flamur Vehapi

I am
Nothing more than
Unsettled dust
From the past
Shaped into a human form,
Frozen in time,
And waiting
For the divine breeze
To blow me away
From this world of dust.
And take my inner self
Back to its Creator,
When and only when
Its time is up.
For now,
I am thankful
For being who and what
I am.

Commit to a Practice
Shahbano Aliani

commit to a practice
even Love
demands
disciplined action

reading and talking
are not enough

whoever heard of arriving anywhere
without a longing to go?
whoever heard of giving up
without first trying

Centerpiece of Meaning
Arthur Skip Maselli

What is knowledge
if it is not shining down upon her face?
Who is to know,
who is to know?
To the canvas from which color leaps,
she is the gesso. I imagine it so,
I imagine it so.

What is rapture
if not the doing of her own work in ascension?
Then creation must be her undoing
of all that is done,
of all she has done.

And love, oh of love,
what is this elusive and lambent specter,
if not her dissolving into a mist
over every morning pond?
She is the stillness in the calm,
the saccharine in the nectar.

What then is mystery's allure,
if not her fleeting morning poem?
When I wake,
dreams are gone,
she remains, yet I'm alone.

What is beauty in the fabric
but the splendor behind the veiling?
She is the light for my reflection,
I'm a ripple in her perfection.
She is the centerpiece of God's revealing.
Oudimentary

Try not to say what is beyond the frame of words
You cannot return the oud oil to the aloeswood.

You cannot tie knots in rays of light
Nor untangle the *nafs* from the *ruh*.

Trust the Alchemist and the burning agarwood
who transforms our ills to liquid gold.
Who can love the wheat of humanity
Without loving the chaff and the mold?

Unspoken One (spoken)
Yusuf Abdalwadud Adams

Which words did we need to describe
The light and the shade as a child?
The motion of sleep mixed with the
Outlines of our parents' voices,
Eternal home shown simply,
Reading existence without words,
With the eyes of hearts still open,
Yet to shut against the intrusion of
The Other.
Am I not Thou?
Scattered pages and random volumes
Scanned by tired eyes and inner sight are seeking
A single voice by design and by choice.
We love to know
You are loving to be known.
The heart knows.
Imagining our smiling infant selves,
Perhaps we will see what is reflected
In our early gaze and in the thick present
Of that time and this or perhaps we
Will learn it from our children who show
Us how to be in a garden which desires
No names by which to grow.
How little we know when we stop at words
To leave the unspoken undiscovered.

Like a Giant Mosque
Yahia Lababidi

Moments when a great silence descends
like a creature of the depths
say, a noble whale swimming through us
—vast and transfiguring everything

Within this experience of grace,
all is like a giant mosque
constructed of crisscrossing
beams of benevolent light.

Mountain Dew
Murtaza Humayun Saeed

A house we will build in the Atlas Mountains
And in the woods the children will play
The goats will provide us milk and cheese
And 'tis to a small mosque we'll go to pray
The air and water will be pure
So drink up lads and be sure
This is where I want to live
So please leave me here, I can't dare go down with you
I've fallen in love with mountain dew
And more God will bless me you'll see
Laila I'll find without trouble believe
A house we will build in the Atlas Mountains
And in the woods the children will play
The goats will provide us milk and cheese
And 'tis to a small mosque we'll go to pray

Bliss
Matthew Bain

In the name of God
the supremely merciful
the compassionate.
I pass through the bower
into the garden.
Aim high! The Prophet
(peace and blessings)
presides over a feast.
Knowers and nobles
exquisitely extend hands.
Their serene manners
confer bliss
as they gently proffer
delectables.
Subtle birds overhead
flit in and out of existence
one wing beat at a time.
Light rainbows over,
in arcfuls of perspective.
Notquite music plays
just out of earshot,
tantalising, it sounds like
"deserving of praise".
Fountains too full
cascade into
rivulets below,
gorging,
satisfying.

sailing in alien waters
Idris Mears

when i come again to home haven
after a life-time of sailing
in alien waters
under a flag of convenience
who will be waiting quayside
to recognise and welcome
the return of the tender child
inside this salt-cured hide

as i step from the gangplank
onto the dock
i will seek out
the faces of near ones
and dear companions
those noble souls
of fair passage
on the trade winds
and battles around the horn
and the heartache of wait
in the doldrums
and others not yet met
but celebrated
in seafarers' yarns
living charmed lives
though life at sea
is always hardship
and once on firm
and lasting ground
i will seek out a mountain tarn
to wash the salt away
and a summer meadow
to lie on to dry on
with the scent of drying grass
and the hum of angel wings

Note to Self
Sukina Pilgrim

Honour your truth
Hold it close to your chest
Like a new born baby.
Find your voice
And sing Freedom songs
To your own soul
To help it grow.
Greet trees with dignity
Stroke leaves lovingly
Tread the Earth gently
And give birth
To brighter tomorrows
Every morning.
Learn the language of the stars
And the cycles of the moon
And strive to see the sunset
It will give you hope
When the darkness lingers.
Speak with mercy in your throat
And truth in between your teeth
Have compassion in your eyes.
Gentleness in your fingertips
And God's Names upon your lips.
Speak with the tongue of your heart
Listen to your intuition
And look beyond
The veils of separation
Until there are no veils
Or notions of separation
Until all that exists is the One.
Treat everyone
As though they are a Friend of God
With a secret for you
Hidden in their chest.
Daydream often

Drift on them
To the sacred spaces
That exist just beneath your surface
Angels are always with you.
Remember that.
Fall in love with your Prophet ﷺ
So deeply
That only God can catch you.
Sit with scholars of the Sacred
Seek out the knowers
Hang out with the lovers
Who graze in God's Garden
And are present in His Presence
With every breath.
Never leave their side, child
Not for the world and all it contains.
Sit amongst them
Until you become them.
Go on pilgrimages
Even in your own city.
Keep a dream diary
Breathe fully
Make art
Wage love
And smile at everyone.
Pray intimately
Even for your enemies.
Love hard
With a soft heart
So full, it could burst
Across the galaxy
At any moment.

41
Daniel Abdal-Hayy Moore
from the poetry collection Transitioning to Zero

Fall deeply into the
arms of sleep

Go ahead
don't fear death

We sleep
but do we give ourselves

to sleep?

Slide deep in?

The scrolls are rolled and
the shelves of them reach

heaven

though they disintegrate in our
hands and shy

away from sunlight

Etched in their DNA
is the entire unravelling

the made plain
the glorious bliss

Take this gladiola
wagging its yellow

tongue

Take a telephone wire
full of birds

When does dream end and
reality begin?

Or is it truly unchronological?

Are our footsteps also etched
in first Sahara sands?

In a dimension that can't be fathomed
down a gray lit esplanade

on invisible Throne sits the awaiting Genius
who makes perfect

sense of it all

no questions asked
no fee required

but our dear unblinking
souls

whose hearts are
safe and sound

in this and the next world
when the

dream awakens

About the Poets

Cherif Abou El Fadl is a poet, rapper, and screenwriter. When he is not writing he teaches yoga, and is the Creative Director at The Usuli Institute. His work is driven by the belief that life is an intricate conversation with Creator: Art is a surrendering to the Divine. The US-born Egyptian/Iraqi resides in California.

Yusuf Abdalwadud Adams wrote, sang and played in bands until architecture took hold as a practice. Writing continues to be a natural reflection of the journey of the heart through life. Currently taking a sufi eco mosque complex through planning in the Midlands UK, he has also made public sculptures as part of the collective the Imaginary Beings. A secret black lava stone house in Sicily is his simplest design, surrounded by low lemon groves and looking out toward Mount Etna. He is honoured to be included in this volume among so many Lovers. He teaches architecture across the UK, and recently completed a PhD on the *adab* of mosque design.

Yasmine Ahmed-Lea is a poet and writer who has given talks and workshops on poetry around the UK. She is an English lit grad with a passion for travelling and also works on the growing Sacred Footsteps podcast about history and travel. She works in marketing and communications and has done so for the past 10 years, but her full time passion is poetry. Yasmine mainly writes about spiritual relationships, family and diaspora.

Mariam Akhtar has been writing since her teens but only in the later part of her 20s felt brave enough to share her words and encourages others to do the same for a cathartic, therapeutic sense of relief and release. She has worked with primary school children for the past 7 years and loves seeing how their little minds work. History, identity, empire and ancestry are just some of the topics which are close to her heart and as such some of her writing is informed by these. She is now living in a village with her husband and trying to do adult life in her early 30s.

Shahbano Aliani (1967 – 2019) *rahimahallah*, was a Shaykha (spiritual teacher) in the Shadhili-Darqawi Sufi order, on the basis of permission from her own Sufi master, Shaykh Ebrahim Etsko Schuitema. Shahbano was born and raised in Pakistan and spent many years studying and working in the United States. Increasingly disillusioned with the mediocrity and futility of her outer endeavours and plagued by a growing disquiet, she searched for deeper purpose and meaning. Her quest brought her to the Sufi path through the Zawia (spiritual retreat) and teachings of Shaykh Ebrahim Etsko Schuitema in 2009. Soon thereafter Shahbano started writing poetry, a collection of which has been published in 2013 by Intent Publishing South Africa and Na'layn Publications, Pakistan entitled, *Set My Heart On Fire*. All the poems in this selection are from this book. Though written in English and in a modern voice, her verse is both a timeless chronicle of and a manual for spiritual transformation in the finest tradition of Sufi poetry. Readers have called Shahbano's work honest, subtle and profoundly moving.

Asim the Poet is an award-nominated spoken word artist and a motivational speaker, delivering a range of topics from hard-hitting stories to light-hearted poems. Asim began his journey as a page poet, with the intent of expressing love of the beloved Prophet of Islam, peace be upon him, spreading positivity and hope through his words. He now continues this through both written and spoken word to engage audiences as he conveys powerful messages to help, inspire and motivate others.

Saraiya Bah is a poet, writer and cultural producer who draws on the traditional West African storytelling style of the griot to wax lyrically about identity, faith, the relationship with self and everything in between. Saraiya is a co-producer of The Black and Muslim in Britain Project, a social engagement initiative that strives to highlight the importance of ensuring that a platform exists to present a plethora of stories, struggles, rich history, challenges, culture, politics, family traditions and the beauty of being Black and Muslim. Through her engagement in the creative arts and social activism, Saraiya has been invited globally to engage in large and intimate performances, panel discussions and facilitating poetry workshops in venues such as The British Library, The British Museum, Amnesty International Head Quarters and The National Poetry Library. She has been featured in articles and productions by BBC One, The Times, Stylist Magazine, Al Jazeera, Amaliah, Dazed.com, Muslim Girl, The Muslim Vibe, Islam Channel and British Muslim TV. Saraiya is a member of ::nana:: Poetry Collective. www.saraiyabah.co.uk

Matthew Bain is a dual English-Australian national and his heart is drawn to Kashmir and Andalusia, which have influenced his poetry as well as his Sufism. Matthew lives in England's Peak District with his wife Diane. He works as a CyberSecurity architect, and enjoys music and dancing 5Rhythms.

Iljas Baker was born in Scotland where he discovered Islam through Subud. He is a graduate of Strathclyde, Aberdeen and Edinburgh Universities. He is a university lecturer, writer and editor and now lives in Thailand.

Eisha Basit is a Canadian writer and artist in her free time when she's not being a mother. She aspires to write poetry that portrays the everyday truths of the wayfarer and to explore the ups and downs of spiritual life through the medium of art. She views sacred Islamic art as a necessity in the modern world and a means of inspiring hearts when combined with the written word.

Rabea Benhalim is a lover of the law committed to finding nuance and truth. She is a seeker of connection, finding the divine in the simple moments between souls. She sustains herself through immersion in beauty. Hybridity is a particular favorite, as she is of hybrid Libyan and Irish American heritage. She works as Associate Professor of Law at the University of Colorado Law School, where she spends much of her day pondering comparative Jewish and Islamic Law.

Suhayla Bewley - English occasional poet and daughter of converts to Islam. Mother of three and a lawyer in her day job.

Yohosame Cameron - 'Yohosame Freeborn Cameron' (as it reads on his birth certificate) was born in Clearlake, California, 1969, at home in the gentle company of just his parents. His first word was "Allah", (his mother says that he used to 'sing' it) and everything else that he has ever said (or sung) pales in comparison. As a child his favorite color was green, favorite animal the cheetah, and he often had vivid dreams of flying. Thankfully, not much has changed since then. Drawn towards nature, music, dance and poetry, he has nurtured his relationship with all of the above, and although he sometimes appears to be clean-shaven, in Truth his beard is much, much longer than yours.

Yasin Chines is a writer, journalist, editor and photographer who lives in Manchester. From a young age, his love for language led him to pursue a higher education in Creative Writing. Yasin studied Creative Writing at the University of Leeds and graduated in 2011. He also studied poetry and nonfiction writing under International writer Rommi Smith. Since then, Yasin has continued to nurture his creativity with his photography, typewriter poetry and short poem series. Covering themes within Sufism that stretch from mysticism, the self, to memory, journeying and repentance, Yasin credits his teacher – author Dr Muzamil Khan (Bury) – from whom much of his inspiration is drawn. As a creative, Yasin has edited books, poems, short stories and numerous newspaper editions. He believes that nothing quite matches the power of creative art and writing in breaking barriers and building familial connections.

H I Cosar is a Sydney-based teacher, bilingual poet and community artist who is interested in writing for the page as well as stage. Her first collection of poems, 'Hijabi in Jeans' was published in 2018 by Guillotine Press. She has also had work published in anthologies 'Poetry without Borders', 'On Second Thought', 'Can I Tell You a Secret' as well as journals, 'Mascara' and 'Australian Poetry Journal.' She likes working on projects of intersectionality, in particular those platforms where poetry meets other art forms. She has performed as a feature in reading circles, 'Live Poets Society', 'Gugubarra' as well as experimental theatre, 'The Prophet - Remix' and 'Night Sky'.

Jessica Daqamsseh is an American poet, writer, teacher and student of Islamic knowledge. Her work on Islamic spirituality and the Muslim American experience is featured on Muslim Girl, a website aimed at amplifying American Muslim Women's voices. She writes in a wide array of formats from essays and poetry to children's fiction and short stories. Daqamsseh's writing centers on Islamic spirituality, self-awareness and discovery, politics, and crafting authentic narratives which dismantle Islamophobic sentiments. Through her writing, she seeks to spark individual's of all ages personal connections with the Divine. She works with young children at a Montessori school and has been blessed with one daughter.

Asiya Sian Davidson grew up on the wildly beautiful island of Tasmania but she now lives in Melbourne, Australia. In 1996 she spent three weeks in the Rif mountain town of Chefchaouen in Morocco, a visit that was to radically change the course of her life. She obtained a Bachelor of Fine Arts from the University of Tasmania majoring in Painting and Art Theory. She is a single mother of five children; Ruqaiyah, Hamza, Mustafa, Hana and Idris. Interested in all meaning systems and religions with a special love for Sufism she finds it difficult to fit 'God' into the boxes and languages that human cultures devise to know 'Him'. She is a student Herbalist with an interest in all forms of healing.

Marissa Diaz is an indigenous activist and community organizer. She was born in New York, grew up in Seattle, and currently resides in California. Her father is Mapuche from Argentina, and she is from a people and land who the conquistadors and long-frustrated colonizers begrudging labeled "The Land of the Giants". Giant in heart, stature, and love for independence and their indigenous traditions, it is this legacy that is at the core of Marissa's work and poetry. Her father fought against the Argentinian government as a guerrilla during one of the most brutal periods of repression in twentieth-century history, and she continues this fight in her work for indigenous communities, MMIWG (Murdered and Missing Indigenous Women and Girls), advocacy for decolonization and for environmental justice. Marissa was raised Muslim by her West African step-father, an accomplished musician and gentle giant from Ghana, who taught her the beauty and poetry of his people, including those songs of praise for the Prophet, everlasting peace and blessing be upon him, and of the saints and *awliya* of his region.

Mohammad Durrani is a Pakistani-born Canadian, with focus on the inner workings of spirituality, steering clear from the outer forms and traditions. Penetrating insight with a deep rooting in philosophy, Buddhism, Taoism, Mohammad considers himself a wayfarer traveling through this temporary world, while attempting to heal and touch as many souls as he can. Where most people are busy building, acquiring and buying houses, wealth, dreams and cars, Mohammad has chosen to focus on ideologies and philosophies that are permanent, that fall outside the scope of entropy and erosion, and therefore, time and space. Having recently lost both his wife and mother to cancer, Mohammad is a firm believer that all things in this life are a blessing, and every experience is a teacher.

Peter Dziedzic is a doctoral candidate studying Islamic literatures, particularly from Morocco and Kashmir. His most recent homes include Jordan, India, Italy, Morocco, and Egypt. His first collection of poetry, titled *Symphonies of Theophanies: Moroccan Meditations*, was published in 2020. More about Mr. Dziedzic can be found at peterdziedzic.com.

Efemeral - It's all ephemeral except the One. Rooted in the Pacific Northwest, Efemeral's multilingual written verse and spoken word performance entwine reflections on faith, language and the human psyche. Her latest works are published in anthologies by Rumi Center for Spirituality and the Arts and in The Puritan's Summer 2019 issue. Her Arabic poetry is currently featured in the public art piece "Weaving Cultural Identities: Threads Through Time" curated by Vancouver Biennale. Efemeral acknowledges the xwməθkwəy̓əm, Skwxwú7mesh, and səlílwətaʔɬ Nations on whose territories she writes and performs. Efemeral can be reached on social media as @poetefemeral or by email at poetefemeral@gmail.com.

Abdalhamid Evans (1951-2018) *rahimahullah*, was primarily raised in the United Kingdom where he was educated and discovered Islam in 1978. He was a creative, a scholar, and a visionary who shared his outlook for a meaningful, ethical and fulfilled life for all through his writings and eloquent speech. In his 50s he found he had poetry and songs in him that needed to be written and played. He proceeded with learning how to play the guitar and recorded two CDs of these songs with deep meaning and published a book of poetry he called *Songs in Search of a Musician* before he passed away in Ramadan, 3 June 2018. *www.fitrablues.com*

Fatima's Hand is a nomad who likes to write and who before becoming a mother of three was in academia exploring themes in Sufi poetry and notions of spiritual 'state' in the work of Ibn 'Arabi. She has lived/studied across the Middle East, taking epic train/bus journeys and meeting with mountains. She can be found in the woods of English shires or exploring Scottish glens in her spare hours. She is a lover of flora and fungi, the old, the analogue and cycling around her beloved Edinburgh. She can be found at highuponahilltop@gmail.com

Rakaya Esime Fetuga is a poet from London of Ghanaian and Nigerian heritage. Her work joins conversations on overlapping identities, faith and culture as self-affirmation. Rakaya won the Spread the Word Poetry Prize in 2017 and the Roundhouse Poetry Slam in 2018. Rakaya has performed internationally and across the UK at venues including the British Museum, Royal Albert Hall, Trafalgar Square and The Ivy. Among others, Rakaya has been commissioned by Bloomberg Philanthropies with Vanity Fair, English Touring Theatre and Kyra TV. Rakaya is a member of ::nana:: Poetry Collective.

Fikasophy is rooted in the South East Asia cosmopolitan city of Singapore. She is a traveller, a soul adventurer and a history lover. Her poetry is inspired by her inward and outward travels. You can find her rocking the bars of lines on Instagram: @fikasophy

Jamila Fitzgerald - Born in Texas, 1947, middle daughter; UCDavis grad in fine arts; painter, gardener, married Michael Abderrahman Fitzgerald, emigrated to Morocco 1976, Tiznit resident one year, Rabat Casbah of the Oudayas resident 7 years; Meriam's mother, Nora's mother. Farm owner near Atlas Mountains, farm house builder, cattle, sheep and chicken cooper. Grandmother of Karima, Abdullah Imran, Amine, Haroun, Youssef, Safiya and Yasin. May they be always in Allah's way. Art teacher, twice Artist in Residence at Frank Waters Foundation in Taos, New Mexico, show of oils in Marrakech; partnership in Center for Language and Culture, Marrakech. Quadrilingual, bi-alphabetic, sometime writer of poems.

Barbara Flaherty, a dual Irish American national, has been a university instructor, a dual diagnosis counselor, a poet, an essayist, a mother, a grandmother, a healer. Her books include the poetry collection, *Holy Madness*, and *Doing It Another Way: The Basic Text*. She has been published in journals, anthologies, and university textbooks and was a winner of the Drogheda Amergin Poetry Award, Ireland in 2005. She was a co-founding companion of a multi-faith spiritual community and is interested in issues of bio-spirituality and the spirituality of sustainability. Her heart explores the way of holy poverty in the borderlands where Christianity and Islamic Sufism meet.

Ron Geaves is better known as an historian of Islam in Britain, especially for his ground-breaking biography *Islam in Victorian Britain: The Life and Times of Abdullah Quilliam* (2010, 2014). He has recently co-edited *Victorian Muslim* with Jamie Gilham (2017) and his new monograph *Islam and Britain: Muslim Mission in the Age of Empire* appeared in early 2018. He has held several chairs at British universities and remains Visiting Professor at the Centre for the Study of Islam in the UK based in the University of Cardiff. He has been writing, publishing and performing poetry since the 1980s, recently appearing at the Bradford Literature Festival along with Ben Okra and others in a session entitled *Modern Mystical Poets*. His first single authored collection of poems *Rumi Weeds* was published in 2017 with Beacon Press.

Dr. Alan 'Abd al-Haqq Godlas is Associate Professor of Religion at the University of Georgia, where he co-directs the Islamic Studies BA, MA, and PhD programs. He received his Ph.D. from the University of California, Berkeley, in 1991, in Islamic Studies, specializing in Arabic, Persian, and Turkish Sufi literature. Dr. Godlas was included in *The 500 Most Influential Muslims in the World* (2009- 2012). He discovered Islam through Sufism and has been guided at times by the Chishti, Ni'matullahi, Maryami, Naqshbandi, and Shadhili Sufi orders. Dr. Godlas' works in progress deal with Ruzbihan al-Baqli's Sufi Qur'an commentary, the relationship between cognition and emotion in Islam, and the calligraphic vision of Islam.

Vedad Grozdanic was born on February 21, 1991. He resides in the city of Sanski Most, Bosnia and Herzegovina. His book of poetry, Aquamarine Earth, was published in 2020.

Randa Hamwi Duwaji is a widely travelled poet, author, and researcher into the linguistic marvels of the Holy Qur'an. Seeing all of humanity on a single plane, she has been conveying the richness of her heritage to the societies she interacts with, building bridges between cultures through her poetry compilations, children's books, and decades-long Qur'anic research, penning her thoughts and findings in both English and Arabic. Growing up as a Syrian diplomat's daughter who was constantly asked about her background, Randa's interest in her faith and her quest to understand and convey its peaceful message has accompanied her throughout life. Randa brings this peace and richness to all her writings, as well as the vision of humankind joined by common values and united in the desire for a better future.

Tazmin H. Uddin is a seeking soul, based in NYC. She is an empath, a lover of Love and life, and a dreamer committed to changing the world one smile at a time. Through courses offered by @rumicenterarts, she has learned to combine her spiritual and poetic journeys and see writing as a form of spiritual practice. You can find her musings on Instagram @soulful_reflections.

Professor Joel Hayward is a New Zealand scholar, writer and poet who has held various academic posts, including Chair of the Department of Humanities and Social Sciences at Khalifa University (UAE) and Dean of the Royal Air Force College (UK). He has earned ijazas in 'Aqīdah (theology) and Sirah (the Prophet's biography). He is the author or editor of many books of non-fiction, particularly in the fields of history and strategic studies. He has given strategic advice to political and military leaders in several countries, has given policy and religious advice to prominent sheikhs, and was tutor to His Royal Highness Prince William of Wales. In 2011 he was elected as a Fellow of the Royal Society of Arts and in 2012 he was elected as a Fellow of the Royal Historical Society. In 2016 he was named as the "Best Professor of Humanities and Social Sciences" at the 2016 Middle East Education Leadership Awards. He has published four collections of Islamic poetry and two books of Islamic fiction.

I.AM.SHAHEED is a writer and spoken word artist, whose work explores the conditions of the heart, the power of vulnerability and the resilience of the human spirit. His debut performance of 'Unwritten Letters' is now the stuff of poetry folklore. This opus has earned him the nickname 'sensei' amongst his peers and bookings at established events such as Flo Vortex, Word On The Street and Mind Over Matter. He has also performed at The Holland Festival in Amsterdam, alongside Umar Bin Hassan of the Last Poets. I.AM.SHAHEED is now in the process of compiling his first book.

Ayesha Ijaz writes to understand the ineffable mystery that is existence. Born in Pakistan and raised in New York, she now resides in Canada with her beautiful family. As an educator, she's interested in alternative modes of learning and can be found mingling with farmers, scientists, and poets on any given day! Grateful for her backstory which allows her to belong 'nowhere and everywhere,' she longs to spread hope and healing to fellow seekers, wanderers, and whiners, in some manner. She can be reached @ineffable_mutterings on Instagram.

Ahmad Ikhlas is an international Dub Poet, reggae and garage musician who draws on his Jamaican heritage and his British upbringing to form a unique style of music and poetry, which he uses in praise of the Prophet Muhammad (PBUH), and to send messages of love and empowerment. Ahmad Ikhlas was born and raised in South London. Although he always had a love of music, a deeper appreciation of music as a means for change and empowerment developed during the rise of the UK garage scene where he was known for his musical abilities and frequented radio stations under his then Moniker Mc Meelos. It was on the Music scene that Ahmad-Ikhlas became good friends with UK-Apache, who then invited him to the Mosque. At the age of 17, while still in school, Ahmad embraced Islam. For the first 10 years of his life as a Muslim, he stopped music to form and focus on his spirituality. Now Ahmad fuses his faith and identity and travels, sharing his experiences and singing songs of praise.

Hanan Issa is a Welsh-Iraqi poet and writer. She has been featured on both ITV Wales and BBC Radio Wales and worked in partnership with National Museum Wales, Artes Mundi, Warwick university, Swansea Fringe, StAnza festival, Wales Arts International and Seren Books. Her work has been published in Banat Collective, Hedgehog Press, Wales Arts Review, Sukoon mag, Lumin Journal, Poetry Wales, Parthian, Y Stamp, sister-hood magazine and MuslimGirl.com. Her winning monologue was featured at Bush Theatre's Hijabi Monologues. She is the co-founder of Wales' first BAME open mic series 'Where I'm Coming From'. She was a 2018-2019 Hay Festival Writer at Work. Her debut poetry pamphlet 'My Body Can House Two Hearts' was published by BurningEye Books in 2019. www.hananissa.com Facebook/ Twitter/ Instagram: @hananiscreative

Hina Jabeen-Aslam - From the clinical corporate world Hina's deep connection to her faith and spirituality has been her therapy in balancing her evolution into the big and incredibly disconnected world she hopes to raise her family in as a metropolitan Muslim mother. Balancing tradition and modernity Hina hopes that her poetry will be what connects those looking to reconnect to their Maker.

Rashida James-Saadiya is a cultural educator, and multidisciplinary artist invested in transforming social perceptions through creative literature. Her work explores migration, identity, and the transmission of spirituality and cultural memory amongst Muslim women in West Africa and the American South. In addition, she is the Arts & Culture editor for Sapelo Square, a digital hub documenting the experience and legacy of Black Muslims in America, and the Creative Director of Crossing Limits, a multi-faith non-profit organization which utilizes poetry as an instrument for social change, highlighting the intersections of faith and social injustice.

Nabila Jameel is currently working as an English GCSE teacher in a secondary school. The main themes in her work are motherhood, childhood, mortality, spirituality, religion, culture, injustice and the rights of women. She describes her poetic voice as nostalgic but also progressive, writing from a place of truth, unapologetically. She enjoys reading and takes inspiration from an eclectic mix of English, Panjabi, Urdu and Persian writers, both classical and modern. Her poetry has been published in various anthologies and journals, including Poetry Review. She has also published articles which contribute to topical discourse in poetry (Poetry News and NAWG's Link poetry magazine). Nabila has a passion for languages and a keen interest in bilingualism, which led her to research Urdu, Panjabi and Persian poetry and run taster sessions in eastern poetry in translation.

Emny Kadri has enjoyed reading and writing poetry since a small child. Growing up in her earliest years in a Sunni/Sufi household, she learnt early to look at the world from a highly spiritual perspective, learning to see Allah's presence in every aspect of life, never believing in simple coincidence and always knowing that everything happens for the most perfect of reasons. One of her most fundamental lessons has come in the reminder of love and compassion. No matter from where it has come, if love and compassion is genuine, its origin is always from the Beloved. Monumental life changes and experiences drove the most recent collection of poetry, for which she is eternally grateful to Allah and His servants (for being a part of the process), and indeed the unparalleled transformation at that moment in her life. With gratitude always for these opportunities of witnessing Allah's manifest Beauty and the poetry that flourished from this divine inspiration.

Mohja Kahf, professor of comparative literature and Middle Eastern studies at the University of Arkansas since 1995, is author of My Lover Feeds Me Grapefruit, The Girl in the Tangerine Scarf, Hagar Poems, E-mails from Scheherazad, and Western Representations of the Muslim Woman: From Termagant to Odalisque.

Amal Kassir is a Syrian American international spoken word poet. She has performed in 12 countries, and over five dozen cities. She has lectured, performed poetry and taught workshops in venues ranging from orphanages to refugee camps to youth prisons to universities. Her work is heavily influenced by her Syrian culture, her experience as a minority in the United States, and the plight of the oppressed all over the world. She designed her own undergraduate major, titled Community Programming in Social Psychology, where she has been able to create programs for a range of causes and communities. She is working on her first book, due for release by the end of 2020, Inshaallah.

Wajiha Khalil is a seeker of sacred knowledge, a poet, and translator. She lives in Brooklyn, New York with her husband and three children.

Asma Khan started writing five years ago after a significant event in her life blew her heart open and words came... since then it has become a therapy and a joy, using language and expression in navigating life situations. She shares with others a deep need to express the Muslim heart, and it is thanks to her insistence that the idea of this anthology as a reality came into being, as a way to share Muslim voices through poetry with a wider audience. She is also a doctor and a mum and works in a peace-making charity.

Yahia Lababidi, Egyptian-Lebanese, is the author of eight books of poetry and prose. His new book, *Revolutions of the Heart*, is an essay collection at the intersection of social activism and mysticism. Nominated for a Pushcart Prize, three times, Lababidi's writing has been translated into several languages, and he has participated in international poetry festivals throughout the USA and Europe, as well as the Middle East.

Khadijah Lacina grew up in Wisconsin's Kickapoo Valley. After converting to Islam and becoming fluent in Arabic, she and her family lived in Yemen for ten years, until the war brought them back to the US. After five years living on a homestead in the Missouri Ozarks with her children and various animals, she has recently returned to her Wisconsin home. Her writings have appeared in various anthologies and many internet venues. *A Slice of Sunshine: The Poetry of Colors* was published in 2012, and her chapbooks *Nightrunning* and *Under the Sky* have been published by Facqueuesol Books.

Ray Lacina is a Professor at Delta College near Saginaw, Michigan, where he teaches writing and a variety of literature courses. He embraced Islam in 1989 and in 1991 he married into a Hyderabadi (Indian) family which has tolerated him reasonably well for the last 27 years. He has written all of his life, starting with his first poem in the third grade ("I like birds/and birds like me/but I live in a house/and they live in a tree"). Over the years has moved on from ornithological verse to "I'm T.S. Eliot. Seriously. T.S. Eliot" verse to fiction, both speculative and mainstream. He lives in Michigan with his family.

Marguerite Lake is a poet, writer and artist. Her poetry reflects her life's journey with self, Soul and the Sacred. Her geometric art expresses the thread of unity that weaves through the multiplicity of forms. Her work is informed by creative imagination and the ancient wisdom traditions. "Mystical poetry and Islamic geometry are archetypal languages expressing the causal relationships of creation. Their beauty lies in the dynamic flow of symmetry, proportionality, rhythm and harmonics in an ordered whole. My work explores the space between the seen and the unseen, the fixed and the fluid, the temporal and the eternal. As patterns are transformed by light and colour, so self is transformed by the light of Soul."

Nargis Latif is a business development manager, poet, writer, feminist, traveller, mother of 5 children and overall loud London girl. She holds a Master's degree in Political Science with over 12 years experience in IT. She travels mostly alone, with an aim to connect to the divine and learn from each experience. Nargis believes poetry, like all art, is a divine expression. We are all paints and pens in the hands of God.

Yacoob Manjoo is a South African writer, blogger, husband, and father of two. Professionally, he works in the communications field, however, he's shared his personal writing for many years via his blog at https://dreamlife.wordpress.com. He has also written articles and produced content for various Islamic media platforms - including Productive Muslim, AboutIslam.net, and AccidentalMuslims.com.

Jessica Artemisia Mathieu is a poet, writer, and slavery abolitionist. She does digital marketing by day and has a Master of Science from New York University in Global Affairs, where she studied the relationship between international political economy, transnational organized crime, and human trafficking. Her work focuses on unity, connection, and exploring the growth of the human soul. She loves solitude, nature, animals, reading, traveling, and meeting people in the inner world.

Aaishah Mayet was born and bred in the City of Gold, Johannesburg, South Africa. She works in the Healthcare sector which, for her, has bridged the frontiers of our shared human experience. As a self-confessed bibliophile of many years, literature remains her teacher and her sanctuary. Her works include Haiku published in the Lotosblute, as well as poetry published online in the Agbowo Limits issue, Poetry Potion, Active Muse, the Brittle Paper and Amaliah.

Tasnim McCormick Benhalim - Growing up in a large Texas family, her earliest memory was *"Why?"*. Light, color, and patterns were - and are - her primary ways of knowing. In her early teens, finding first one - Rumi - and then others who spoke the same language guided her, over time, to Islam and her larger *family*. Through her company, DiversityWealth, Tasnim works to build bridges across cultures and generations, creating community and belonging. Through her independent trainings and her facilitation of Brené Brown's Dare to Lead™ program, she helps others answer the *"Why"* in their work and lives. Tasnim feels awash in grace and gratitude for life and our wealth of *family* and connections. *...here we are breathing, the sky deep and endless, and the night full of stars.*

Idris Mears was born in Cornwall in 1951. He moved with his parents to Bahrain in 1954 and it became his family home till he went to read English at Oxford University in 1970. He entered Islam in 1973 and has travelled the breadth of the Muslim World since then, building up a network of contacts and a catalogue of experiences. As a teenager, he wrote poetry and won a national poetry prize adjudicated by the then poet laureate, Cecil Day-Lewis. He returned to writing in the last few years but does not identify himself as a poet but as a chronicler of his life and times as a Muslim.

Malika Meddings is a Craniosacral Therapist with a love of plant and Chinese medicine. Her poems are an expression of gratitude for experiences with people and nature that have been transformative. She finds words a medium for healing, and real expression a gift that helps us to find solace in ourselves. www.harvestcalm.com

Abbas Mohamed has a huge appetite for life and what is beyond. He is involved in community projects focused on food, poetry, and the arts with organizations that include GAMA, Compassion Crew, and Halalfest. Abbas has been writing poetry since 2008 and humbly presents his stanzas as an offering of peace and blessings. You can find him on Instagram at @babashamss.

Daniel Abdal-Hayy Moore (1940-2016) *rahimahullah*, was born in 1940 in Oakland, California. He had his first book of poems, *Dawn Visions*, published by Lawrence Ferlinghetti of City Lights Books, San Francisco, in 1964, and the second in 1972, *Burnt Heart/Ode to the War Dead*. He created and directed *The Floating Lotus Magic Opera Company* in Berkeley, California in the late 60s, and presented two major productions, *The Walls Are Running Blood*, and *Bliss Apocalypse*. He became a Sufi Muslim in 1970, performed the Hajj in 1972, and lived and traveled throughout Morocco, Spain, Algeria and Nigeria, landing in California and publishing *The Desert is the Only Way Out*, and *Chronicles of Akhira* in the early 80s (Zilzal Press). Residing in Philadelphia since 1990, in 1996 he published *The Ramadan Sonnets* (Jusoor/City Lights), and in 2002, *The Blind Beekeeper* (Jusoor/Syracuse University Press). He has been the major editor for a number of works, including *The Burdah* of Shaykh Busiri, translated by Hamza Yusuf, and the poetry of Palestinian poet, Mahmoud Darwish, translated by Munir Akash. He has been poetry editor for *Seasons Journal, Islamica Magazine*, a 2010 translation by Munir Akash of *State of Siege*, by Mahmoud Darwish (Syracuse University Press), and *The Prayer of the Oppressed*, by Imam Muhammad Nasir al-Dar'i, translated by Hamza Yusuf (Sandala). In 2011, 2012 and 2014 he was a winner of the Nazim Hikmet Prize for Poetry. In 2013 he won an American Book Award, and in 2013 and 2014 was listed among The 500 Most Influential Muslims for his poetry. You can find out more about his life's work at https://www.ecstaticxchange.com.

Muneera Pilgrim is an international Poet, Cultural Producer, Writer, Broadcaster and artist who works across disciplines and form with words and text as her stimulus. She conducts expressive-based, purpose-driven workshops, shares art, guest lectures, hosts and finds alternative ways to educate, exchange ideas and grow. She is a co-founder of the Muslim female Spoken Word and Hip-Hop duo Poetic Pilgrimage, and since that point has been exploring narratives and stories that are rarely centralised. As a writer and broadcaster Muneera regularly contributes to BBC Radio 2's Pause for Thought and has written for The Guardian, Amaliah, Huffington Post, The Independent, Al Jazeera Blog and Black Ballard and many more. Muneera holds an MA in Islamic studies and an MA in Women's Studies where she focused on intersectionality, spirituality, auto-ethnography and methodologies of empowerment for non-centred people. For her academic work and use of poetic enquiry, she won the Ann Kolaski-Naylor award for creativity. Muneera is the current Artist Associate with The English Touring Theatre where she is writing her first play, and she is a Resident Creative at Pervasive Media, a hub of creatives, technologists and academics. If she were asked to describe herself in three words, she would say "Just Getting Started".

Bushra Mustafa-Dunne is a poet, writer of mixed Iraqi and Irish parentage. Her poetry explores gardens, imagined homelands, womanhood, uprootedness and the sanctity that draws these imaginings together. When she is not in her grandmother's garden, Bushra pursues a degree in Comparative Literature with Arabic, and hopes to write and translate in her mother tongue in the future.

Nimah Ismail Nawwab - Descending from a family of scholars from Mecca, Saudi Arabia, Nimah is an English poet, writer and photographer, an international lecturer whose work and writings span issues on spirituality, empowering youth, diversity and mutual respect for genders and races. Her poetry has been featured in documentaries and film. She is also a poetry judge and is engaged in mentoring writers, journalists and young poets through interactive workshops on the arts of writing and verse. Her best-selling poetry volume *The Unfurling*, with over 7000 copies sold worldwide, is the first book by a Saudi poet to be published in the United States. She had a major ground-breaking book signing in Jiddah, the first ever such signing in Saudi Arabia by a male or female writer, and a historic signing at Barnes and Noble, Washington DC. Her last book to date *Canvas of the Soul: Mystic Poems from the Heartland of Arabia*, promotes Islamic arts including calligraphy, Turkish miniature art and *ebru* with reviews by acclaimed scholars and artists. She has been a featured poet at schools and colleges in the East and West with readings, presentations and lectures at major institutes, forums and venues. Her poems on women, spirituality, Arabian society, and global issues, as well as the universal themes of love, loss, and simple joys have been taught at schools and universities in Arabia, the U.S., Canada, Venezuela, Singapore, Japan, India and others. Her poetry has been translated from English into numerous languages and her work has been included in numerous anthologies. Some of her work is featured on www.nimahnawwab.org.

Miroku Nemeth was born to hippie mother and a father who was a combat veteran in Vietnam who was a member of Vietnam Veterans Against the War. Born and raised in Michigan, he moved to Fresno, California at 15, which at that time had the highest per capita murder rate in the United States. After trials that many youth in America face growing up, he worked to extricate himself from negativity through the study of art, comparative religions, and mystical poetry. Inspired by Sufi love poetry, at 22, he converted to Islam near the gates of Yosemite National Park at the hands of a Sufi of the Shadhili lineage. Marrying a Muslima of Nubian origin three years later, he traveled to Egypt with her to meet her extended family, including in the rebuilt ancestral village of Ballana, where her people had been resettled after the construction of the Aswan High Dam destroyed the land that had been her people's for time immemorial. His first son, Omar, was born on June 5, 1998, and seeing his eyes open and calling the *adhan* and *iqama* in his ears on that day changed his life forever. His second son, Yusuf, was born while he was on Hajj in 2002, and is forever his Eidiyyah from Allah. Miroku has academic degrees in Linguistics and English Literature from C.S.U., Fresno, and owes much to working with poets locally, though more to the Sufi poets who first connected him to his own heart and Creator in a way like never before. He has taught high school and college locally for decades, always with an eye and heart for social justice that is sorely needed in California's Central Valley, one of the most impoverished and desperate regions in the country. Many of his students are from Huron, often the "poorest city in California" in ratings, from hard-working immigrant families who work the industrial agricultural fields of the region. Working with such communities has been a gift, and seeing former students succeed and even become activists has been a blessing. Miroku's eldest son passed away unexpectedly on January 3, 2018 at the age of nineteen and a half. He hopes to be reunited with him and his Nubian ancestors in Jannah.

Nile Mystic is a lover of words and feelings. She was conceived in the longest kiss, the confluence of the Blue and the White Nile. And she was nurtured in the rich cultures of the Persian/Arabian Gulf. Her artistic heart has been blooming in the beautiful coasts of North America. Her love for poetry started when she was a toddler listening to her two grandmothers in Sudan improvising beautiful lullabies full of poetic praises. Then her love grew more when she came across the poetry of Mevlana Rumi. Rumi's poetry helped her turn her feelings into poetry. Through poetry she found an avenue to express her hidden feelings and discoveries.

Rabia Saida is the founder of Lote Tree Press which developed from an online poetry forum she started ten years ago. She is a British American second generation Muslim whose parents hosted weekly *dhikr* gatherings during her childhood. This tradition of *dhikr* and *qasida* singing has inspired a love for devotional poetry in the original, especially when sung. Rabia Saida studied Arabic and Persian at university and is a translator and sometime teacher and journalist.

Sabila Raza, based in the North West of England, is British born, of Pakistani heritage. Her creativity is centred in expressing the complexities of human fragility, hoping to open consciousness, empower and convey the shared vulnerabilities within the many shades of being human. Sabila has featured in The Tempest and shares writing in her online blog and Instagram named A Million Thoughts A Minute, amtamblog. Sabila envisions to continue and develop in sharing her perspective through storytelling and writing in different mediums.

Zakriya Riaz is a British Pakistani Muslim, born in East London, with a great appreciation for the creative arts. He has performed poetry all over London at a range of events, exploring the plight of young disenfranchised people on stage. He performs as a form of therapy, as it allows him to vent his pain, as well as cover important topics like racism, feminism, Islamophobia, and personal tribulations. He is the founder of the Muslim Arts Movement campaign, designed to empower young disadvantaged people through open mic events, allowing them to tell their stories. He is a politics graduate, and expert on Islamophobia, having written a first-class dissertation on the question: "Does Islamophobia have the same meaning in the US and the UK"?

Murtaza Humayun Saeed was born in 1977 and has been engaged in an entangling yet fruitful journey in his mind and heart about how to determine what is true since his school days. Not realizing early on that he was grappling with what is described as nihilism, considered by thinkers as one of the modern world's root crises, he has emerged more confident about matters of religion and spirituality. Gifted with the ability to draw, paint and write, his findings find expression in his work. He is a Business and Law graduate from Lahore where he has lived since 1991, having been raised in Dubai and London. He is one of the Executive Producers of the Documentary: Blessed are the Strangers (2016) (www.thestrangers.co.uk) and an Art of Seeing traveller (www.artofseeing.org). He teaches the Beautiful Patience Class at Zaawiya Trust School in Lahore (www.zaawiya.org) and has been a contributor for Sacred Footsteps (www.sacredfootsteps.org). He can be reached at murtazahsaeed@yahoo.com.

Abdus Salaam is nobody, son of nobody. He found poetic inspiration after meeting a wandering dervish who mirrored to him his Selfhood. Ever since he has been journeying on the horizons and within as a process of unveiling.

Mai Sartawi is a lawyer, poet, and artist who currently lives in Kuwait. Poetry has become an essential tool for her to explore deeper within self the roots of injustice, its ironic beauty, and to witness the marvels of the Creator. She seeks to awaken, heal, and connect with her soul family.

Toneya Sarwar is a lifelong student. Writing poetry gives her emotions wings and her mind a place to explore and ponder the world around her. A British Muslim living in Dubai she draws on all her experiences for inspiration. Her three children are a constant source of gratitude and she hopes that one day they too will unlock the gifts that both reading and writing poetry give. Toneya's teachers are Khalil Gibran and Moulana Rumi, may they continue to move the hearts of those who follow them.

Novid Shaid is an English teacher and writer of novels, short stories and poetry. Born and brought up in Aylesbury in the UK, Novid developed a love for writing stories and reading English literature as a child, which culminated in him later becoming an English teacher in local secondary schools. In 2014, Novid published his first novel, the mystical thriller, The Hidden Ones and thereafter he published a book of short stories and poetry. He shares short stories and poems on his website: www.novid.co.uk

Sidd is a spoken word artist/creative, using spoken word poetry as an outlet, to express his own political views in his early 20s. After slowly becoming more religiously conscious, his writing began to reflect a more Islamic perspective. He now produces content based around the Islamic creed, covering aspects like the afterlife, prophetic stories, etc. His long-term goal is to make Islam more digestible for the Muslim youth and for it to be easier to understand for those that are not Muslim themselves.

Arthur Skip Maselli lives with his two teen children in Northern Virginia, near Washington, D.C. He is an initiate on the Mevlevi path of Sufism, with Shaykh Kabir Helminski. His books, "A Sparrow Who Ate the Universe" and "Twenty Five Words Toward the Truth, #25wtT" can be obtained through most major book outlets. While completing several poetry manuscripts, he occasionally blogs at www.phosphorimental.com. A part-time student of the ney, triathlete, businessman, and amateur event organizer; Skip seeks collaborations for spiritual gatherings and writing opportunities.

Abdul Kareem Stone - Getting on in the UK, a not so new Muslim, father of three children nearly all adult. Can only write poems with the rare internal season of inspiration. Still searching for a voice. No real accomplishments but a relish for the divine.

Sukina Pilgrim is a Poet, Spoken-Word artist, Playwright, Workshop Facilitator and Event Organiser and co-founder of Muslim female Hip Hop duo, Poetic Pilgrimage. She has facilitated creative writing workshops across the world empowering communities to use the written word as a tool for dialogue and as a means for accessing their authentic voice. She has launched a workshop series called The Art of Speaking from the Heart and that she has delivered around the world. She has played an intrinsic role within the British Muslim creative communities as a performer and events organiser and has created platforms for many national and international Muslim artists to express themselves and launch their careers. She was the Project Manager of a Muslim Sufi centre in London called Rumi's Cave where she organised Islamic courses, lectures, workshops and retreats. Her work has been featured on the BBC News, World Service and Asian Network, ITV, Channel 4 and Al Jazeera and has been written about in the Huffington Post, Daily Mail, The Voice and many other international media outlets. In March 2015 Al Jazeera screened a documentary about her group called Hip Hop Hijabis. Sukina made her theatre debut in 2016 in a production called Malcolm X at the Royal Flemish Theatre in Brussels which was critically acclaimed, and her first play will be premiered at the Theatre in 2020. In 2017 she delivered a Tedx Talk on the healing potential of poetry. Sukina holds a BA (Hons) Degree in English Literature and Caribbean Studies and is currently pursuing an MSc in Creative Writing for Therapeutic Purposes.

Paul Abdul Wadud Sutherland - British-Canadian poet Paul Sutherland (b. 1947) embraced Islam in 2004, receiving the name Abdul Wadud from Shaykh Nazim Al Haqqani of the Naqshbandi Tariqat. He turned freelance, and married Afifa Emutallah. His *Poems on the Life of the Prophet Muhammad* was published in 2014, *A Sufi Novice in Shaykh Efendi's Realm* a bilingual Romanian-English book followed, re-published in English only in 2016. A new edition, with 30 extra pages, is due from Beacon Books with the title *Servant of the Loving One.* In 2017 Valley Press published his monumental *New and Selected Poems,* covering 45 years of his writing. It was listed by PBS, and the *Morning Star* selected it as one of the year's top ten books. The University of Lincoln archives his work.

Nura Tarmann was born in a village in Austria and travelled as a child with her mixed family through several countries eventually settling in Medina, Saudi Arabia in 1978 where she married and had a son. She moved to the UK in 2009 where she writes to express her faith and sort out her impressions and feelings. She finds language a beautiful tool whose use she is still trying to perfect. She trained to be a counsellor and volunteered at MIND for several years. She now works with young people in care and her goal is to make them feel they are valuable members of society.

Aasifa Usmani is an immigrant originally from Indian occupied Kashmir with a background in Literature and Human Rights issues. She works in London with a feminist organization and raises awareness with healthcare professionals about domestic violence and abuse, working in partnership with them to holistically support victims/survivors. Working in this field has enhanced and expanded her insights into the impact of trauma due to gender violence and at the same time has taught her about the resilience of human spirit and women's agency. As a full-time working mother she feels that poetry strengthens her, and is interested in issues of exile, grief, trauma, love and endurance. She describes poetry as a *rooh* (soul), *najaat* (salvation) and *noor* (light) of life.

Flamur Vehapi is a researcher, poet, literary translator, academic and a leadership and success coach. He received his A.A. and B.S. in Counseling Psychology with a minor in History, and in 2013, he received his M.A. in Conflict Resolution from Portland State University. In 2009, Vehapi received the Imagine Award for Community Peacemaking. Currently, he is an Education and Leadership PhD student at Pacific University. Vehapi taught social sciences at Rogue Community College and Southern Oregon University, and more recently he taught at various institutions in the Middle East. His publications include The Alchemy of Mind and A Cup with Rumi, both collections of spiritual poems, and his most recent books are Peace and Conflict Resolution in Islam, The Book of Albanian Sayings and The Book of Great Quotes, and two translations of Sami Frashëri's books. He has worked as a contributing writer for the PSU Chronicles. Vehapi and his family currently live in Oregon.

Medina Tenour Whiteman was born in Granada, Spain, in 1982 to American English Muslim parents. She graduated from SOAS, London, with a BA (hons), 1st class, in African Language and Culture in 2005. Since then she has written freelance for organs including Critical Muslim and Permaculture Magazine on topics such as history, culture, religion, sustainable agriculture, and the arts. She is the author of a collection of poetry (Love is a Traveller and We are its Path), Huma's Travel Guide to Islamic Spain, and The Invisible Muslim. She also writes documentary scripts and short stories, translates, and composes and performs music. She lives near Granada with her husband and three children.

Glossary

aşk - love

adab - appropriate behaviour, etiquette, spiritual courtesy

adhān - the call to prayer

ahlen - welcome

Ahlul Bayt - The family of Prophet Muhammad, also sometimes applied to the family of Prophet Abraham, peace be upon them.

akhira - the Hereafter

al-fatiha - the first seven verses of the Qur'an, which are repeated in the daily prescribed prayers.

al-Musawwir - The Fashioner, one of the 99 Names of God.

alhamdulillah - Praise be to God - often used as an expression of gratitude

alhamdulillahi washshukrulillah Praise and thanks be to God

Allahu akbar - God is greater – recited in the call to prayer and said repeatedly in the daily prescribed prayers. Used in many different contexts, often as an expression of gratitude, celebration and wonder.

Allahumma salle wa salim wa barik alay – O Allah, bestow blessings and peace upon him.

ash-hadu an la ilaha illa Allah - I bear witness that there is no deity but God - The first part of the Islamic testimony of faith.

assalamu alaikum wa rahmat Allah - Peace be upon you and the mercy of God - this is said to greet people, and it is also said at the end of the prescribed daily prayers and is directed towards those sitting to the right and left of the worshipper and towards the recording angels.

astaghfirullah - I ask God for forgiveness

awliya - saints

Ayat ul Kursi - the Throne Verse, verse 2:255 of the Qur'an - often recited for physical and spiritual protection.

Baraka - blessings

barzakh - used to mean the space where souls reside after death, and also a phase between death and resurrection. It is also described as a place for unborn souls in the lowest heaven, where an angel blows them into wombs. Some consider it to be a place the soul can visit during sleep and meditation.

basma - smile

bismillah - in the Name of God

deen - religion

dhikr/zikr - remembrance - a form of meditation remembering God, often through the repetition of devotional phrases. This is central to the Islamic relationship with the Divine and appears in the Qur'anic verse {Remember Me and I will remember you. And be grateful to Me and do not deny Me} 2:152.

duas - supplications - prayers made often with palms raised.

durood - sending blessings upon the Prophet through repeating devotional phrases

fajr - the dawn prayer

ghusul - greater ablution

Hu - He - a name for God

huzoor - witnessing

ibadah - worship, devotion

ihram - the clothes worn to perform the pilgrimage - in the case of a man this is two unstitched pieces of cloth. Ihram also refers to the sacred state entered into on putting on this clothing, in which one must abide by various conditions and restrictions.

ihsan - benevolence

inna lillah wa inna ilayhi rajioun - Verily to God we belong and to Him we return - said in times of difficulty and upon someone's death.

insaan - the human being

iqama - the second call to prayer

isra' wal-mi'raj - the night journey and ascension through the heavens of the Prophet Muhammad, peace be upon him

kun fayakun - Be and it is - this phrase appears several times in the Qur'an, for example in verse 36:82
{His command is only when He intends a thing that He says to it, "Be," and it is}

la ilaha illallah Muhammadun rasulullah - There is no deity but God and Muhammad is His messenger - the Islamic testimony of faith.

lughat aḍ-ḍād - the language of the letter *ḍād* ض

lutf - grace

maghrib - the prayer after sunset

malamiyya - "the path of blame" whose disciples incur the blame of others as a way of becoming detached from their reputation and subduing the ego.

mihrab - niche in mosque wall indicating the direction of prayer

miqat – the boundary within which one must be in a state of *ihram*.

Mustafa - a name of the Prophet Muhammad, peace be upon him, meaning Chosen.

nafs - the self, the ego.

PBUH - Peace be upon him

qari' - Qur'an reciter

qasida - a poetic form originating in pre-Islamic Arabia which spread throughout the Islamic word, used in many contexts, including devotional poetry.

qibla – the direction of prayer facing the Kaaba in Mecca.

Rabi' al-awwal - The month of the Prophet's birth

rahimahullah/rahimahallah – May God have mercy on him/May God have mercy on her

rahma - mercy

rak'ah – a unit of the prescribed prayers consisting of a series of devotional recitations said in different positions. The five daily prescribed prayers have different numbers of *rak'ahs* depending on which prayer is being prayed.

rasool – the Messenger

rasūlullah - the Messenger of God

ruh – spirit/soul

sabr - patience

salaam - peace

salat - prayer

salawat – prayers upon the Prophet

sallallahu Alayhi wa Sallam - the peace and blessings of God be upon him

sama' - a gathering of dhikr – the word literally means "listening"

subhanallah – Glory be to God! - often repeated as a devotional formula and also used in conversation as an exclamation of praise, gratitude or amazement.

sibha/subha - prayer beads

suhūr - the pre-dawn meal before fasting

sujood - prostration

sunnah – Prophetic tradition

tajweed – rules of Quran recitation

tasbih/tasbeeh – prayer beads

umma/ummah – the Muslim community

wudu – ablution

Acknowledgements

Thank you to my brainstorming buddies Asma Khan and Medina Tenour Whiteman for the discussions and organisation that got this anthology in motion. It would not have come into being without your ideas and thoughts and your final editing and proofreading. Thank you also to Nura Tarmann for furnishing the title for the anthology in her poem Kaleidoscope, to my sister Lateefa for allowing her artwork to be used for the cover and to my mother for her editing and proofreading. My thanks to Baraka Blue for introducing me to a number of the poets included in this anthology through the Rumi Center for Spirituality and the Arts inaugural poetry anthology *Opening the Eye of the Heart*. Finally my thanks go to all the amazing poets who contributed to this anthology and who have made it what it is.

Poems of Daniel Abdal Hayy Moore (1940-2016) are listed with the poetry collections they originally appeared in, available from www.ecstaticxchange.com. Thank you to his wife Malika Moore for agreeing to the inclusion of his poems in this anthology.

All the poems in this anthology by Shahbano Aliani (1967-2019) originally appeared in the book *Set My Heart On Fire*.

Most of the poems in this collection by Abdalhamid Evans (1951-2018) first appeared in *Songs in Search of a Musician*. Thank you to his wife Salama Evans for agreeing to the inclusion of his poems in this anthology.

Previously published poems in this anthology include:

"After Ramadan Comes Thanksgiving" by Mohja Kahf first published in Critical Muslim.
 "Light Upon Light" by Mohja Kahf - first published in *Prosopisia: An International Journal of Poetry & Creative Writing*, Vol. XI:1 2017

"The Inner Tablet" by Nimah Ismail Nawwab originally appeared in *Canvas of the Soul, Mystic Poems from the Heartland of Arabia*

Yahia Lababidi's poetry has previously appeared in his collection: *Balancing Acts; New & Selected Poems (1993 - 2015)*.

A number of poems in the anthology appeared originally in the Rumi Center for Spirituality and the Arts inaugural poetry anthology *Opening the Eye of the Heart*

Efforts have been made to trace and contact relevant copyright holders. However, if any have been overlooked the publisher will be pleased to rectify any errors or omissions at the first opportunity.

Index of Poets

Printed in Great Britain
by Amazon